I0119195

paul mallett is a tender-minded social-justice activist, policy thinker, and servant leader with more than three decades working alongside communities too often overlooked or left behind. His career spans health and fitness, educational research, homelessness prevention, children, family, and disability service leadership, and workforce development across the care economy and public service. He maintains a consistent focus on early intervention, upstream thinking, and building systems that treat people with dignity.

He's known for people-centred leadership, clear policy thinking, and programs that challenge inequality and injustice. Much of his impact has been behind the scenes, where persistence matters more than profile. His practice is shaped by research and by the lived experience of people navigating inequity; he uses anti-oppressive practice, implementation science, and collaboration to turn evidence into outcomes.

paul founded **vibrantnation.au** to host ideas for upstream thinking and kind politics — prevention-first reforms grounded in empathy, fairness, and shared action. He lives in northern Tasmania with his family, close to rivers and communities that keep him grounded and hopeful. When not writing or reading, he's usually out walking or riding, scheming ways to shift social policy from the bottom of the cliff to the top.

VIBRANT CITY

TWELVE UPSTREAM INITIATIVES TO RESHAPE LAUNCESTON'S FUTURE

VIBRANT NATION TRILOGY
BOOK 1

PAUL MALLETT

vibrant nation

ALSO BY PAUL MALLETT

BOOKS

Book II

vibrant state: ten kind policies to transform Tasmania

Book III

vibrant nation: eight citizen-led movements to advance Australia fair

WEBSITE

www.vibrantnation.au

CONTENT WARNING: The *vibrant nation trilogy* contains references to human suffering, including physical and mental abuse, bullying, suicide and suicidality, grief and loss. Mild adult language appears. Reader discretion is advised.

DECLARATION: This book blends memoir and fiction. Apart from paul mallett and clearly identified public figures and institutions, the characters and events are invented or used fictitiously. Any resemblance to real persons, living or dead, is purely coincidental.

CONTENT CREATION: This work draws on human imagination, conversation, and research, with occasional help from AI tools to refine prose and prepare footnotes. The tools were instruments, not authors. All ideas, interpretations, and final responsibility remain with paul mallett.

vibrant city

Book I of the vibrant nation trilogy

Copyright © 2025 paul mallett

All rights reserved. Except as permitted under the Copyright Act 1968 (Cth)—including fair dealing for research or study, criticism or review, news reporting, and parody or satire—no part of this publication may be reproduced, stored in a retrieval system, or transmitted in any form or by any means (electronic, mechanical, or otherwise) without prior written permission of the author. The moral rights of the author have been asserted.

First edition, September 2025

Print ISBN: 978-1-7642922-0-7

Ebook ISBN: 978-1-7642922-9-0

Subjects: Political Science / Public Policy / Social Policy; Social Science / Sociology / Urban; Social Science / Future Studies; Architecture / Urban & Land Use Planning; Education / Educational Policy & Reform; Business & Economics / Urban & Regional; Nature / Environmental Conservation & Protection

Published by paul mallett, Launceston, Tasmania, Australia.

For permissions and rights enquiries: www.vibrantnation.au

Cover design: paul mallett

Cover photograph: *Launceston Fireworks* © 2022 Arya Shahrdami. Used with permission. Instagram: @arya.s.photography

This work presents general information and informed opinion. It is not legal, medical, or financial advice. Readers should seek professional guidance where appropriate.

Every effort has been made to identify and obtain permission for copyrighted material. Any omissions are unintentional; rights holders are invited to contact the author.

All trademarks are the property of their respective owners and are used for identification purposes only.

Legal deposit: A copy of this publication will be lodged with National edeposit (NED) and Libraries Tasmania in accordance with legal-deposit requirements.

*For **Maitreya** and **Xolani***
— and for every child yet to come,
who will inherit the world we choose to build.

CONTENTS

ACKNOWLEDGEMENT

Before we travel forward together, we must first look back — with open eyes and an honest heart.

For over two thousand generations, the confluence of the North Esk, South Esk, and Kanamaluka (Tamar River) has been a place of deep meaning and meeting. The palawa/pakana peoples — including the Panninher, Tyerrernotepanner, and Letteremairrener clans — gathered here to trade, heal, resolve conflict, and celebrate. Ceremony, kinship, and custodianship flourished long before asphalt roads and colonial names marked the land.

This story does not begin with colonisation — and it cannot be complete without truth. The city now called Launceston was founded on dispossession. Its streets, buildings, and institutions sit atop stolen land. Yet through invasion, violence, forced removals, and cultural suppression, palawa/pakana people survived. And they continue — not as relics of the past, but as sovereign custodians of living Country.

Truth-telling, land return, and shared power are not symbolic gestures. They are necessary acts of justice. Returning land does not erase history — it restores agency, affirms culture, and helps build a future where all people can live well on Country, respected in community.

Leadership in this space must be more than performative. It must be courageous enough to confront harm, and compassionate enough to imagine repair. And it must be structural: embedded in law, budget, land titles, and the shared reimagining of what fairness demands.

The future cannot be built on denial. It must be co-created — through deep listening, mutual respect, and ongoing stewardship of the lands, waters, and stories that hold us all.

My commitment — to truth, to justice, to shared stewardship — is the foundation of this book, and of the entire trilogy. Therefore, I seek:

To honour what was.

To reckon with what was taken.

And to imagine what might still be shared.

Because a nation built on prevention and kindness must first be grounded in honesty, courage, and care.

AUTHOR'S NOTE

"I can't accept not trying" — Michael Jordan[1]

For most of my life I've worked behind the scenes — in service of community — listening, building, and helping vulnerable people solve problems before they spiral. Again and again I saw the same truth: so much harm could have been prevented if we had acted earlier — and if we had found the courage to confront the systems that hurt and harm people in the first place.

That is why I wrote this book.

vibrant city is the first in a trilogy about building a better future — not just for some, but for all. It is for people who care deeply, act locally, and are tired of politics that slaps on band-aids instead of addressing root causes. This is not a policy manual or a party platform. It is part memoir, part speculative history, part hopeful act of political imagination. It weaves memory, ideas, and futures to spark conversation and inspire action — an experiment in fiction as civic intervention.

The approach draws on futures traditions. Damien Lutz calls it "future scouting" — designing tomorrow's inventions and embedding them in story to provoke change today[2]. Speculative design and design fiction (Dunne & Raby) speak of "future prototypes": artefacts and scenarios that seem to arrive from another time[3]. In these pages, Launceston's Tamar Lake and people-first City Bridge, its mural trails, its "teenagency" vertical school, and its Statue of Equity serve as such prototypes. They are not predictions; they are provocations—made visible enough that citizens can debate their desirability.

In futures scholarship, Hancock and Bezold's Futures Cone[4] describes four zones of imagination: the probable, the plausible, the possible, and the preposterous. This book moves among them. Some chapters remain in the probable, grounded in current trajectories. Others step into the plausible, consistent with today's knowledge but requiring deliberate choice. Still others venture into the possible — even the preposterous — to stretch imagination and seed inspiration.

The narrative also traverses familiar archetypes: dystopia, utopia, and protopia[5]. There are dystopian shadows here — inequality, exclusion, lost opportunity. There are flashes of utopia. But the dominant orientation is protopian: not perfection, but steady improvement — step by step, reform by reform, culture shifting toward inclusion and care.

This work also sits within fictional intelligence (FicInt): research-informed fiction used to explore policy and prompt strategic reflection[6]. Where FicInt is often short-form, this book stretches it into long narrative.

To make the reading practical, the book blends four elements:

- *Personal Reflections (Memoir)* — stories drawn from lived experience, showing what has shaped my values and decisions over a lifetime of public service.

- *Leadership Tools* — footnoted throughout the book are the frameworks, concepts, and theories that have helped me make sense of complex issues and lead change.
- *Evocative Futures Writing* — set in the year 2064, imagined conversations that show what a better future might look like. This isn't about prediction but possibility: by looking back from the future, we see more clearly what choices matter now.
- *Policy Calls to Action* — at the back of the book you'll find practical next steps (things we can do—or should do—now) and chapter summaries that set out each initiative in words and numbers, with indicative estimates from the fictional Avoidable Costs Unit (ACU). These are starting points, not prescriptions.

The ideas explored in this book are not soft slogans or what some dismiss as 'woke'. They are structural. They are about the deliberate design of kinder systems, and the pursuit of fairness and justice. They are about the choice to act early — to prevent harm, save lives, and invest resources where they make the greatest difference.

I sometimes think of politics like a shadow-puppet play. Most of what the public sees is the shadow — the announcement, the budget line, the headline. What you don't see are the hands behind the screen — the people, the process, the slow, difficult work of turning vision into focus. In these pages, I want you to see both: the shadow animal and the hands that made it; the process and the product; the future — and the hard work required to build it.

This book was written with care.

I hope you read it with care.

A city worth fighting for.

A future worth building. Together.

INTRODUCTION

"In a gentle way, you can shake the world." — Mahatma Gandhi[1]

What if we designed our cities not just to function — but to care?

This is the first book in the *vibrant nation trilogy* — a hopeful future told in stories, where harm is prevented, not patched, and where kindness is woven into the foundations of daily life. It begins not with national policy or global movements, but with something smaller — a walk by a lake that wasn't always there.

In vibrant city, we start close to home — on the streets of Launceston, Tasmania — imagining what becomes possible when upstream thinking meets local leadership. Here, in one regional city, a different kind of transformation took root. Quiet at first. But powerful.

The chapters that follow trace twelve bold initiatives seeded at the local level — each grounded in care, each shaped by lived experience. Together, they offer a model for what local government can be when it listens deeply, plans wisely, and dares to think in the *long now*[2].

We begin with water — and the upstream metaphor made real. Tamar Lake, once a vision laughed off as impossible, becomes a living example of restoration, climate resilience, and community imagination. A few steps away, a bridge reconnects the city's past and future — a symbol of equity, access, and shared journey.

Then come the children — whose wellbeing becomes the central test of our civic design. We explore early years reforms, cradle-to-career education, and a shift toward empathy-centred schools. And we see how local government helped bring families and communities into that work — not as clients, but as co-creators.

We walk through parks and murals, encounter play streets and sport loops, and pause at the vibrant public spaces that quietly transform public health, social trust, and mental wellbeing. We visit a new kind of school — Changemaker High — and imagine a civic culture where curiosity, collaboration, and citizen science are part of the curriculum.

Along the way, we talk work — how cities can value care, support young people into purpose, and cultivate enterprise and renewal. And we celebrate festivals, stories, and the public rituals that connect us — not as consumers, but as contributors to a shared civic life.

These local shifts may seem modest — but their ripple effects are profound. Because when we redesign the places we live to prioritise health, connection, equity, and joy, we don't just improve services. We reshape culture. We change what feels normal. And we make kindness visible, tangible, and contagious.

At the heart of this future is a young woman named Willow. She was born long after these reforms began — but her life is shaped by them. Through her eyes, we walk the city — not as it was, but as it became. We pause, reflect, and remember how the tide turned.

Beneath every chapter runs a deeper current — three shared principles that shape this trilogy:

Upstream Thinking[3] — the logic of prevention, foresight, and structural redesign. It asks us to stop pouring resources into the bottom of the cliff and instead change the conditions that push people over the edge in the first place. Upstream thinking is both pragmatic and humane: it saves money, but more importantly, it reduces human suffering and saves lives.

Kind Politics[4] — the courage to lead with empathy, and design with dignity. It resists the pull of fear and division, choosing instead to build policy that affirms worth, nurtures connection, and treats fairness as infrastructure. Kind politics is not soft politics; it is the harder path of listening, including, and choosing justice over expedience.

Power Threat Meaning Framework[5] **(PTMF)** — a model that shifts our lens from "what is wrong with you?" to "what has happened to you?" It helps name how power is used and misused, how threats are experienced, and how people create meaning and survival strategies in the face of adversity. PTMF rejects narrow biomedical labels and instead offers a systemic, socially aware approach that recognises human responses to oppression, trauma, and inequality. At its heart, PTMF insists that personal distress must be understood in the context of wider social conditions — making it both a tool for practice and a compass for justice.

Together, they form a lens — not just to understand harm, but to prevent it. To unpick systems that wound, and reweave systems that heal.

This is not a policy manual. It's a storybook for the future. A speculative memoir of a city that turned toward care.

If you've ever believed that local government could be more than roads, rates, and rubbish — this book is yours.

If you've ever wondered how small changes, well designed, could transform whole communities — this book is for you.

And if you've ever been told that kindness isn't serious politics — this book dares to prove otherwise.

Let's begin the walk. Toward a vibrant city.

And a nation worth growing into.

IT'S TIME TO STAND

Remember tonight, while we sleep tight,
A child curls up in fear and fright.

No food, no heat, no loving glance,
No safe room where dreams can dance.

No story read, no blanket tight,
No calm voice to guard the night.

No giggle shared, no goodnight kiss,
No promise whispered: "You've got this."

So you and I must act today,
Bring hope and kindness, lead the way.

Bring change for kids both near and far,
To light the dark where shadows are.

So every child can dream out loud,
Stand tall, stand free, stand safe and proud.

Across this city, across this land,
For fact's sake — it's time to stand. [1]

TECHNOLOGY GLOSSARY

The future imagined in this book takes place in 2064 — a time where technology is seamlessly woven into everyday life. Willow, one of our central characters, is native to this world: a future that is vibrant, community-oriented, and deeply grounded in empathy, equity, and civic participation. This glossary introduces key technologies that shape that world.

Synapstra. A neural interface installed just behind the ear, enabling users to access networks, information, and communication tools through thought alone. Standard from age 12 in most regions, Synapstra is as commonplace in 2064 as Wi-Fi or air travel is today. It can be muted, paused, or set to *Mindful Mode* when needed. When paired with LumenView, it has replaced the need for handheld devices. Callers only hear spoken words — not private thoughts.

LumenView. An augmented reality system that projects digital content into the user's field of vision through contact lenses, smart glasses, or retinal implants. Maps, data, media, and messages appear as contextual overlays in the surrounding environment, or hover discreetly in the user's peripheral vision. Content can be shared with others, always with explicit consent.

Clara *(Contextual Learning and Recall Assistant)*. An adaptive AI embedded within Synapstra. Clara acts as a quiet cognitive companion, offering emotional support, memory prompts, and conversational guidance. It helps users regulate tone, reflect on difficult interactions, and navigate relationships with empathy. Clara is not a replacement for human connection — more like a mental health coach, conscience, and translator rolled into one. Only the user can hear what Clara says.

CivicLoom. A civic participation platform where residents help shape policy through interactive forums, proposal voting, and AI-powered future simulations. CivicLoom replaces traditional town halls and consultation processes with a more inclusive, co-creative approach to democracy — grounded in memory, equity, and place.

MemoryLoom. An open-source, AI-enhanced historical record that stores public speeches, civic events, environmental data, and social change movements. Citizens can verify claims, trace decisions, or revisit turning points. Within MemoryLoom is **DeepSeequence** — a tool that models how different decisions might shape future outcomes.

PerceptaNet. A vast network of ambient sensors embedded in public infrastructure — streets, buildings, trees, even public transport. PerceptaNet collects and shares real-time data on air quality, traffic, noise, and safety. Though invisible, it is fully accessible: anyone can query it through Synapstra or LumenView to get instant, local information.

GrowthLoop. A lifelong, adaptive education system where learners co-design their pathways around interests, strengths, and community needs—and share their work publicly. Core strands include storytelling, critical thinking, civic engagement, and real-world problem-solving, building a culture of continuous, purpose-driven learning.

CitizenEcho. A location-based memory archive that links personal and public stories to physical places. A park bench might trigger the message: *"This bench was funded after the 2044 grief rally, designed by Isla, age 9."* CitizenEcho helps communities stay emotionally grounded in shared history and place.

KindraPass. A universal digital identity system designed for equity and inclusion. Unlike systems based solely on income or address, KindraPass adjusts access to services based on factors like trauma history, caregiving roles, or lived experience. It also supports time-banking and community credit systems — fostering participation, dignity, and mutual care.

Avoidable Costs Unit (ACU). A transparent, public metric that tallies the dollars a community doesn't need to spend when it invests upstream—fewer ambulance call-outs, cleaner air, stronger school completion. ACU estimates are expressed as annual gross costs avoided and paired with human outcomes. It's not a new currency but a civic yardstick, updated through MemoryLoom and DeepSeequence to help communities compare options and choose prevention with clarity. *Note: ACU figures in this book are indicative and speculative; they have not been independently verified and are provided for illustration only. Further economic modelling would be required to validate assumptions and ranges.*

PRELUDE

THE CONNECTION

"It is in the shelter of each other that the people live"
— Irish proverb[1].

paul hadn't expected to outlast them all.

Ninety might be the new seventy in body, but friendship doesn't follow biological trends. One by one, his circle had gone — some quickly, some after long farewells — until only echoes of their laughter remained. He never imagined it would be him left to carry so many memories alone.

Mornings were for movement — weights, stretching, lake walks — anything that kept his limbs honest and his mind from drifting too far. Afternoons belonged to words. Most days, he pedaled to the university library, a ritual born from loss. With his friends gone, the quiet rows of books became a refuge, a place that didn't ask him to explain the ache.

There, he filled pages with half-formed notes, still arguing — softly — with the world. He felt... unfinished.

It had been four years since the last funeral. Ten years since he'd spoken in public. Only last month had his GP — a young, earnest man with kind eyes and a belief in social prescribing — convinced him to join the Intergenerational Pathways program. Not just for the walks, but for the company.

"You need others, paul," the GP said. "Grief doesn't dissolve with time, but it softens in company."

MemoryLoom was part of the prescription.

"Your story matters," the GP added. "Upload it. Reflect. You'd be surprised how many young people read these."

At first, paul scoffed. Who would want his hesitant recollections of community service and policy battles? But MemoryLoom didn't want perfection — it wanted texture: memory, feeling, regret, the unvarnished truth of living through consequential times. Slowly, entry by entry, Clara coaxed him to speak again — not to crowds, but into the net.

Across the bridge and only minutes away, Willow scrolled her morning stream — a blur of climate models, ethics debates, and the strange internet nostalgia currently fixated on 2026.

Today's task was grounded in reality: verifying elder uploads for MemoryLoom. The role of AusCorps Community Data Guardian wasn't glamorous, but it covered Willow's living stipend, paired neatly with her History and Political Science majors, and kept her debt-free.

One profile caught her eye:

paul mallett — Age 90 — Launceston, Tasmania.
Status: New Contributor.

Willow frowned. "I know that name — the social change guy from Civics, the one who insisted on spelling his name in lower case.[2]"

Scrolling further, headlines flickered past: The Interdependent Candidate. Fair Go. No-Pokies. No-Poverty.

She stopped, eyebrows raised. "What? Even The Naked Politician? He must have a story or two."

A deeper cross-check pulled up his official record:

> paul mallett — Community service leader, politician, political strategist and adviser, speechwriter, published author, thinker, futurist. Career span: 1988–2054.

His entries were sparse but layered — a mix of policy notes, reflections, and journal-like fragments. They weren't polished, but they were honest. And something about them suggested a turning point — a shift from silence to reckoning.

The pattern matched a hunch forming in Willow's own thesis: that the transformation of the late 2020s to the 2060s wasn't sudden but seeded by local actors with bold, upstream ideas. A kind of politics now at risk of fading under austerity.

This wasn't just data. It was history speaking.

The pairing was formalised a week later. Community Data Guardians were matched to elders by locality, record complexity, and — strangely — something called mutual benefit scores. Whatever algorithm drove it decided that paul needed Willow, and Willow, it seemed, needed someone like paul.

At first, they messaged. Willow challenged timelines, asked for sources, pressed for clarity. paul replied with patient humour, rarely defending himself but always giving more.

He had been reluctant about the Intergenerational Pathways program, dismissing it as structured connection dressed up as wellbeing. But the idea of pairing his walks with MemoryLoom reflections softened him. Two tasks, one ritual. Efficient, as always.

Then Willow suggested they meet by the lake. He almost said no. But something in her tone — curious, grounded, hopeful — reminded him of old colleagues. He agreed.

So paul sat on his usual bench, facing Tamar Lake, letting its calm surface hold the weight of his thoughts.

Willow arrived late, carrying her hemp bag and a recycled paper notebook scrawled with questions.

And that is where this story begins.

Two people walking the edges of memory.

One searching for meaning in the past.

The other unsure if he left any behind.

Together they retrace the choices that shaped their city — river repair and bridge building, urban greening and population growth, thriving children and community festivals.

In conversation they explore the messy, beautiful truth of living in service to something larger than oneself.

This is their reckoning.

This is their remembering.

This is vibrant city.

ONE
THE LAKE
A FRESHWATER FUTURE

"Water is life's matter and matrix, mother and medium. There is no life without water." — Albert Szcnt-Györgyi[1]

23 January 2064

It was high summer at Tamar Lake, and the midday sun blazed in a sky rinsed clear of cloud. paul sat alone on the bench, the lake gleaming like a pane of glass — clear freshwater, now held permanently at river-edge level. Sunlight flashed across the ripples as black swans drifted in the shallows, and somewhere beyond sight, a child's laughter carried from Riverbend Park.

His right arm rested along the backrest, fingers idly tracing the edge of a small bronze plaque screwed into the recycled plastic slats. He didn't read it. He never did. But his fingers knew every ridge, every groove. They moved like memory.

Above him, eucalyptus leaves whispered, stirred by a warm breeze that smelled of freshly cut grass.

He'd arrived early. He always did.

A woman approached from the northern track, her stride steady, a hemp satchel slung across her shoulder. She was taller than he'd imagined — early twenties, a neat dark braid, eyes alert. She paused before speaking, her gaze sweeping across the lake.

"You're paul?" she asked.

He looked up, squinting slightly beneath the brim of a baseball cap. "I am."

"I'm Willow. Community Data Guardian, assigned to your Memory-Loom stream."

With a quiet ease, he raised his right hand to the rim of his cap and gave it a gentle tap[2] — a simple, old-fashioned gesture of respect. He nodded once, offered a soft smile, and motioned for her to sit.

"Nice to meet you."

"It's so beautiful here," Willow said, a little nervously.

She took another moment to take in the lake, then sat beside him. The bench creaked softly under the shift in weight. After a pause, almost apologetically:

"I read your entries last night."

"I hope they made sense."

"They did. More than most. And I think that's why I'm here."

paul waited.

"They've asked me to fact-check as usual," she said. "But I'm also... considering a thesis. On citizen-led change — collective action. Your stories of 'kind politics' really stood out."

paul gave a soft chuckle.

"Careful. Most of what I remember, I've only just started saying out loud — after a lifetime of making it up as I went along." He paused, then added, "Well, maybe with a little inspiration from Chomsky, Freire, and Dr. Seuss. If you're chasing citizen-led change, you'll need all three — the critical, the hopeful, and the playful."

Willow smiled politely, not really catching the first two names — though Dr. Seuss, at least, rang a bell. "That's what MemoryLoom is for, I guess."

He nodded. "That, and cognitive health incentives."

She tilted her head slightly. "Social prescription?"

"Weekly walks. Shared stories. Mild embarrassment. Keeps the heart going… and wards off short-term memory loss. And, um…" — he paused — "short-term memory loss."

Willow laughed — not politely this time, but genuinely — and glanced at the plaque beneath his hand. "I'm meant to meet each of my elders regularly," she said, "for fieldwork and source triangulation."

"That's quite a mouthful."

"I didn't write it. The department did."

She looked out at the lake again, letting the silence settle. "It's peaceful here."

"It wasn't always."

She turned toward him, curious. "I'd like to understand that."

paul stood slowly. "Let's go!" He gestured to the path. "Walk with me."

They set off together, following the curve of the shoreline. The gravel crunched gently beneath their feet.

After a minute or two, Willow spoke again.

"My grandfather used to bring me here to paddle and play on the beach when I was little. I didn't know the history — just that it felt safe."

"That's how you know it worked," paul said.

She glanced at him.

"The change was upstream," he continued with a faint smile. "Literally — they built the weir at Point Rapid and turned the tide into a lake. But the other kind of upstream change... that's harder to see. Not obvious at first. But once it arrives, it changes everything quietly."

Willow nodded. "I'm learning to spot that pattern. The slow policy moves — the ones that last."

They passed the eastern pier, where a row of ice cream, coffee, and souvenir huts were just opening for business.

Further along, the walking path was framed by reeds and sculpture installations.

"What was here before?" Willow asked.

paul raised his eyebrows.

"Honestly? A three-meter tide, ugly and smelly mudflats, sunken boats, and a hell of a lot of shopping trolleys."

Willow blinked. "Hard to picture."

Willow gestured to her ear — a familiar sign that she was about to share a Synapstra experience.

"Want to see what it used to look like?"

paul smiled.

A faint shimmer flickered across her pupils as LumenView engaged — the contact-lens tech that layered shared visuals into the user's field of view. With a knowing glance, paul simply nodded to accept the reel and his glasses pulsed once in sync.

In an instant, the vibrant lake scene dissolved. The water darkened. Movement slowed. Around them, the clean boardwalk and shimmering lake were replaced with silted sludge and weed-choked banks. The iconic jet fountain vanished. In its place, two rusting yachts keeled over in the mud like forgotten bones.

The air — imagined but vivid — felt heavier, brackish. The tide had dropped, revealing a landscape trapped somewhere between neglect and collapse.

Willow spoke softly. "This was the yacht basin. It says it was Summer low tide. Late 2026."

She pointed to a vast sea of dark brown sludge.

"Evidently that's monosulfidic black ooze[3] —M-B-O. On a bad day you could smell it from Launceston College."

paul nodded, jaw tight. "For fact's sake, it was an eyesore—our river choking. And still, some said, 'It is what it is.'"

The simulation hung around them a moment longer — stagnant, still, suffocating.

No scent reached her; still, something in the dark sheen made her stomach dip. She cleared the overlay and the lake returned: sunlit, vibrant, breathing.

Willow let out a breath she hadn't realized she'd been holding.

They resumed walking, and paul gestured north with a tilt of his head.

"We had good science — funded by locals[4], not government. A small group of committed people who had a belief in something better," he said. "After generations of turning our backs on the river, we understood the cost of doing nothing — a stalling regional economy, and a stinking, embarrassing mess of a waterway."

He paused, then gestured toward the lake again.

"But building that weir didn't just clean things up. It created a beautiful freshwater lake — stable, secure, and right in the heart of our valley. Suddenly we had a place the community could gather, play, swim, paddle — even drink from, if we damn well chose to."

Willow smiled at that.

"It gave irrigators confidence to plan. Laid the foundation for new crops — like industrial hemp. Opened the door for new industries too — clean hydrogen, water-intensive processing, things we couldn't do with the salt water and tidal mud still here."

He looked out across the water.

"And more than anything, it gave the region a shot in the arm — jobs in construction, jobs in what came after. And pride. Real community pride. A belief that we could do something bold and get it right."

Willow looked out over the water, taking it in — not just the view, but the community effort it took to make such stillness possible.

"This feels like a good place to start," she said. "For my thesis. For understanding citizen-led change – for understanding what came before."

paul offered her a sidelong glance. "And for you?"

She hesitated, then met his gaze. "My grandfather passed away last year. He was the one who first brought me here. I didn't think I'd miss our walks this much."

paul looked down briefly. "I'm sorry."

She nodded. "I think I'm here for more than the thesis."

paul didn't reply. Instead, he matched his stride to hers, the pace softening. They followed the curve of the path until the shoreline opened to a gentle rise — a quiet bend where the new waters met the old contours of the riverbank. Below, the lake shimmered gold, its surface catching the bright summer light. Distant birds wheeled above the reeds.

Near the crest, an old park bench sat uphill from the path. Its slats were weathered but solid, the concrete legs bolted deep into the earth.

Beside it stood a slender metal pillar, unobtrusive except for the soft blue halo glowing at its crown.

Willow tilted her head toward it. "CitizenEcho?"

He nodded. "One of the early ones, I think. Want to hear it?"

She stepped forward and tapped the top of the pillar. A soft chime sounded. Above the bench, a projection unfolded — first as mist, then slowly sharpening into colour and sound.

"The flood came through here like a freight train. June 2029. You wouldn't believe it if you hadn't seen it. That lake down there? The water surged all the way up here. This bench — it stood right where the flood turned. Waist-high water on this rise. That's how far it reached. Most things were swept away. But not this. A boy slipped in and was carried by the raging water — fast. But he grabbed hold of the side of this bench. Clung to it, half-submerged, until help reached him. That little boy was me."

The image faded to an archival photo: floodwaters curling around the embankment, the path submerged, the bench half-covered but holding firm. Then a newspaper clipping — the boy at the time — and finally the man he became when making the recording.

Willow lowered herself onto the bench, resting a hand on its edge. CitizenEcho had been part of her world since childhood — place-tied layers of memory you could pause to hear or add to yourself. People recorded their stories, others could respond, annotate, build another layer.

"I still use the Aboriginal Civic Record all the time," she said.

paul glanced toward the lake. "That record's one of the best things we ever built together. Memory, but on people's terms — given freely, able to be taken back. No exploitation. Just belonging, held in place," he said. "It gives place texture. You don't just walk through a city anymore — you walk through a chorus. And sometimes... it's enough to sit. To listen. And remember that even a riverbank has history."

They stood quietly. From farther along the bank, another CitizenEcho was activated — a child's voice laughing, recounting the first time they learned to ride a bike beside the lake.

Willow closed her eyes, letting the sound wash over her, recalling her mother and grandfather walking with her on the other side of the lake. Clara gave her a gentle nudge to stay with the moment.

"This place remembers. I remember," she whispered.

paul nodded. "That's the idea. The lake invited us back to land, water, nature—to slow[5] down, just enough in a busy world, to grow."

They moved on, passing the roundhouse café and the kids' amphitheatre, the city humming with activity.

At the next bend, Willow spoke again. "You use the phrase 'upstream thinking[6]' in a lot of your entries."

"Yes."

"What does it mean to you? Beyond metaphor."

paul smiled gently. "It means asking different questions," he said. "Not just what's wrong? — but what's missing? What didn't happen that should have? What support wasn't there before the wheels came off?"

He paused, watching the ripples catch the light. "Upstream thinking is about meeting human needs before they harden into harm — and doing it in ways that respect the limits of the environment. It's early help instead of emergency response. Preventative health instead of just more hospital beds. Stable housing instead of rising prison numbers. It's not soft — it's smart. It costs less in the long run, gives people what they need to thrive, and saves lives along the way."

Willow nodded, letting it settle. "That's a shift in thinking — it wasn't always rewarded."

"No," paul said. "But that shift changed things. Once you think it through — really think it through — you can't unthink it: the logic of prevention, investing early, stopping harm before it starts. It's what people expect from politics I think."

Willow leaned in. "You were an early voice?"

"I wasn't the first, but I staked my whole political career on it," paul said without hesitation. "I put my heart into arguing for upstream thinking — and kind politics."

"I've seen the slogans — 'Interdependent candidate.' 'Fair go.'"

"Took me a few goes," he admitted. "Interdependent was too cute by half. Most people thought I'd misspelled 'independent.' And 'fair go' — as Aussie as it gets — didn't give people enough detail."

"And the 'naked politician' line?"

paul let out a guffaw. "Haven't thought about that in a long time." He grinned. "I was chasing a bit of free media—cheeky way to say my politics were stripped back to basics: simple, no spin, fresh ideas. It was a hook for a book and podcast I was trying to make, not a literal dress code."

Willow laughed. "Didn't catch on?"

"Nope."

"You persisted with the decapitalisation of your name. That kind of became your trademark."

"Inspired by feminist scholar, bell hooks[7], actually—and hardly anyone honoured the request, especially the rules-bound media. But I wanted the spotlight on the ideas, the policies, the issues—not on me."

"Didn't the unique styling do the opposite?"

"Well, yes and no. I wanted people to ask why. To wonder who makes the rules—many we've never questioned—and which ones we should, if we're serious about change."

"You're not talking about your name anymore, are you?"

"No. I wanted people to know I wouldn't automatically accept convention; that I'd swim against the tide if it meant speaking truth to power and building a fairer, more decent world—especially for the most vulnerable."

Willow offered a gentle smile and let his words sink in.

They stopped at a viewing platform. Another school group was arriving — pairs carrying brightly coloured kayaks, even brighter backpacks, their chatter light and easy.

Willow turned to him. "Next week, could we talk about that?" she asked, nodding toward the bridge. "You mentioned it in MemoryLoom – one of the big four investments in the city."

paul nodded. "Yes— and these three here: the City Bridge, the Lake, the Statue — they were game-changers. For the city. For the economy. For our community."

"Same time?"

"Yep," he said, touching the rim of his cap with a quick hat tip.

As she walked away, Willow activated LumenView, the faint chime sounding in her ear. She began scanning his archive again — not for errors, but for signs. Clues. Questions worth chasing.

paul watched her go, then turned back to the lake. Mist from the fountain in the yacht basin shimmered in the sunlight, casting a faint rainbow across the water.

TWO
THE BRIDGE
CONNECTED COMMUNITIES

*"Bridges become metaphors for everything
that connects us."* — Jeanette Winterson[1]

8 February 2064

The February heat rose early over Tamar Lake, but the bridge's midpoint was cooler, shaded by tall solar trees that lined the pedestrian lane like quiet sentinels. Above them, the structure arched in a sweep of smart glass and native climbers, gathering sunlight by day and casting a kaleidoscope of colour over the lake each night.

paul was already seated when Willow arrived, his fingers twitching faintly in the air like he was playing an invisible piano. A slight crease furrowed his brow, lips moving in silent calculation. As she approached, he looked up, offered a mock-serious hat tip — and then glanced back into the middle distance.

"Morning, paul. Uh… are you okay?" Willow asked.

He didn't look up. "Word game thingy. Third guess. Um, I've got this."

She grinned. "You still do that every day?"

He nodded, eyes flicking across the LumenView interface hovering before him. "Every morning. Haven't missed one in fifty years. Longest streak in the Commonwealth."

Willow raised an eyebrow. "That's… oddly impressive."

"Ritual matters," he said simply. "Besides, it reminds me of hangman from primary school. Just fewer chalkboards. And no one dies."

Willow laughed. "Hard to believe we called that a literacy activity."

paul gave a dry smile. "Hard to believe we called half of my childhood 'safe.'"

The word clicked into place. He blinked, dismissed the interface, and finally turned to her.

For a moment, they sat quietly, looking out — south to the Statue, east to the new suburb stretching into the hills, and west to the softened grid of Riverside. Below, paddleboards were already tracing slow circles on the lake.

"You know it turns thirty this year?" paul said, his gaze still on the water.

Willow turned. "What does?"

"The bridge." He tapped the bench beside them. "But it almost never was."

Willow raised an eyebrow, "Show me."

paul activated Synapstra. A faint shimmer crossed his vision as Deep-Seequence spun up, syncing with Willow's contact lenses. The present peeled away.

They were on another bridge—and in another year.

Ahead, a narrow concrete span stitched the Tamar near Pomona Road. No architectural flourish, no lookouts, no paths for bikes or feet—just two lean traffic lanes hemmed by waist-high barriers and the odd road sign rattling in the wind.

A single truck rumbled past. Too heavy, too fast, too close.

"That's it?" Willow asked.

"That's it," paul said quietly.

The scene shifted — Riverside's bottleneck still clogged in peak hour. Traffic choked tight suburban streets never meant for freight. Emergency vehicles crawled. Active transport plans had been shelved. Pedestrians and cyclists were advised to steer clear of the crossing altogether.

At the northern entry ramp, graffiti scrawled across a maintenance box read: "Nice one, Robin."

Willow frowned. "Robin?"

"In this scenario, locals must've given it a nickname," paul said, half-smiling. "It's a pun. The first Tamar crossing was called the Batman Bridge back then. So naturally… Batman and"

"…Robin."

"Exactly. But it's layered. I reckon people felt robbed."

"Robbed of what?"

"Of a real solution. Of vision. Of community voice. In this version of the bridge, cost pressures won. And probably election timing too."

Willow studied the structure in silence. "There's no room for expansion."

"No. Built to minimum spec. Cheap, fast, politically tidy. But not future proof."

The LumenView shimmered, then paused, offering an Avoidable Costs Unit (ACU) summary overlay.

Traffic Reduction: Marginal
Pedestrian Access: Nil
Cycling Access: Prohibited
Economic Benefit: Limited
Public Sentiment: Disappointed
Projected Upgrade Cost (2065): $2.7 billion

Willow winced at the last figure.

"They saved money early... and paid twice later."

"Classic false economy," paul said. "The community warned them."

The overlay faded, and the real lake returned — bright, open, breathing.

Willow stood quietly for a moment, then stepped toward the guard rail — the kind designed to prevent jumps, not just accidents. Her eyes tracked the curve of the shoreline below.

"No one celebrates bridges like that," she said softly.

paul nodded. "That's the thing. Infrastructure isn't just concrete. It's belief. It's what you choose to connect — and who you bother to include."

Willow folded her arms, still processing. "Wow. We really could've been short-changed," she said. "I've known nothing but this bridge — this beautiful bridge. I used to lie down there as a kid and watch the boats pass underneath."

She walked a few steps ahead to one of the glass panels offset from the pedestrian path — large, clear squares that let locals and visitors alike feel like they were walking on water.

paul watched her fondly. "It could've been worse," he said.

Willow glanced at him. "Worse?"

He gave a tight nod. "I'll run the scenario where we never built it at all."

He activated LumenView again. The DeepSeequence shifted.

The lake dimmed.

Launceston re-emerged around them — but smaller, greyer, heavier. A drone of traffic hung in the air. The sky seemed duller, the city slower. The simulation zoomed to ground level, pausing at major arterial routes: the East Tamar Highway, backed up from Landfall to the heart of town; the West Tamar corridor, gridlocked from Legana Primary to Launceston College.

The air shimmered with captured heat. Noise. Frustration.

The 20th century bridges still bore the weight of a growing region. The city had grown — but its infrastructure hadn't.

paul narrated softly as the images played out.

"With no second crossing, there was no relief route. If the community hadn't stamped their feet, the 'We can't afford it. Too hard. Too risky' brigade would've won the day. A second bridge would've slipped from priority... to proposal... to footnote."

The scene zoomed in on Charles Street Bridge. Ambulances crept forward between utes and hatchbacks. A fire truck veered away from peak-hour traffic, rerouted through Invermay to buy minutes it didn't have.

"Transport studies showed that by the late 2030s," paul continued, "emergency response times would've increased by minutes. For fact's sake. Not because we didn't care — but because we didn't act."

Willow turned slowly, taking it in.

Pedestrian counters showed a steady decline. Local businesses reported footfall down 18%. New developments on both the East and West Tamar had stalled. Some freight operators bypassed Launceston altogether, citing delays and unreliability.

Digital ACU overlays appeared across the simulation:

Second Bridge Status: Abandoned (2041)
Projected Cost of Delay: $3.1 billion (cumulative)
CBD Congestion (AM Peak): +42%
Access to Education & Health Services (West Tamar): Declining
Community Satisfaction (Transport): 8%
Public Health Index (Air/Noise Impacts): Deteriorating
Housing Growth (Northern Corridor): Flatlined

Willow exhaled, low and slow.

The simulation lingered a moment longer on the skyline — static, stalled, boxed in by its own caution.

Then, paul shut it down. The LumenView faded. The breeze returned. The lake sparkled.

Willow turned to paul, her eyes wide with renewed perspective. "I can't even imagine Launceston without this bridge," she said. "How much did it cost?"

paul shook his head gently. "Can I reframe your question, Willow? It's not what it cost — it's what we invested... and what it's returned in thirty years."

Willow blinked, then activated her Synapstra.

A moment of silence passed — her gaze unfocused, flickering as she scanned the incoming ACU data stream:

Second Bridge Status: Completed (2034)
Capital Investment: $840 million
30-Year Net Return: $5.4 billion (estimated cumulative economic & social benefit)
CBD Congestion (AM Peak): –36%
Access to Education & Health Services (West Tamar): Improved
Community Satisfaction (Transport): 81%
Public Health Index (Air/Noise Impacts): Improved

Housing Growth (Northern Corridor): +48%
Mode Shift (Active Transport): +61% in bike/pedestrian traffic
Tourism & Civic Engagement: Increased visitation; bridge cited in 1
in 4 Tamar region travel reviews
Energy Offset: Net positive from solar-integrated infrastructure

Willow stood quietly, absorbing the numbers. "So, the bridge was an $800 million investment... but the economic return was five or six times that?"

"That's the splash and ripple effect," paul said. "The splash is the build — workers, materials, immediate jobs. But the ripples? They last for decades. Faster commutes. New businesses. More housing. More tax revenue. And for the first time, residents of the northeastern suburbs had direct access to the better medical and recreational facilities on the western side of the lake."

Willow nodded. "There you go — it wasn't just a bridge."

"No," paul said. "It was belief — made concrete."

They stood together, looking out at the bridge — just taking it in. Proud of what their community had dared to build. A bridge that rose from the water like it had always belonged — a sweeping arc of steel and light, linking the city's future to its forgotten edges.

The alignment solved what decades of plans hadn't. It pulled pressure off the old corridors, opened growth across the Tamar Valley, and stitched together what the river had long kept apart.

But it wasn't just a road. It was a statement.

Four lanes of traffic moved cleanly across its spine — freight, buses, and electric vehicles gliding between east and west. Alongside, a wide, separated corridor offered cyclists and pedestrians their own space, fully integrated with towering solar trees. Their sculptural forms captured sunlight by day and released it by night — illuminating the bridge in stunning colours, telling timeless stories[2] through light. Visitors gathered at dusk just to watch it change.

Inlaid along the pedestrian lane were transparent panels — "walk-on-water" glass — revealing the gentle swirl of the river below. Artists had etched community names, poems, and shared histories into the path. The bridge had become both gallery and gathering place.

And on the inner edge — running quietly, never yet activated — sat the light rail corridor. Future-ready. A promise built into the foundations.

People didn't just cross it. They lingered.

Tourists walked it for the views. Locals jogged it, biked it, met on its landings. Schools brought classes to study its engineering. It was photographed millions of times — the solar canopy beaming across the world, offering Launceston endless moments in the global spotlight.

It was more than infrastructure. It was identity.

The bridge didn't just carry people — it carried belief.

That a regional city could dream big. Build well.

And make connection itself into a landmark.

paul leaned against the rail, watching a first-time visitor pause at the inset glass walkway, hesitate, then skirt the solid edge instead. "Connection isn't just what bridges do," he said quietly. "It's what they mean."

Willow glanced over.

"They remind us that distance isn't permanent. That the gaps between us — between ideas, suburbs, people — can be crossed. If we choose to build."

She hesitated, then leaned in. "Can I ask you something personal?"

paul nodded.

"You wrote about a bridge in your MemoryLoom entries. You didn't mean this one, did you?"

He drew a slow breath. "No, Willow. I meant the people who gave me the foundations to cross any bridge. My parents. A few great teachers. They built me as much as any structure ever did."

Willow smiled. "You wrote beautifully about them."

"I was lucky. Not with money — we had just enough — but with people. Mum was a full-time carer, endlessly generous with her time and love. Dad worked shifts and taught me hard work and problem-solving. Neither had much formal education, but they were whip-smart. They knew the value of school and sacrificed plenty so I could have a chance at a good life through a good public education."

"And the teachers?"

He spoke carefully, almost reverently. "Mrs Hinks, who helped me wrestle with literacy until it became a strength. Mr Denton, who nudged me toward technology when the whole school shared one computer. Mrs Stanley, who showed me that service mattered as much as success. And Mrs Calister, who opened up critical literature and taught me how to read power itself."

"You speak of them like it was yesterday."

"For me, it is. Their lessons haven't aged. That's the power of great teachers — they keep walking beside you, decades later."

Willow tilted her head. "So when you wrote about a bridge... it was a bridge to a good life?"

He smiled, eyes distant. "Exactly. Built out of sacrifice, patience, and belief. Stronger than steel. My parents, my teachers — they helped me find my passion."

Her voice was gentle. "Which was?"

paul didn't hesitate. "The success of every child — especially those from hard places. I wanted to pay it forward, to make a difference the way my mentors once did for me."

He looked out across the lake, then back at her. With a quiet hat tip, he said, "Let's begin there next time."

THREE

THE CHILDREN

EVERY CHILD SUCCEEDS

"There can be no keener revelation of a society's soul than the way in which it treats its children." — Nelson Mandela[1]

20 February 2064

The day was warm and dry, late-summer heat settling like a soft haze over Tamar Lake. As Willow reached the bench, paul rose and tipped his hat. "Let's go!" he said with a smile — his long-retired campaign slogan, a line he'd worn smooth over years.

They began walking the Seaport Loop, their steps unhurried. For a while, neither spoke — just the sounds of children running, climbing, and shouting across Launceston's premier play space – Riverbend Park.

Willow slowed, noticing paul's hands clasped behind his back, his eyes fixed on a small child who had frozen midway across the high ropes: caught between climbing higher or turning back.

She leaned slightly. "You said last time you wanted to pay it forward — to give every child the best start in life, especially the kids from hard places. That was what drove Every Child Succeeds? But it wasn't just another education program, was it?"

paul exhaled, gaze steady on the water. "No. It was born out of resistance. For decades — right up until the late 2020s — a book and training package called Bridges Out of Poverty was everywhere: councils, emergency services, community agencies, even schools. It was sold as insight, but it was deeply flawed[2]. It claimed poverty could be explained by so-called 'hidden rules' — noisy households, poor time management, wrong priorities. It treated every poor person as if they were the same. Homogenised. Broken. It invited readers to naturalise stereotypes — to believe that families in hardship were defective, and that their deficits explained their circumstances."

Willow frowned. "That sounds… demeaning."

"It was worse than demeaning," paul said, his voice tightening. "It was discrimination dressed up as professional development. People of colour were disproportionately depicted as poor, as problems to be corrected, while whiteness was equated with normality and success. It was patronising. As if a two-day workshop, sprinkled with Americanisms about 'old money' and 'new money,' could transform life chances for local kids. It was dishonest."

Willow flicked her LumenView through the archives. "It seemed popular here. Wasn't there evidence behind it that appealed to agencies?"

"Evidence?" paul barked a laugh, sharp and bitter. "For fact's sake — there was none. Just anecdote dressed up as research — no peer review, no credible scholarship. Payne published her own books, sold them through her own company, and built a for-profit training empire on stereotypes. And it was dangerous. Teachers were told to expect less of children in poverty. Service workers were trained to 'correct' families instead of challenging the inequities that trapped them. It shifted responsibility away from systems and onto the most vulnerable."

"Sounds assimilationist and paternalistic," Willow said quietly.

"Spot on. It was a manual on how to 'teach the poor' middle-class manners, speech patterns, and priorities — as if that were the key to mobility. Meanwhile, the real determinants — housing, wages, racism, trauma, broken systems — were ignored. It was uncritical. Self-serving. Pseudo-scholarship. And people bought it — literally. Millions of dollars flowed through Payne's business while whole communities were treated as projects to be fixed."

He shook his head, the edge still sharp in his tone. "That was the line in the sand. No more paternalism. No more snake-oil theories that excused the system and blamed the victim. What we needed was to confront inequity directly — so we built a different approach. One rooted in evidence. Critical theory. Trauma-informed care. Frameworks like Power Threat Meaning. We shifted the gaze from deficits to structures — from 'fixing families' to fixing inequities. From blaming individuals to reshaping the systems that held them back."

Willow looked at him, eyes wide. "And that became Every Child Succeeds?"

He nodded. "Exactly. It was a direct, evidence-informed answer to that prejudiced mindset. Instead of labelling children, we lifted them. Instead of teaching families to perform middle-class respectability, we created the conditions where they could thrive as themselves. Equity. Dignity. Tackling inequality at its roots. That was the promise we tried to keep."

Willow nodded slowly. "You wrote that you'd tried to establish it years earlier but couldn't get traction?"

"Yeah. A bunch of us — early-years professionals, community service workers, neighbours who cared. We'd been pushing ten, maybe fifteen years earlier," paul said, a hint of frustration rising. "Dig around and you'll find the original State of Launceston's Children Report[3]. Not the 2028 one — the very first, around 2014. I was up the front of the bus with that one, Willow. My teams had their hands on the wheel, their hearts in the engine. That was my wheelhouse — trained as a teacher, working with vulnerable kids and families. I was just channeling my passion."

Willow stayed quiet, letting him continue.

"You know what kept me up at night? The data was always there. One in four kids — worse in some suburbs, one in three — not thriving by age five. Falling behind again by high school. And then, predictably, not finishing by eighteen. We tracked it. We reported it. Year after year, the same outcome. No shock. No urgency. Just… inertia. Like someone, somewhere, had decided some kids just weren't meant to make it."

"That's brutal. But… it wasn't personal, right?"

"Wasn't personal?" paul snapped. "It was deeply personal."

"These weren't just 'poor outcomes' on a spreadsheet," paul said, voice tightening. "These were children — kids with chronic health conditions, untreated speech, hearing or dental problems, vision issues that made it hard to read a page. Children battling anxiety and trauma before they even had words for it. Kids starting school hungry, without the language or social skills their peers took for granted. Falling behind in literacy and numeracy and never catching up.

"Children who went without stable housing, who shifted schools three times in a year because the rent was unaffordable. Children who missed out on sport or music because their families couldn't afford the fees or the uniforms. Kids carrying the weight of caring for younger siblings because their parents worked whenever they could pick up a shift.

"By adolescence, too many were disengaging completely — drifting out of school, turning up in youth justice, or self-medicating with alcohol and drugs. They were the ones missing critical health checks, the ones with undiagnosed learning difficulties, the ones sitting in classrooms but not learning.

"They were locked out of further education. Shut out of stable work. Caught in cycles of insecure jobs and insecure housing. And dying younger — sometimes by as much as ten years for Aboriginal community members[4] — from illnesses that should have been preventable. Worst of all, their children were set to inherit the same fate."

He shook his head. "We had brilliant people in schools, in neighbourhood houses, in frontline roles — doing heroic work. But as a city? As a state? As a system? We let it happen. We acted like postcode was destiny. Like the birth lottery was a legitimate policy setting."

Willow frowned. "But you pushed for change. You built programs. You didn't give up."

He exhaled, sharp. "Yeah — but for too long we were downstream. Triage. Crisis response. Patch and repeat. That's failure demand[5], Willow. The costs we rack up because the system fails in the first place. Costs that should never have existed. Avoidable costs.

"Every time a child drifts out of school, every time someone is pushed onto income support for life, we spend far more than it would have cost to prevent the harm. Economists in the 2020s put the average lifetime social-security bill at more than two hundred thousand dollars per person — and up to six hundred thousand for those with complex support needs across their lives. Six hundred thousand, before you even count the extra load on hospitals, courts, and child protection[6]." He held her gaze. "And that's just the fiscal ledger. The human cost — the suffering — is worse."

He tapped his temple with one finger as they walked.

"Now picture this: take just a fraction of that money and invest it upfront. Give that child what they actually need to thrive. They do well in school. They step into decent work. They pay taxes. They contribute. That small investment is returned a dozen times over — and the system saves the six hundred grand it would otherwise burn reacting to failure. That's the difference, Willow — between Payne's snake-oil and the Launceston Promise. Between empty aspiration and practical sense. Between charity... and justice."

He softened, but the fire stayed in his eyes. "The tragedy was the buy-in wasn't there. Not early enough. Too many kept calling prevention 'unaffordable,' while quietly signing off on the even bigger bill for failure."

"Some pilots limped along. But the full vision — what we modeled on collective impact initiatives like Harlem Children's Zone[7] and Wrap-around Milwaukie[8] — never got the scale it needed. Not in the 2010s. Not in the '20s. The politics just didn't match the evidence. You could get quasi-city deal of $130 million for an elite sports facility upgrade without blinking. But ask for that kind of money to break intergenerational poverty?" He laughed without humor. "Suddenly it's: 'Let's do seven feasibility studies.'"

Willow frowned. "You needed a City Deal for kids."

"Exactly." He smiled. "With $260 million from the first City Deal we rebuilt the central city streetscape. Revamped Civic Square. Moved the university. Built the beautiful Riverbend Park. All good — but what if we'd put the same energy behind every vulnerable child? Imagine if that had been our infrastructure priority. Imagine where we'd be now — two, three generations later."

He slowed, breath catching in the wind. "I was angry then. And I'm still upset. Because our delay cost lives. It cost futures."

Willow paused, then turned toward him. "But something changed, didn't it? You made progress. I know you did. I've seen it myself."

"I'm glad you have," paul said. "Because we finally found the courage to go where we'd never gone before — to tackle intergenerational disadvantage at its roots. To be bold, to be ambitious. We dared to succeed."

He looked out across the lake toward the city's outer suburbs. "It took a shared commitment. A twenty-year financial deal. Co-designed. Community-led. Evidence-based. A real promise — not just words — that every child would be backed. Every single one. Every single time."

Willow triggered Synapstra, the overlay of datasets, clippings, and academic citations unfolding in her LumenView as she walked. She filtered for outcomes of Launceston's Every Child Succeeds initiative, tracing its arc from 2028 onwards.

A gust off the lake lifted her hair, the shimmer of data overlaying water and sky.

The first layer opened from the tenth State of Launceston's Children Report, 2060. She clicked into the section titled Cradle-to-Career Continuum. Numbers pulsed before her: nine in ten children entering kindergarten assessed as school-ready by age five. It marked a dramatic shift from the years before the reforms, when barely six in ten reached that milestone. Launceston had forged a strategy that pushed it well above the national norm for cities of similar socio-economic profile.

Another headline flashed: High school completion surged. From the late 2030s onwards, nearly every eighteen-year-old in Launceston — including those from the northern suburbs — finished Year 12, and more than nine in ten went on to tertiary study or skilled apprenticeships. Willow cross-checked the peer-reviewed citations: for two generations now, Launceston's public school outcomes had stood shoulder-to-shoulder with the best in the nation. Doors once closed to young people had been thrown wide open.

Scrolling further, she paused at the section tagged Post-School Navigation. Since 2035, five hundred of Tasmania's most vulnerable students had been supported into university or TAFE each year; scholarship funds leveraged had climbed past $200 million across two decades — and was higher again once matched contributions from employers offering earn-and-learn pathways were counted. She blinked — all of it seeded by the "City Deal for Kids," the long-term tri-partite funding pact. Scaled further through Social Impact Bonds[9] that tied financing to results, Tasmania's ambition for every young person was paying dividends year after year — for investors, yes, but far more importantly for the students themselves. And even at Tasmania's smaller scale, the queue of ethical investors never ran dry.

Somewhere nearby a child laughed, the sound cutting through the web of statistics.

The place-based saturation map drew her eye: concentric rings of service hubs around child and family learning centres, schools, early learning centres, health clinics, and youth centres. Three out of four children and young people in Launceston engaged with at least one program each year. The pattern was unmistakable — international evidence showed that saturation at this level marked the tipping point. Willow smiled. This wasn't just borrowed rhetoric. The numbers proved it: saturation wasn't theory; it was lived reality.

Finally, she opened the longitudinal summary. By 2060, the income gap between Launceston's north and the rest of the city had more than halved; intergenerational welfare reliance had dropped by over 80 percent; teen pregnancy and youth offending had fallen to historic lows. Achievement gaps in maths were closed, and halved in English. Researchers confirmed a significant and sustained narrowing across class and postcode.

Willow kept walking, the shimmer of LumenView overlaying the sounds around her — children calling encouragement across the ropes course, gulls lifting from the shoreline, paul's steady steps matching her own on the gravel path. What began as a trawl for evidence now felt like watching history unfold in numbers. These weren't abstract statistics — they were proof the city had bent its trajectory. Launceston had taken international best-practice models, refined them, stretched them across its own soil, and written its own success story.

Her eyes fluttered as she continued to scroll LumenView. "There it is — Rumbles Quest[10]. I remember playing it, I just couldn't recall the name."

paul grinned. "That was the first domino. We started using this gami-fied survey software with kids in public schools. Then expanded city-wide. It gave teachers immediate insight into their students' wellbeing — and gave the city a map, anonymized and aggregated, of how six-to-twelve-year-olds were really doing."

"We built programs around real need — not guesswork," he added. "We tracked progress with Results-Based Accountability[11]. We learned what worked — and what didn't."

Willow nodded, scrolling further. "Says it ran for almost twenty years."

"Eventually replaced by something better," paul said. "But it sparked a collective impact movement[12] — grounded in evidence, not charity. And yeah, it was a significant investment. But the return? It made economic sense."

Willow squinted at the figures. "Looks like every dollar spent returned more than four — and severe childhood obesity and chronic asthma presentations down more than thirty percent. Youth justice referrals cut by sixty-five percent across the city."

"Those in power knew the economics long before I was rabbiting on about it," paul said. "James Heckman[13] spelled it out back in 1999 — invest early, stay the course, and the returns are enormous. And yet it took us another three decades to ditch Payne's nonsense and finally listen."

He slowed his pace. "That was the Launceston Promise. Not a pamphlet. A pact. From birth to a good job — or even before birth — we backed every child. With dignity. With consistency. No wrong doors. We pooled funds. We built wraparound models. We anchored hubs led by locals."

His eyes brightened with memory. "I saw a kid suspended three times go on to become school captain. I saw teen parents finish Year 12 because someone finally believed in them. I saw schools become second homes — safe, warm, alive. We supported the state to establish innovative new models too — like your own alma mater, Change-maker High."

Then he stopped and looked directly at Willow. "The problem was never the kids. Never. It was the system. And we bent the curve in their favour."

Willow's expression tightened as new headlines flickered in her LumenView. "I can see you had plenty of opposition," she muttered. "Even when the harm was falling away. MemoryLoom shows you had some pretty fierce critics."

He paused, then: "I'd stand my ground again. The evidence was compelling then. Still is."

Willow kept scrolling, filtering fragments of old news reports and op-eds.

"Opponents said if you give people support, they'll stop trying — that welfare just breeds dependency."

"Nope," paul shot back, slipping easily into the rhythm of a familiar defense. "Most people don't want handouts — they want a fair go. Support helps them get back up, not stay down."

"What about the bludgers? The rorters? The ones gaming the system?" Willow asked, her tone light with disbelief.

"Fraud rates were tiny. Always have been. The bigger cheats wore suits, not track pants. People just wanted dignity — not punishment."

"Some said, 'It's their own fault. Bad choices. Bad habits...'"

"Wrong. No child chooses poverty. Most adults didn't either. It was trauma, racism, insecure jobs, low pay, no safety net — that's the real setup."

She tilted her head. "And the ones who said it was too expensive — that taxpayers were footing the bill for someone else's poor choices?"

paul leaned forward. "The math was clear. We couldn't afford not to act. Prevention saved money. The real waste was waiting until people broke. And the real injustice was thinking you could punish someone into wellbeing."

Willow raised an eyebrow. "What about the classic — 'Just get a job'?"

"Sure," paul said. "If it's safe, pays the rent, and fits around caring for kids or elders. And never forget — unpaid carers are working."

"And the one about free stuff killing ambition?"

He grimaced. "Stability fuels ambition. Being unhoused and hungry never helped anyone concentrate."

Willow leaned back, arms crossed. "Last one. Some people reckoned the poor were just... different. Like there was a whole underclass."

paul shook his head. "The only real difference was luck. Don't kid yourself — most people were one sick kid or rent hike away from needing help."

He let it hang there, just long enough.

"I could do this all day. But here's the thing: we were all in—no excuses. It wasn't just the right thing; it was the smart thing. Healthier kids learn better. Better learners get better jobs. Better jobs pay better. Better pay lifts the economy. Stronger economies build stronger communities."

He paused, then added softly, "And upstream investment? Every dollar saved four downstream. More than that—it gave people their lives back. It was kind policy."

Willow smiled. "My mum was the first in our family to graduate uni," she said, voice catching slightly. "She's proof." She glanced toward the playground. "I'm proof."

paul smiled, pride in his eyes. "You're proof, squared. That's the beauty—this stuff compounds. Like interest, but better. Not just dollars in a bank; lives transformed."

Willow's gaze lingered on the children playing nearby. "Mum got into the care-workforce pathway," she said. "She started with a Certificate, then finished the Diploma and kept going to train as a registered nurse. She always said she wouldn't have made it without the early support—without someone seeing her as more than a tired kid with a struggling dad."

paul turned to her, voice quieter now. "That's the bit people miss. It's not just the kids. Families rise with them."

Their walk circled past the ropes course. Willow touched paul's elbow. The same child from earlier was back on the high ropes, cheeks streaked with the stubborn shine of almost-tears. Below, a parent called up, steady as a metronome: "One step at a time. I've got you."

The child hovered, toes searching for a hold that felt like certainty. A hand from the ground didn't lift them; a voice did. "That's it. Left foot. Yes—now move your right."

paul exhaled, the fight returning to his shoulders. "People said this work was too ambitious, too expensive, too early," he said, almost to himself. "They called it overreach. They said 'resilience' like it was a substitute for scaffolding." He shook his head. "Resilience isn't leaving kids on the wire and hoping. It's building supports—the scaffold; surrounding them with caring adults who can help them take the next step."

Above them, the child edged forward—one small move, then another —until the small body uncoiled into motion. The wobble didn't vanish; it was mastered. "You're doing great," the parent called. "Again."

paul's voice settled into its familiar, flinty calm. "The chorus was always the same: wait, trim, test, prove it first. My answer was the same too: children get the first dollar, not the leftover dollar. We don't lower the course to meet them; we build the scaffold, we address the inequity, we raise the net."

A breath later, the child reached the top and slapped the post—half triumph, half disbelief. A whoop from below startled two gulls; the parent laughed and clapped. The child looked down, eyes bright with the shock of having done it, and waved.

Willow saw the corner of paul's mouth lift.

"That," he said, nodding upward, "is policy in real life: a patient adult, a safe system, the next foothold named out loud. No child left frozen halfway because we were too timid to build the way across."

They watched the careful descent, the last jump, the fierce hug — then turned back to the path.

"A person's a person, no matter how small[14]," paul murmured.

"Dr. Seuss?" Willow tilted her head.

Another faint smile. "Some truths don't age, Willow."

He walked a few steps, then turned to her. "That's what drives me: building a fairer system — a healthier, happier, more liveable place. Not just help after things go wrong, but the right help, at the right time, for what matters. Keep people well. Lift early. That's the work."

paul touched the brim — real or imagined — and dipped it her way. "Every child succeeds," he said. "Not as a slogan — as a standard."

Willow nodded—then, for the first time, tipped her lid in return.

As they walked on, a sun shower drifted in, thin as gauze, bright in the low light. The first drops freckled the path; then, as the rain thickened, rain-activated art[15] bloomed beneath their feet.

"I absolutely love this part of the park," Willow said.

Colour woke under their feet. From the wet path, butterflies lifted — cobalt, lemon, cherry — wings mid-beat as if the surface were about to fly. Flowers opened in neat bursts of coral and green. Vines threaded the edges. Kids squealed and chased the painted trail.

"This is what I mean," paul said quietly. "Design that meets you where you are. Even the rain gets to be useful."

"It's joyful," Willow said. "And it's public. No ticket required."

They followed the butterflies along the curve, footsteps soft in the new shine. As the shower moved on, the colors began to fade back into plain concrete, but the lift in the air stayed with them. They walked on, light and unhurried, the path still bright in their minds.

FOUR
THE PLEDGE
HEALTHY TOGETHER

"Our only goal is to live longer and live better — to outlive."
— Peter Attia[1]

2 March 2064

It was the first week of autumn — though in Tasmania, this was often the warmest part of the year. The air carried a golden haze, and Tamar Lake lay unruffled, a sheet of light broken only where the breeze worried the edges. Near the meeting bench, paul stood in his hat and sunglasses, ready for their walk, watching the recreated beach where families spread towels and kids engineered moats in the sand.

Willow's footsteps crunched along the path. She slowed when he didn't turn. "You okay? You look a little distracted."

Without taking his eyes off the sandy embankment, he answered dead-pan, "No, this is my resting beach face."

Willow groaned, then laughed despite herself. "Have you been saving that?"

paul finally tipped the brim in greeting and glanced her way. "Morning, Willow."

"Morning."

They fell in beside each other, the lake to their right, the small beach alive with squeals and splashes. Conversation found its usual rhythm as they set off, the kind that clicks back in like a well-worn path.

A little further on, Willow stopped in front of a sculpture that caught the morning light. Three metres tall, built from glass and chrome, it seemed to bend and warp as though something once solid was surrendering to heat. At first glance, it resembled a giant set of bathroom scales, but stood upright, balanced precariously on a melting corner. The base, a puddle of distorted chrome, hinted at the weight that had once pressed down — the burden a city had learned to shed.

A large flat faceplate invited passers-by to pause and catch their reflection — to see themselves in the transformation. It was part artwork, part mirror, part memory.

The inscription at its base was simple: The City That Lost 500,000kg.

"So, it's true then?" she asked, teasing. "You were the driver behind the City Pledge?"

paul laughed, softly. "I might have been up the front of the bus on this one Willow. We were facing an obesity time bomb[2]. We pledged two outcomes: more movement, less loneliness. But that's not quite the full story."

She turned, curious. "But it worked, right? Steps, stories, shout-outs. Whole suburbs competing. People actually got healthier -together."

He nodded, then paused before answering. "Yes, that bit did work. But not because of slogans or leaderboards. What made it work was the part that few really understood at the time."

Willow raised an eyebrow.

paul tapped gently on the sculptural base. "Before we became the city that moved, we became the city that listened. That measured. That paid attention."

He paused again, more serious now.

"It started with a survey. Purposeful and authentic. A carefully designed survey that asked the right questions. And as a council we positioned ourselves to actually listened to the answers."

Willow tilted her head. "So... not just weight loss and steps?"

"No," paul replied. "The Preventative Health Survey[3] – it ran for three maybe four cycles before it was folded into CivicLoom — but every three years we asked thousands of residents how they were doing. Physically. Mentally. Socially. Did they feel safe? Were they lonely? Were they eating well? Did they have time to play, space to move, anyone to call on?"

He shifted slightly, watching a school group pass by. "It wasn't perfect data. But it was honest. And it helped us see patterns we'd never mapped before — postcode by postcode, street by street. We paired it with the other survey data, from Rumble's Quest, for kids under 12 too. Ultimately, what got assessed finally got addressed."

Willow was quiet, then murmured: "So the weight loss stuff... that came after?"

paul nodded. "The weight campaign made headlines. But the survey made change. It shaped where we put parks. Where we built courts. Where we lit walking tracks or funded tai chi in shopping centres. It gave permission for council to care about things we used to think belonged to hospitals."

He smiled wryly. "We had a good look at what worked elsewhere[4]. We had grounded our plan in evidence. And we got creative and — made it ours."

Willow slowed as they reached a shaded bench, the plaza quiet behind them. "So where did this all come from?" she asked. "The upstream thinking. The weight loss campaign. The obsession with survey data."

paul smiled, then sat down slowly, stretching one leg out. "It started long before politics. I trained as a health and phys ed teacher. That was the first time I realised that health isn't just about diet charts or gym drills. It's about what surrounds you[5] — your housing, your income, your sense of belonging."

He paused, more thoughtful now. "And I spent a lot of time listening to kids. Really listening. Their stories told you more than any hospital data set. If a child was too tired to learn, too anxious to join in, or didn't have shoes for sport — that was health data too."

Willow nodded. "So it wasn't just about getting people to move more."

"No," paul said. "It was about dignity. About what it takes to live well. About giving people the conditions to thrive. And if you're lucky enough to sit on council, or in government, then you have a democratic obligation to act on what you hear."

He leaned forward slightly. "It's not enough to collect feedback and file it away. If people trust you with their truth, then you owe them action — not just a nod. That means targeting dollars well. Funding what works. Scaling what matters. And doing it all with a bit of humility and a lot of kindness."

Willow smiled. "So that's your secret? Data, dignity, and upstream kindness?"

paul laughed. "Sounds like a weird tattoo, but yes. That's the heart of it."

Willow leaned back, watching a pair of toddlers chase each other across the grass near the footpath. "You know," she said slowly, "in my political theory class last semester, we talked about governance as systems of control — rules, compliance, regulation. But this..." She gestured toward the lake, the plaza, the court nearby. "This feels more like stewardship. Like care."

paul didn't interrupt.

Willow continued, more animated now. "You took health — which most governments treat as someone else's job — and made it local. Not through mandates or fear campaigns, but through listening. Investing where it counts. Building trust."

She looked over at him. "And the crazy thing is, it worked."

paul smiled. "You sound surprised."

She laughed. "I am. I know the long history of top-down policy approaches — national, bureaucratic, usually reactive. But this... this feels personal. Placed. Democratic in the truest sense. People spoke. Our city leaders responded."

Then, after a beat: "So leadership is partly the act of asking good questions and what? - staying long enough to listen."

paul gave a big nod, eyes still on the lake. A light breeze stirred the reeds along the edge. "Not that hard to grasp really," he said quietly. "Honestly, the hard work is in the follow up and follow through. The real credit on this one belongs to the council — not just the elected members, but the officers who did the work behind the scenes. The data analysts who turned spreadsheets into insight. The health planners who saw possibility, not just problems. The community development teams who knew every face, every postcode."

He paused. "And the community — they didn't just answer the survey. They kept showing up. To consultations. To workshops. To the smallest walking group on the coldest Tuesday morning."

He turned to Willow. "That's the thing about this kind of work. If it's done well, no one remembers who started it. They just remember that something changed — and they felt part of it."

He leaned back slightly. "What matters is that we listened. Then we moved."

Willow grinned. "Okay. Can we talk about it now?"

paul raised an eyebrow.

"The campaign," she pressed. "The City That Lost 500,000 Kilos. The step trackers. The leaderboards. The suburb challenges. You can't tell me that wasn't your idea."

He smiled—slow, a little sheepish. "It was never meant to be that big. We started with one question: how do we make health collective, not just personal? The weight-loss line—catchy, sure—was just the hook."

"And people bought in."

"They did," paul said. "Streets formed walking groups. Workplaces added movement breaks. Schools turned steps into maths problems. Every suburb had a pedometer scoreboard outside the local shop."

"The HMI is still taught at school, you know. I keep it in mind," Willow said.

"I'm glad. We had to make it simple enough to stick. It was originally called the Launceston Heart–Move Index[6] — L-HMI! Either way, it was a masterstroke from the community development and comms teams: average daily steps divided by average daily heart rate. Wearables did the measuring; a bit of easy maths gave you your score."

"Score of 100–149 is the green zone," Willow recited. "I'm still there! I want to reach 150+ and stay in the gold—maybe after I finish my thesis."

"It was the people in the red, scoring less than 60, and amber zone, 61-99, who made the biggest gains," paul said. "Another 1,500–2,000 steps a day nudged them towards that magic 100. And, just like cricket—everyone wanted a century. Simple, motivating, and it used the data on their wrist or phone."

"Sounds like you're proud of that one?"

He nodded. "Yeah. We started by listening—and scaled what was already working, like Active Launceston and parkrun."

"What do you mean?"

"parkrun was growing, but not everyone knew about it or could get there. So we lowered barriers: small subsidies and help with transport. We pushed new parkrun sites to transport-poor suburbs and funded the Tail Walker role—so nobody finished last. KindraPass and social prescribing made it easier later, but even then, we tipped in seed funding."

"Results?"

"On a few fronts—more participants, and plenty who found their tribe as volunteers. Running or walking wasn't for them, but the hi-vis and helping out became the social highlight of the week."

"What else?"

"Rolling Active Launceston programs into the outer suburbs was a hit."

Willow opened LumenView, searched "Active Launceston," and flicked through the clips. She paused on a video titled Walking Football.

"What's this?"

paul laughed. "That was big for a while. Modified rules—no running, no contact—on school ovals. It kept older adults moving together, and the post-game chat was non-negotiable."

She scrolled again: photos of yoga and tai chi outside the Palestra on the lake foreshore, and activation sessions using the equipment under the pavilion roof.

"They were called Seniors' Exercise Parks?"

"Yep—co-designed with older residents," paul said. "Balance, strength, and social ties. GPs loved referring people."

"So social prescribing helped?"

"Definitely. Like rocket fuel. GPs loved referring to the Seniors' Exercise Parks—balance, strength, conversation. When the Social Impact

Bond trial let doctors prescribe a gym membership and covered the fee, participation jumped again."

Willow tapped into grainy footage of Launceston's Open Street Days—CBD streets closed on Sundays, people moving and playing where cars usually ruled. Dancing, buskers, markets, kids everywhere.

"Oh, I remember these—roads blocked off, chalk everywhere, dancing till I collapsed."

"They ran in the suburbs too—PlayStreets," paul said. "Council handled closures, insurance, even roving entertainers. Locals just brought chairs—and each other. We did the bump-in and bump-out; the community had the party."

"And got to know each other?"

"Bingo." paul smiled. "Once momentum built, council chipped in for regular street BBQs, and locals coordinated their own block."

He paused. "We had no trouble making the 30 km/h Slow Streets permanent. Locals practically demanded them—so they could use streets as places again."

Willow swiped to an image of a conga line of kids walking to school, parents chatting at the tail, then closed LumenView. "Did all this happen at once?"

"It was contagious," he said. "One suburb got something going; the next asked for the same. It snowballed."

"The competitive spirit kicked in," Willow teased.

"It sure did. In just the first two years, the city logged more than 120 billion steps."

"Billion?" Willow raised an eyebrow.

"Yes — over 40,000 people joined in at some point of the campaign. The headline was something like a hundred trips to the Moon and back," paul said.

"Hundred and twenty-five," Willow corrected, fact-checking in real time.

paul waved it off with a grin. "Anyway... hospital data showed modest drops in obesity-related admissions. But the bigger shift? People moved — together. For the first time, movement wasn't punishment. It was pride."

Willow paused. "And after the 500,000 kilos?"

paul smiled. "We stopped counting weight. Started measuring strength. Sleep. Connection. It became about quality of life."

She turned back to the path. "Still," she said, "it started something."

paul nodded. "It got the city moving. That was the point—not just our bodies, our mindset."

"So mental health improved too?" Willow asked.

"Well, social isolation and loneliness were just as pressing as inactivity."

She grinned. "Let me guess—another data point?"

paul nodded. "The 2032 survey showed one in four residents felt lonely. It jumped to nearly two in five among older men and full-time carers. We knew isolation was dangerous—on par with major risk factors[7]—but we hadn't acted at scale."

"So you did?"

"We funded connection like we fund roads. Morning teas, walking groups, story clubs, even the intergenerational mentoring program— slow to start, but it worked."

Willow laughed. "Like what we're doing right now?"

paul shrugged. "Loneliness wasn't just a feeling. It was a public health risk. We treated it like one."

"Another favourite was the on-Country activities that opened after the State returned land to the Aboriginal community," he added. "The

Guided Walks program was brilliant. That, and establishing Thera-peutic Gardens, wove movement in nature with cultural learning."

Willow's thought caught up with her: maybe this is what policy looks like up close—chalk dust, borrowed trestles, names learned on the nature strip.

They sat for a moment on a low stone bench at the edge of the plaza, the mid-morning sun casting long slants of light across the court. Chil-dren's laughter carried from the playground, punctuated by the soft thump of a basketball drifting wide.

Willow turned slightly. "Do you ever think about what you'd do differently?"

paul didn't pause. "Food," he said. "Access to healthy food. We didn't move fast enough."

Willow nodded, thoughtful.

"We built paths, funded programs, lit courts. Got the city walking, even dancing. But too many people were still skipping meals. Too many parents choosing between petrol and groceries. We should've treated food like infrastructure."

He paused, then added more quietly, "We talked about dignity a lot. But hunger — that's the sharp edge of indignity."

Willow looked at him. "So... what stopped you?"

He exhaled. "Politics. Budgets. Maybe fear of getting it wrong. I don't know. But if I had another run at it, I'd start with the soil."

She raised an eyebrow. "The soil?"

He touched two fingers to an invisible brim and smiled. "Come back next week—I'll show you the garden that changed my mind."

FIVE
THE GARDENS
GROWING SLOW

"The best time to plant a tree was thirty years ago.
The second best time is now." — Unknown[1]

19 March 2064

Willow spotted him from twenty metres out: paul, head bobbing slightly, shoulders loose, hands relaxed. His eyes were half-closed behind the lenses, the ghost of a smile at the edges.

She sat beside him. "Morning. Clara got you on a meditation? Rain sounds?"

He cracked a big grin, tipped an imaginary brim. "Midnight Oil, actually."

Willow raised her brows. "Wasn't expecting that — and that is definitely... not rain."

"Depends on the song," he said. "Earth and Sun and Moon[2] — it's about cycles, renewal. Felt right for a day about propagating, planting, produce, and, people.[3]"

She laughed, trying to keep the alliteration going. "Perfect, paul — please proceed past the pergola, along the pollinator path, to the permaculture plots."

He stood, still laughing. "Not bad. Let's Go! Let's talk soil, shade, and supper."

They set off along the shoreline path, the city humming around them. As they neared the entrance to Republic Park — once known as Royal Park, a name now mostly remembered by those with grey in their hair — Willow paused beneath a majestic Swamp Cypress triggering the CitizenEcho:

> "Trees are elegant, masterful, life-supporting systems. They make oxygen, sequester carbon, fix nitrogen, distill water, create sugars and foods, change colour with the seasons, and self-replicate[4]. This Swamp Cypress is 128 years, 11 months, and 14 days old. One day it will fall to the ground — and become soil again."

Willow stood quietly for a moment, letting the words settle. She glanced at paul, a wry comment on the tip of her tongue about him being as old as the tree — the kind of thing she would have said without hesitation to her grandfather.

Clara chimed in gently, "Humour's a lovely bridge, Willow — but maybe this time, let the silence speak. paul's a good listener — especially when you need someone to truly hear you."

Willow let the moment pass, saying nothing.

paul looked at the tree, then at her, and grinned. "Beautiful specimen. I planted it myself... back in 1836." He gave a mock-serious nod, as if recalling the day in detail.

Willow half-smiling, half-shaking her head, muted Clara for 60 minutes. A small glyph at the edge of her vision dimmed. Then she gestured for paul to join her at the wide stone entrance, where bursts of greenery spilled across the path like an unrolled welcome.

"The garden's bigger than when I was here last," she noted.

"And louder," paul added, as the chatter of families and the clatter of garden tools filtered through the trees.

Just ahead, a young boy climbed into a wheelbarrow, feet poking out one end, giggling as he pretended to lather himself with imaginary soap.

"Bath time!" he shouted to no one in particular, before tipping over sideways in a tangle of limbs and laughter.

paul slowed. His eyes followed the boy, then drifted — aflicker of memory passed over paul's face — one of those images that lives longer than it should. He was caught by something deep inside.

His father, in worn overalls, lying in the wheelbarrow in the middle of his childhood home's veggie patch. Work boots still on. A Polaroid captured it once — tired eyes, the morning sun low behind him. Just home from night shift. Just happy to be there.

The ache arrived before he could stop it.

Clara pulsed gently. *"Would you like to sit with this for a moment?"*

paul acknowledged the message and then let the quiet settle.

Sometimes, memory wasn't about words. It was about staying long enough to feel the love inside the loss.

Then smiling, almost to himself. "Now that barrow reminds me of a photo I haven't seen in years," he said.

Willow tilted her head. "Of what?"

"My dad," paul replied. "After night shift. Still in his overalls, dead tired. Laid out in the wheelbarrow — hands behind his head, boots dangling, grinning at the sky like he'd finally made it to paradise."

Willow grinned. "That sounds like a good dad."

paul's eyes softened. "He was. Taught me a lot about gardening, building, taking pride in your handy work. And about stopping to rest when it's earned."

They continued along the winding path, dappled sunlight catching the edge of a scarecrow — someone's child had dressed it in a commemorative Tassie Devils jumper, celebrating last year's back-to-back AFL premierships.

Willow glanced sideways. "Was your garden like this?"

paul smiled softly. "Yeah. My childhood garden in George Town — nothing fancy, but it had balance. One third for the house — a modest little eight-squares. One third for lawn and backyard cricket — my friends called it the 'M-C-G': Mallett Cricket Ground. And about a third fenced off for the garden and orchard."

"A veggie patch and an orchard?" Willow said, surprised. "Nice."

paul nodded.

"'Pink Lady' and 'Lady in the Snow' apples, raspberries, pumpkins, carrots, and heaps of beans — runner beans, yellow beans, broad beans. And peas — we'd pod them at the kitchen table and talk... Oh, and we had a plum tree that shaded the chook pen. It grew so much fruit that we'd interrupt our summer fishing trips at the lakes just to come back and harvest.

Mum would bottle tonnes of plums in jars. We didn't think it was anything special. It was just what you did."

Willow looked around at the kids playing near the apple trees. "Was that common back then?"

"Absolutely," paul said. "Every second backyard had something growing. Even rental places had a patch. Gardens were practical. Shared. You swapped pumpkins over fences."

Willow frowned slightly. "So what changed?"

paul exhaled, looking out toward the lake. "I don't know… We lost a few things. Intergenerational knowledge for one. Fewer kids learned how to grow stuff — schools stopped teaching it, parents got too busy. But the big shift? Housing. Prices went up. Land shrank. Took two full-time incomes just to service the mortgage, and house sizes grew – they swallowed the block. No time, no space. No garden."

Willow was quiet a moment, then asked: "Have you been back? To your old place?"

paul nodded, slowly. "Yep. The old shed and the cricket pitch and the veggie patch? Gone a long long time ago. Three units have been on that block for decades. Not a garden in sight."

Willow winced. "That must've felt strange."

"It did," paul said. "But it also reminded me why we fought for community gardens — urban food forests, edible playgrounds. So kids today — kids like you once were — didn't have to be lucky to have green space and a full belly. We tried to make it normal to be free range[5] again."

Willow smiled, watching them. "You know… I never thought about these gardens when I was growing up," she said. "They were just… there. Like footpaths. Or a set of swings. Every neighbourhood had one."

She plucked a leaf of mint and rolled it between her fingers.

"We didn't think of it as a program or policy or anything. It was just part of how a suburb worked. You'd meet your friends, pick your favourite fruit, run around. Someone's dad would be pruning, some-one's nan would be dropping off cuttings. It wasn't special. It just *was*."

paul chuckled. "That's the magic of upstream thinking. When it works, the problem never arrives. You got fresh fruit, daily exercise, a social hub — and no one had to invent a program to 'tackle childhood obesity' or 'build community resilience'. The garden *was* the interven-tion — and it didn't feel like one."

Willow nodded slowly, thoughtful now. "And it didn't need much looking after, either. Just… happened."

paul smiled. "Once the garden was in, the community carried it. Not council. That was the point. Ownership. Pride. People thought it would be vandalised, poisoned, stolen from — I heard it all."

He shook his head, eyes narrowing slightly in memory. "But when was the last time you saw someone vandalise a telegraph pole? Seriously. I argued, back then, that we had to stop peddling in fear. That policy should be built on trust in the *best* of our people — not suspicion of the worst."

Willow leaned back, letting the sunlight filter through the canopy overhead. "Well… you were right."

paul raised an eyebrow. "Say that again?"

She grinned. "Don't push it."

Willow thoughts drift for a moment, before: "Still. I'm glad I grew up thinking they were just part of life. That means someone upstream did their job."

paul gave a faint, thoughtful nod. "Well, that's how it ended up. But it wasn't how it started. In the beginning, the gardens were mostly seen as a fix for poverty — a way to stretch tight budgets and ease food insecurity."

"A bit of a Band-Aid solution?" Willow asked.

"Exactly," he said. "But that was just the seed. What grew was something far more powerful."

Willow looked up, curious.

"They became social spaces," paul continued. "Not just plots of soil — but places where people actually gathered. Social pathways. As normal and expected as a letterbox or playground. From East Launceston to Ravenswood, you could smell the earth, hear compost bin chatter, see fruit trees so heavy with fruit they needed propping."

Willow smiled. "So it wasn't just about food anymore."

"No," he said. "The food was the invitation. But what we really culti-vated was trust."

They turned a corner where an older man was showing a young girl how to save seeds from a pod.

"Elders passing on knowledge beside kids. Recipes shared across languages. Former refugees planting things they hadn't seen since childhood, offering them to neighbours they didn't yet know. The gardens blurred all the lines."

"We built the gardens," Willow said softly, "and they built us."

paul nodded. "And that mattered more than ever when new commu-nities arrived. When the world felt like it was pulling people apart, Launceston chose to do the opposite. We made room to meet — on our knees, in the dirt, under fruit trees and sunflowers."

Willow glanced up at a ripe peach hanging overhead. "The fruit fed our bodies," she said.

paul smiled. "And the conversations fed our humanity."

They rested for a moment on a low stone wall at the edge of the garden — a semicircle of raised beds brimming with herbs, fruit trees, and autumn pumpkins. A sparrow warbled nearby as a group of kids darted between the citrus trees, laughing, pockets full of mandarins.

"Did you ever think it'd work this well then?" she asked.

paul gave a slow nod. "Yeah… but it wasn't guaranteed. The idea nearly died in committee half a dozen times. A small group had to argue hard to get it into the City Deal for Kids. That was the chance."

"Wasn't that funding meant for, like… the 'poor' suburbs?" Willow asked, air quoting.

paul sighed. "Exactly. That was the bloody 'Bridges Out of Poverty frame' — a deficit frame. Fix the broken bits. But the group pushed back. We argued, if you want long-term impact, you don't just plant a garden for the postcode that's struggling. You create *norms*. Make it something every child expects to see when they walk out the door. So we got clever."

Willow's eyes lit up. "What'd you do?"

paul smirked. "The city bought in bulk. Timber, compost, fruit trees.

Said it was more 'efficient' that way. And it was — technically.

But really the surplus was always going to go toward extra builds.

One garden in Youngtown became two. Two in West Launceston became three. Next thing you know, Trevallyn, Riverside, Summerhill… they all had a couple too."

Willow laughed. "Ultimate guerrilla gardening!"

"Quiet subversion[6]," paul said, smiling. "Once it started working — and it *did* work — everyone wanted in. And the Commonwealth Government contract auditors? They suddenly wanted to claim the whole city roll-out as theirs. 'National pilot success', they called it."

Willow rolled her eyes.

"Classic. But hey — if the fruit's ripe, who cares who planted the tree."

paul chuckled. "Worked for me. We always looked for others to blame the good work on."

Willow turned, eyebrow raised. "That a strategy?"

"One of the best," paul said. "Let others take the credit, and the good ideas keep moving. Less ego, more momentum."

They resumed walking again and strolled past a hand-painted garden sign — *"Grow together, grow forever"* — Willow paused beside a bed of freshly turned soil. "How many of these plots ended up across the city, do you reckon?"

paul raised an eyebrow. "I lost count to tell you the truth. But I know only a fraction were formally set up as community gardens."

"So the rest…?"

"Managed themselves, mostly," paul said. "Some started with a bit of help — tools, mulch, starter seedlings — but once they were going, people just kept turning up. Tending them. Owning them."

Willow glanced down the row of plots — some neat, some wild, all alive. "And that actually saved city money?"

paul smiled. "Ironically, yes. The same plots we used to mow, weed-spray, and complain about — the ones we saw as cost burdens — became cost savers. Maintenance went down. Engagement went up."

Willow nodded. "The community did the work."

"They did," paul said. "And they did it better than we ever could've from a depot."

Willow paused beside a row of late-season tomatoes, fingers brushing one of the ripest.

"You know," she said, "this one patch alone has probably saved the health system a fortune — and ratepayers too."

paul chuckled. "You think?"

She grinned and activated Synapstra. "I know."

A soft glow appeared above the garden beds — figures from the Preventative Health Survey and other Avoidable Costs Unit reports hovering like a holographic harvest:

"Loneliness down 11% in neighbourhoods with active community gardens. Mental health presentations down nearly 6%. Elders reporting higher mobility — fewer falls, fewer hip replacements. Obesity rates dropped. Diabetes stabilised in key groups. Kids showing up to school nourished, focused. Even crime rates down — especially where young people helped build and tend the gardens."

"From garden beds to balance sheets", paul said.

Willow nodded. "And not just cost savings — real lives improved. Because people talked. They moved. They shared. They belonged."

paul stopped to lean on the fence rail, thoughtful. "Funny how the kindest policies turn out to be the smartest investments."

Willow closed the overlay. "Not everything needs to be fast to be effective."

They wandered on, watching kids race through the citrus grove.

Then paul offered a quieter reflection. "Truth is," he said, "the community gardens were a damn sight easier than the canopy[7]."

Willow looked over. "Easier how?"

"Smaller scale. Immediate payoff. People saw the veggies and the neighbours and thought — great idea. But trees? Trees take time. Years. Decades. People said it was too slow, too expensive. That we should wait for better economic times."

"But we did it anyway?" Willow said.

paul nodded slowly. "Eventually. But only just. There was a real push to scrap the greening program in 2029, again in 2033 — pre-election years. Candidates trying to score points by winding it back, promising to shave a few bucks off everyone's rates. Believe it or not — it came down to one or two votes each time."

Willow gestured toward the side of her head again. "You logged the MemoryLoom?"

"Of course," paul said. ""It's one of the earliest simulations we built. Watch what happens when Council votes yes — and when it doesn't."

Willow smiled. She loads DeepSeequence 1: *The City in a Garden – Council Votes Yes*.

The world around them reshapes. The sun shifts, and the garden dissolves into light.

They stand on Cimitire Street. Towering trees and deciduous shade trees arch overhead, dappling the pavement in soft light. The air smells of jasmine and eucalyptus.

Elderly residents sit on curved bus stop benches beneath fruiting trees. Teenagers ride through misted cooling zones. Vertical gardens scale century old apartment façades. Bees hum. People linger.

Willow breathes in. "It's cooler — fifteen degrees cooler. Literally."

paul smiles. "We called it the 'City in a Garden' vision. Took three decades. One tree at a time across the entire city. From an 19% canopy to over 60%. In some parts of the CBD we planted a tree in every third on-street parking space. You bet it was controversial then — but look at it now."

From the Launceston Museum and Art Gallery at Republic Park to the Albert Hall at City Park, a continuous green canopy shades the street.

They nod to a courier topping up her e-bike beneath a solar pergola.

A young boy plucks a passionfruit from the inner-city public orchard trail.

At the corner, volunteers guide new migrants through their first planting day.

"This," Willow says, "is what shared effort looks like."

"Okay—now the counterfactual," paul says, gesturing for Willow to reset the scenario.

She loads DeepSeequence 2: *Concrete and Cost Cuts – Council Votes No.*

The scene resets. Same street. Different world.

The trees vanish. The temperature surges. The footpath shimmers under the glare. Willow flinches.

Bitumen stretches in every direction. Cracked pavements. No shade. The few remaining trees sit wilted, squeezed between faded parking bays.

A child clutches her mother's arm, crying as they rush toward the Museum through the belting heat. No shelter. No colour. No joy.

Willow winces. "This feels... brutal."

A man in his seventies struggles with grocery bags. His hand recoils from the searing metal at the bus stop.

A heat alert flashes overhead: *38°C. High UV. Limit Exposure.*

paul shakes his head, his voice thick with frustration. "They thought they were saving money. But in doing so, they stripped the city of everything that made it liveable."

The scene refreshes. Autumn. paul continues.

"In autumn, the leaves barely came. A few isolated maples in wealthier pockets clung to color, but most suburbs stayed brown and bare. Parks felt sparse. Playgrounds cracked and faded. Instead of rustling leaves, the wind lifted dust. There was no burnt orange in the hills — only haze."

Another refresh, the scene transforms.

"In winter, the sun finally reached the pavement — but there was no comfort in it. The trees were too few to filter the wind, too far apart to frame anything beautiful. Instead of quiet silhouettes, there were rusted poles and dying shrubs. The sky felt too close. The streets too empty. And people... people got angrier."

Another refresh.

"In spring, the blossoms didn't bloom together. They came in scattered, lonely bursts — a rogue plum here, a stubborn peach there. Bees struggled. Yields dropped. Kids no longer played blossom-tag; they stayed inside. The old gardeners said the soil wasn't what it used to be. And neither were the people."

Smash cut back to summer.

"In summer, the city burned. Footpaths shimmered. Shop awnings sagged. Ambulance callouts spiked. Concrete radiated back at you with quiet fury. Walking anywhere felt punishing. Bus stops became furnaces. Pedestrians learned to cross the road, not for safety, but for the shadow of a street sign. A city once known for its festivals and street life now wilted by noon. People went home. They shut their doors. The city stopped breathing."

Willow glanced around. "We baked our own city. It's like all the soul was stripped out."

"Fifteen percent canopy. Same city. Different logic." paul's voice was quiet now. "They called it 'budget responsibility.' But they forgot to count the ambulance calls. The isolation. The energy bills. We traded a living city for a lower rates notice. A false economy. A lost canopy. A betrayal of the kind of city we could have been. They saved cents and lost decades."

A bus passed. Its tires kicked up heat haze.

Willow ended the simulation. The trees of the real garden flickered back into place. Birds returned to song. "That second version felt... like punishment," she said.

"It was," paul replied. "Not intentional. Just the inevitable punishment of small, downstream thinking — the belief that we can pay later, after the damage is done."

"How close did we come to getting that?"

paul exhales. "For fact's sake, it came down to just two votes a few times. One bad budget cycle. That's all it would've taken."

Willow looks out toward the gardens now integrated in Republic Park. "I'm glad someone fought for the first version."

paul smiled. "It wasn't just someone. It was thousands of someones — our community, their voices... and a few hopeful seedlings."

They walked slowly now, the shadows of the fruit trees reaching across the path. Behind them, the garden hummed with quiet life — bees drifting deliberately from blossom to blossom, a child's laughter rising near the apple tree.

Willow brushed her fingers across a hedge of lavender as they passed. "It's wild to think this used to be a bowling green," she said.

paul nodded. "But just remember, this didn't build itself," paul said.

"Our city needed people. And the people needed good work."

Willow looked out across the garden, where an older woman knelt beside an infant, pointing gently at a row of sprouting greens.

"So… we grew the workforce like we grew the gardens?" she asked.

paul smiled, running two fingers along his hat's brim. "Exactly. Next time, I'll show you who helped build all this."

As they parted, paul glanced at a wheelbarrow by the tool shed and smiled. Some work you sweat for; some you let grow. Either way, you earn the rest.

As Willow walked into the distance, she queued up a fresh Growth-Loop via Synapstra — an assignment uploaded that very morning by a local student from Changemaker High, part of their reflection on history, place, and gratitude:

GrowthLoop: Launceston — City in a Garden
(Submitted in partial fulfilment of course requirements. Public access consent granted.)

Launceston is a city in a garden. Not a slogan. Not a brochure tagline. A lived reality. A place where nature isn't something you escape to — it's something we live within.

The canopy — once patchy and under siege — now stretches wide and generous, a living roof above streets, schoolyards, and suburban crescents. From just 19% cover in the late 2020s, we've grown to 68% in 2064. A full, functional, breathing system. Every neighbourhood. Every postcode. No one left out.

In autumn, the hills blaze with colour. Burnt orange. Ochre. Claret red. Leaves fall in slow spirals, layering footpaths like nature's confetti. Children kick them skyward. Elders walk a little slower, just to savour the rustle. Cafés extend tables beneath golden branches. The whole city shimmers — like it's been dipped in honey.

In spring, everything sings. Blossoms burst — plum, apple, cherry, wattles glowing. Suburbs carry the scent of renewal. Bees move like punctuation marks through the air. School kids compete to spot the first magnolia bloom. The gardens aren't just beautiful — they're edible, seasonal, and social. You can wander Invermay and pluck a lemon, trade herbs in Mowbray, or picnic beneath pears in St Leonards.

In summer, the canopy holds the heat at bay. Streets that once scorched bare feet are now dappled and cool. Walking feels like retreat, not endurance. The city glows — not with heat, but with green. Cooling corridors connect every suburb. Mist gardens soften every plaza. You don't need wearable aircon when you've got a canopy like ours.

And in winter, even the bare trees serve a purpose. Their silhouettes reach skyward like quiet sentinels, letting soft light warm the pavement. Vitamin D soaks in. People walk in winter — they don't hibernate. Beneath skeletal limbs, the first shoots emerge, preparing to bloom again.

Every season tells the same story in Launceston: We are proudly green. Not separate from nature, but held within it — Sharing space, giving care, growing together.

We honour the early-century stewards who planned not just for roads or buildings — but for life. We thank them for choosing, long ago, to invest in trees, in shade, in beauty, in each other, and in me — planting what they might not live to see.

SIX
THE WORKERS
GOOD WORK FOR ALL

"Caring is not just an emotion. It is a practice, a politics, a way of being in the world." — bell hooks

2 April 2064

A breeze moved gently through the turning leaves, scattering gold across the path like confetti from some quiet celebration. The sun hung lower now, casting a soft glow through the canopy — that particular kind of autumn warmth that lingers just long enough to be noticed.

paul was already at the bench, one foot resting on the stone base, hands pinned under his thighs. His gaze drifted for a moment — the tell-tale sign of Synapstra. He blinked back into the present and offered a hat tip as Willow approached.

"Oliver Burkeman," he said, tapping his earpiece. *"Four Thousand Weeks* on audiobook — a reminder that life is short." He tilted his head. "Or, as Henry Rollins sings: *'No such thing as spare time, no such thing as free time, no such thing as down time. All you got is life time. Go.*[1]*'"* He smiled wryly. "I'm ninety now — north of four and a half thousand weeks. If Burkeman's right, I'm deep into overtime."

Willow tilted her head. "I have a feeling the final siren is a long way off for you, paul."

"Well, they say only the good die young," he quipped.

"So... eight thousand weeks for you?" she teased.

paul laughed, stood, and straightened his jacket as he fell in step beside her. "Makes you think though. You're a thousand weeks in, Willow, just finishing your first tranche of study. Reminds me that the point isn't busywork or make-work — it's the good work. The kind that gives life meaning and makes it liveable."

She nodded, scarf flicking in the breeze. "Which is exactly what you dropped into MemoryLoom the other day: *'A strong city is founded on good work for all.'"*

He chuckled. "That's the entry I never finished."

"Well," she said, nudging him as they walked, "let's finish it now. I want the long version."

They continued walking along the shoreline path, the crunch of gravel underfoot punctuating the rhythm of their thoughts.

"I know none of this was neat, or linear, or yours alone," Willow said.

"It wasn't. It really wasn't. This was deep system work, and it took a big cast", paul offered.

Willow nodded. "So... where did it start?"

The leaves swirled around them as they walked, and the conversation — like the season — turned toward change.

paul took a breath. "I think it really began with a mindset shift. As a community — and as leaders — we made it our job to grow our own. And we backed them, every step of the way. Good training, a good job, and good pay - that's how you leave no one behind. Especially in a city like ours."

He glanced across the lake. "We trained the people we needed — especially in the care economy. Because caring for each other is real work. And it had to be valued."

Willow raised an eyebrow. "So what tipped it? When did we start getting serious about workforce expansion?"

paul exhaled slowly. "Around the time of the first pandemic. I was working in workforce development — trying to untangle the wicked problem of how to attract, recruit, and keep people in our city, in our region, in our state. Doctors, nurses, allied health workers, child safety officers… really, it was every sector. Everyone was short-staffed after COVID, and no one had easy answers."

Willow frowned. "I thought unemployment was the issue back then?"

paul gave a half-smile. "It's a fair question. The straight answer is there was both – workforce shortages while those without skills and training were experience the brutal impact of income support while unemployed. It was a wicked problem by all definitions.

paul paused. Then, "But I'll stick to my knitting — the care economy is where I was focused. I know almost all other sectors like construction and hospitality were struggling too. We had a few things driving the crisis - the data told a very clear story."

Willow blinked twice, Synapstra flickering. "Health Workforce 2040[2]," she said, scanning the archived document. "Published in 2021."

paul nodded. "We were facing a perfect storm. Demand for services was skyrocketing — more people were sick, ageing, needing complex care. The National Disability Insurance Scheme was maturing and needed staff. And just as all that hit, our workforce pipeline was faltering. The people we had were burning out, or ageing out. We were losing decades of experience — and not enough was coming through to replace them."

Willow narrowed her eyes. "That sounds like the definition of a crisis. So what did you do?"

paul gave a knowing glance. "What did we do?" He smiled. "Well, you're probably spotting the pattern by now. We looked at the data. We listened to community. We tackled the root causes — the system failures. And then we started walking upstream. Investing early. Acting with purpose. Building the systems we actually needed."

Willow kept walking, Synapstra scrolling quietly beside her. "Um, paul... are your dates right? I mean, the workforce reports from the late 2020s and early 2030s show the shortages getting worse — not better."

paul nodded. "Correct[3]".

Willow frowned. "Now I'm really confused."

paul smiled gently. "Willow, it took decades to get ourselves into the mess. It wasn't going to turn around overnight. But don't miss the seeds of change. We listened. We challenged the status quo. We tried new things. And slowly, we started to move the needle. The State and the Feds — with Flexicurity — helped us accelerate this work later."

Willow shook her head. "Still confused."

paul stopped walking and faced her. "Okay. Let's back up. Leading in complex systems[4] — it's not about finding the fastest answer. It starts with defining the problem properly. The simple slogans from some politicians at the time were way off. They distracted attention — and diverted resources away from what actually worked."

He paused. "Here's the headline version: First — there was a mismatch between what training providers were offering and what industries actually needed. Second — a geographic mismatch. The workforce was clustered in places far from where care was needed most. Our city was challenged and it was felt even more acutely in the smaller remote communities.

"And third," paul continued, "we made it far too hard for people without formal qualifications to train, retrain, or re-enter the workforce.

Affordability. Access. Support. All of it needed serious work."

Willow raised an eyebrow. "So how did the city tackle that?"

paul nodded slowly. "We activated community. We shook off the old constraints and stepped into a new role — as facilitators and catalysts for change. We brought people together across the three tiers of government, across sectors, across silos. And we got bold. We hosted pilots. We tested ideas right here that had relevance for the rest of the country eventually. Because when you're dealing with complexity, you don't wait for perfect — you experiment. You go first. You learn as you go."

Willow scrolled through the data again, Synapstra flickering. "But paul... the reports say not much changed."

"Not at first," he said. "Upstream leadership is often low and slow. You've got to go slow now to go fast later."

He paused, then gestured ahead. "Run the DeepSeequence. Take out the roundtables. Mute the community voice. Delete the data-informed pilots from the late 2020s and early 2030s. See where it leads."

Willow activated the scenario. The path ahead of her shimmered, then shifted.

She walked now through a version of their past defined by relentless crisis. Headlines scrolled across the sky like warnings[5]:

Health system
Grim state of ambulance ramping revealed
Ambulance ramping crisis under scrutiny
Hospitals battling record-breaking ambulance ramping crisis

Early childhood and education
Children forced away from childcare due to staff crisis

Dozens of childcare centres closed due to staff shortages
Early childhood education crisis deepening as 60% of workers plan to leave

Disability (NDIS)
NDIS providers under compliance pressure
New data reveals 'worst year ever' for disability providers
NDIS in the balance: How changes are shaking the foundation

Child protection
At risk children's 'broken' child protection system harming kids
Inquiry launched into 'failures' of child protection
Child protection system failing vulnerable kids across Australia

Aged care
Aged care homes facing major bed and staff shortage
Australia's residential aged care sector facing 'crisis in care availability'
Elderly dying while waiting for home care
New year, same aged care crisis: Longer wait times, facility closures and hospital strain

Every cluster carried a different name, but the headline was the same: crisis upon crisis, stitched across the fabric of care. Across every sector — nurses, social workers, early educators, support workers — the same pattern: too few hands, too much harm.

Governments scrambled, throwing money at the fire front — crisis after crisis — but the flames only spread.

Then Willow noticed something else.

"No Pathway Program," she murmured. "Wait — my mum doesn't become a nurse?"

She scanned deeper.

"No Timebanking."

"No AusCorp."

"No Social Impact Bonds…"

She turned to paul. "Hang on. All of that… it's gone? Because we didn't listen? Because we ignored the data? Because we stayed downstream?"

paul met her gaze. "Correct."

He exhaled. "We can talk about State reforms – like portable entitlements, and the big national Labour Market reforms another time — Flexicurity, Income Guarantee, Life Long Learning credits, AusCorps, all of it. But their origins? They weren't grand announcements. They began when leaders listened. When they matched what people truly needed with what the evidence told us worked. Then we tested. We learned. We scaled."

Willow let the scenario fade, the lake path reappearing around them.

She nodded slowly, brow furrowed. "Slow now, fast later."

paul smiled. "Correct."

Willow glanced sideways as they walked, ducks scattering ahead. "This is still feeling kind of abstract. Can you give me an example?"

paul nodded. "Sure. Let's take George Town — my old hometown. Back in 2025, workforce modelling said the town needed to train 40 new care workers a year for a decade just to meet growing demand for care services."

Willow tilted her head. "And?"

"They were training almost none. The system was misaligned."

They rounded a bend, the lake shimmering to their right.

"What do you mean, misaligned?" Willow asked.

paul gestured with one hand. "Millions had been invested in a care training facility — in Launceston. Fifty kilometers away. The assumption was people would travel there to study."

Willow raised an eyebrow. "And they didn't?"

"They couldn't," paul said sharply. "Transport costs, childcare, time. Life."

Willow shook her head. "So what did the community want?"

"They'd been asking for years to refurbish the old automotive shop at the George Town Trade Training Centre. Turn it into a mock hospital — train local support workers, right there in town. If you train them locally, they are more likely to stay locally."

"And?"

paul gave a wry smile. "The system kept saying no. Even though that auto shop hadn't trained a mechanic in over a decade, they insisted it might one day be reactivated. So the cracks stayed — and people fell through."

Willow frowned, brushing a leaf from the toe of her shoe. "That's maddening."

"And it wasn't just George Town," paul added. "This story was playing out across the state. Probably the nation."

Willow narrowed her eyes. "Did it ever get fixed?"

"Eventually — but not quickly. And each time we patched one gap, another appeared."

They slowed as a jogger passed. The gravel crunched beneath their feet.

"Okay," paul continued. "We finally secured a $300,000 grant to convert the old auto space into a proper mock hospital. It was ready. Local people were keen. There was just one problem."

Willow grinned. "Let me guess — no teacher, no trainers?"

paul laughed. "Correct."

"So what did you do?"

"Not a quick fix. We pushed to train more trainers, build the whole pipeline."

"Did that work?"

He winced. "At first? No. The system sent a trainer from another town — which just robbed Peter to pay—"

"Paul?" Willow smirked.

paul laughed. "Exactly. But then we found our rhythm. We aligned the funding, the ideas, the trainers, the spaces. And we finally backed place-based solutions."

Willow nodded. "You listened to community — and acted."

paul smiled. "Spot on."

They kept walking, leaves scattering ahead like quiet applause.

Willow kicked a loose pebble. "I can see why it took so long to turn the ship."

"We picked up speed as momentum built," paul said. "Once you have a few wins, it gets easier to convince people. But the secret was staying close to the ground — always listening to local, always adapting in line with evidence – looking at what worked elsewhere – experimenting – taking risks."

Willow tilted her head. "How so?"

"Well," paul said, "once we started training more support workers — for aged care, disability support — the sector had shifted. A lot of those jobs were now part of the gig economy."

Willow frowned. "Wait — you mean they had to run as sole traders?"

paul nodded. "Yep. They were essentially micro-businesses. But the training programs were focused on care — as they should be — not bookkeeping, invoicing, superannuation, Business Activity Statements and tax."

"Oh my," Willow murmured. "So, what did you do?"

"We pivoted. Set up small business incubators. Paired people with mentors. And we supported other local enterprises to handle the 'back of house' admin — so newly trained workers could actually focus on caring."

He paused as they reached a bend in the path, ducks drifting quietly below.

"Tech platforms helped," he added. "But again — the big shift came when we listened. And responded."

Willow smiled. "Bottom up, not top down."

They walked in quiet rhythm for a while before Willow glanced at her overlay.

"It says that in 2026, Tasmania had 89,000 people in unpaid caring roles. Is that right? 89,000 — out of 550,000 people?"

paul nodded. "Spot on. The hidden workforce. Family members, friends, neighbours — sometimes even kids — saving the economy billions. Quietly holding things together. Through love."

Willow frowned. "And that's not even counting the tens of thousands of volunteers doing 'the work'."

"Correct," paul said. "That's why we had to support and celebrate carers and volunteers. They were — and still are — the backbone of our communities. I never forgot that."

Willow tapped her Synapstra again. "And you're saying every sector — hospitality, construction, agriculture, mining, higher education — was dealing with the same shortages, mismatches, training gaps?"

paul nodded. "Correct."

Willow let out a long breath. "Honestly? It's overwhelming. I don't know how I would've coped back then. Just imagining it feels heavy."

paul looked at her, steady. "It was heavy. But that's what leadership is. Real leaders lean in. They step up. They take a stand. They roll up their sleeves — because it's hard."

He paused.

"And the good ones? They listen. They learn. They adapt. They own their mistakes. They pivot. They keep showing up — not for legacy, not for applause, but for community. To build a better future. For everyone."

"And I never stopped trying to draw attention to — and support for — the health care and social assistance sector. It had been overlooked and under-resourced for far too long. Mostly because it was, and still is, a predominantly female workforce.

I said it so often that one of my team members printed me a T-shirt for Christmas, parodying the old Bill Clinton line: "It's the Care Economy, stupid!"[6]

Willow's Synapstra flickered as she scrolled forward — like a student checking the answers at the back of the textbook. Data rippled across her vision. Her eyes widened.

"Wait... hang on. When it took off — it really took off."

She turned to paul. "The job numbers, the revenue, the wellbeing scores — it's like everything lifted at once."

paul smiled, resting his hands on the rail. "That's the thing about upstream investment. It looks slow... until it isn't. Like a sports star or a movie star people call an 'overnight success.' Very few see the years of hard slog — the false starts, the quiet grind, the hard yakka behind it all."

Willow grinned. "Can we unpack that next time?"

paul nodded. "Yes we can."

They turned back toward the bench, golden leaves swirling behind them.

SEVEN
THE BOOM
A WELLBEING ECONOMY

"The greatness of a community is most accurately measured by the compassionate actions of its members."
— Coretta Scott King[1]

9 April 2064

A stubborn low front had rolled in overnight, casting the city in shades of grey and drumming rain against windows across the valley.

Willow blinked awake to the sound, then blinked again — Synapstra syncing her half-formed intention to check the forecast. Heavy rain. Intermittent storms. Poor visibility.

Their walk was out.

She reached out via Synapstra, her thoughts forming a quiet message to paul, "Still on for this morning? Or shall we wait it out?"

A moment later, his reply floated back — warm, unbothered. "Let's pivot. How about a drive into the Valley instead? I'll pick you up same time."

Willow smiled. Classic paul. Always adapting.

By the time she reached the kerb, the car was already waiting — sleek, silent, driverless. The doors lifted open as paul gave a hat tip from the passenger seat. Willow placed her hemp canvas bag in the footwell and slid in beside him, rain tracing soft lines down the glass.

As they glided across the bridge, the world beyond softened — mist settling over Tamar Lake, solar trees pulsing gently in the haze. The Statue shimmered in the distance, half-veiled, like memory.

They turned north, the road rising gently as the East Tamar unfolded ahead.

Willow tapped lightly on her armrest, then spoke without turning. "Hey... I found this on MemoryLoom." She rarely played old clips in front of him — preferring to follow protocol, letting paul lead with his own recollections. But this one felt different. Worth it.

The LumenView activated, stretching across the windscreen in a translucent overlay. A woman's voice — clear, firm, familiar — filled the car.

The Honourable Sulapa Jaswal, Premier of Tasmania, appeared: calm, composed, and mid-speech:

> *"This city — and the beautiful Tamar Valley — are open for business. But make no mistake: this is not business as usual.*
>
> *We're building a wellbeing economy: growth that works for everyone, prosperity that lifts every household, a fair go for every business, dignity and safety for every worker, and families that don't just*

survive — they thrive. And the beauty that sustains us is protected for generations to come.

Our test is regeneration[2].

Environment regeneration: we restore ecosystems and biodiversity — not just conserve what remains.

Energy regeneration: we build renewable, resilient, community-owned systems.

Health regeneration: we shift from treating sickness to creating wellbeing.

Housing regeneration: secure, sustainable homes are a right, not a commodity.

Income regeneration: fair work, dignity, and shared prosperity.

Transport regeneration: human-centred, clean mobility that connects communities.

Education regeneration: lifelong learning that renews creativity, citizenship, and resilience.

Each "R" signals a bigger shift: from extraction to regeneration; from capital accumulation to human potential; from short-term growth to long-term flourishing.

In a wellbeing economy, rivers matter. Air matters. Soil matters. Ecosystems matter — because thriving people depend on a thriving planet.

Greater Launceston stands for secure jobs, fair wages, clean industries, and real opportunity — not just for today, but for the long term. We won't rest until every local business is backed, every worker respected, every family supported, and every decision honours the land and water that sustain us.

That's how we rise — together. Right here in Launceston. Right here in the Valley. Right here in Tasmania."

paul exhaled softly. "Blast from a distant past. She was so good at that. I reckon that was just after the council amalgamations."

"Yep, spot on." Willow grinned, always a little awed by his encyclopedic recall. "The file tag here suggests you might've penned that speech."

"I may have offered a word or two. But the Premier's communication skills rarely needed my pen," he replied.

"Was that the foundation of the 'wellbeing economy mindset'?" Willow asked, watching an agrivoltaic farm blur past the window — solar panels gleaming above a paddock of grazing sheep[3].

paul shook his head gently. "No. Not at all. The City was well on the way before then — it just came into sharper focus because of the Premier was building momentum. The old ways were being transformed years before then. People were calling for something more balanced, more human."

Willow nodded.

paul continue. "The pursuit of a wellbeing economy was about balancing people and planet. It was about making sure everyone has what they need to live — food, shelter, education, health, connection — but without pushing our environment beyond its limits."

Willow raised an eyebrow. "So... not too hot, not too cold?"

"Exactly," paul said. "The Goldilocks zone. Doughnut Economics[4]. The safe space between social foundations and ecological ceilings. You meet human needs, but you stay within what the place can handle."

"Just right," Willow murmured, half to herself.

paul nodded. "That was the shift. Economic growth was no longer the sole goal. It became about people and planet — thriving together."

Willow sipped from her cup, watching the landscape roll by as the driverless car curved north through the valley. A cluster of solar panels glinted through the trees — then another, and another.

CitizenEcho stirred softly to life, its voice low and unintrusive:

"Launceston's northern fringe hosts over 300 hectares of multi-use solar farms[5] — home to pollinator meadows[6], shaded mushroom rows[7], and elevated panels above premium vineyards[8]. Each site contributes clean energy, biodiversity, and local produce."

Willow glanced out the window as wildflowers shimmered beneath the panels and a hillside vineyard rippled with late-season colour.

They travelled a little further. A broad irrigation dam came into view beside the highway, sunlight catching the grid of panels floating[9] quietly on its surface.

Willow nodded slowly, still taking it in.

"Bricks," paul muttered with a short laugh, shaking his head.

Willow turned to him, puzzled. "Where? What do you mean — bricks?"

"No, no - electrified bricks[10]. he said, still smiling. "We had solar everywhere, but we needed storage. Something clean. Scalable. Batteries were scarce. Pumped hydro was too slow to bring online. So..."

"So?"

"Thermal bricks," he said, nodding. "We adapted emerging tech — Bell Bay became a global case study. Those bricks stored solar energy as heat and released it cleanly to the heavy industries that needed it. No rare earths. Just heat. Just science. We solved a huge problem — by doing what we always did best: looking at what works elsewhere and making it work here."

Willow stared at the dam. "I thought those had just... always been there."

paul smiled.

There was a beat of silence between them.

"So the boom of the '30s? Can you tell me about that?", Willow asked quietly.

paul chuckled, shifting slightly in his seat. "That's right. *The boom.*"

He glanced out to the bushland as it blurred past the window.

"Funny... back in the '20s, we talked about the promise — the promise of the 2030s. A boom was just a hope then. A vision. But once we got momentum, almost every sector took off."

Willow smiled. "So... where do you want to start?"

"Oh, how about my favourite..."

"The care economy!" Willow jumped in, finishing his sentence. "I'll check MemoryLoom."

Her Synapstra flickered to life. "Alright... wow. Every major indicator — up. Wages, workforce participation, productivity, community well-being, even tax returns."

paul played along. "And don't forget Timebank and KindraPass. Or the new arrivals reforms. That care-led growth brought more people to our shores than ever before."

Willow made a note through Clara to return to each of those initiatives. As she scrolled, her eyes moved across the glowing dashboards — trendlines, heat maps, and embedded human stories. Then, within the Care Economy overlay, a familiar training pathway title surfaced.

"Care Pathways," she murmured, surprised. "That one helped my mum... wow."

paul nodded gently.

"She was one of the first to complete the full stream," Willow said, her voice quieter now. "Paid to train as a support worker, then an Enrolled Nurse, then Registered Nurse... then Nurse Practitioner."

"Like most of the Pathways participants — they earned while they learned," paul said. "And they didn't do it alone. That pathway was built to remove barriers — every step scaffolded. Placement support. Mentors. Peer networks. Communities of practice. Flexibility for carers. It wasn't magic. It was kind policy. Wrapped around real lives."

Willow paused, letting the screen hover. Clara's quiet prompt surfaced in the corner: "Maybe give your mum an extra hug." Willow smiled and nodded.

Outside the window, a sleek farm drone zipped low over a row of orchards, dropping nutrients with pinpoint accuracy. A second followed, scanning tree health in real time. Willow barely glanced at them. That kind of quiet precision — it was just her native world.

With a quick swipe, she shifted overlays. "Okay... let's move onto the construction sector."

"Ah yes — economic multipliers," paul said, his tone lifting. "To build the big three, we needed workers, materials, trucks, tools, lunch vans. That meant more houses. Which meant more builders. More childcare. More gyms. More everything. For fact's sake."

Willow's Synapstra filled with graphs and projections of the "big three" – the lake weir, the second Tamar bridge, and the Statue of Equity.

"Returns of $2.70 for every dollar spent.", Willow reads.

"Then came the growth in training organisations, industry hubs, schools..."

Willow was about to swipe again when paul gently raised a hand.

"Before you jump — follow the report there."

She clarified. "This one? 'Final Report on Construction Pathway'?"

"That's the one. This is really what kind politics looks like."

With a glance, the report opened. Line by line, the conditions became clear — State and Commonwealth funds tied to wraparound supports for young people who might otherwise fall through the cracks. A parallel system of care, built alongside the infrastructure itself.

Willow was curious. "Didn't that ramp up the cost to build?"

"Not a cost, Willow — an investment," paul said. "An upstream investment in our people. The maths on failure demand and avoidable costs was solid. We knew — just like the generation before us knew — that every young person who didn't finish school and didn't work would cost the system more than a quarter of a million dollars across their lifetime."

"So we added $20,000 — sometimes $25,000 — per young person into the bridge, dam, and statue builds. In total? Seven or eight million a year inside a $3 billion decade long package."

He paused, letting the numbers settle. "Two and a half percent, Willow. That's all."

"And that money...?"

"Got hundreds of kids — many from tough beginnings — into trade training. Not just jobs, Willow — lives. Families. Taxes. Stability. Some of them grew up and passed the trade on to their own kids. That's intergenerational change.

$30,000 invested upstream instead of a quarter mill' lost downstream. I'd take that win every day."

Willow sat quietly, letting it land. "Clara. We're coming back to that to."

She flicked forward. "Okay. Agriculture?"

"Not yet," paul said, gently. "Go back. You skipped something."

She rewound. "There?" she asked, as a section glowed.

"Arts and Entertainment."

"Really?"

"Yep. This is the interdependence of everything in a mature economy. Build the weir, create the lake; the lake irrigated the valley, and it attracted the green hydrogen mob[11], it attracted recreational fishing[12]... it even caught the attention of streaming services looking to make digital content."

"What?", Willow puzzles.

paul, "Right, the city's annual budget was about $170 million at the time."

"$173 million," Willow corrected, grinning.

"We carved out $8 million — controversial at the time. The policy pooled funds with Screen Tasmania, the State and the Feds to lure the production of *Still Water World* here."

Willow blinked. "Oh, that's right. That was filmed here, wasn't it?"

"On the lake. It all came about in a business-community Roundtable discussion. We were trying to find away to beat the winter lull in tourism. We worked with local hotels for winter discounts — those rooms were sitting empty. Some revenue's better than none."

He smiled. "The production crews — scores of them — stayed seven, maybe eight weeks. Turned fog into magic. And that film became a postcard to the world."

"Do you know the returns?" Willow asked.

"Not exactly. Maybe a 12% or 15% return on investment."

Willow glanced at her Synapstra. "Hang on... accounting for accommodation, production spend, and induced tourism benefit... it was 17.8%, actually."

paul chuckled. "There you go. Anyway, it almost didn't get up. Might've been one vote in it. But leadership isn't always about guarantees. Sometimes, it's about backing what might work."

He paused, then added, "Hobart got the spin-off production base — we lost that round. But a few of our kids were extras. Some of them ended up working in film and media. That's the thing about investments like this... the returns aren't just economic. They're social. Generational."

Willow tilted her head. "Now agriculture?"

"Yes, alright," paul said, smiling. "But let's turn off here and go have a look IRL."

"Where we going?", Willow queried.

He pointed to her bag.

She looked down. "This? It's just my market bag."

"Exactly," he said. "Industrial hemp. Grown here. Woven here. Sold here – and across the globe."

She tilted her head, intrigued.

"We didn't just grow the crop here," paul said. "Some really clever investors and some very smart farmers — with a bit of help — built out the value-adding parts of the industry. From seed to fibre to finished goods. We united science with soil, economists with funders. We aligned policy with purpose. And it all hinged on one thing."

Willow grinned. "Clean water."

"Exactly. No lake, no water.

No water, no irrigation.

No irrigation, no farms.

No farms, no hemp.

No hemp, no downstream industries.

No industries… no jobs."

The car eased to a stop beneath a timber-and-glass archway, its sign etched with fine latticework: Hillwood Hemp Precinct.

Willow stepped out first, breathing in the earthy scent of soil and fresh rain. paul followed, adjusting his hat against the light drizzle. Around them, rows of hemp swayed gently in the breeze — tall, purposeful, and unmistakably alive with potential.

"This way," Willow said, already making her way toward the visitor centre.

Inside, they stepped onto a glass-fronted viewing platform. Below, robotic arms moved with elegant precision, sorting hemp fibres into neat bundles. Overhead, a circular display hovered, slowly rotating through the site's main product streams.

From seed to stem, leaf to fibre, the precinct produced:

- Bioplastics for packaging and industrial parts
- Textiles for clothing, home furnishings, and durable outdoor gear
- Hempcrete panels for sustainable housing
- Nutraceuticals and omega-rich hemp oil capsules
- Protein powder and plant-based meat extenders
- Pet bedding and mulch from processed stalks
- Paper and recyclable packaging
- Carbon-sequestering insulation and soundproofing panels
- Biochar for soil health and carbon drawdown
- Natural dyes and inks for artistic and industrial use

Willow paused by a vertical display showing rotating case studies — Tasmanian homes built with hempcrete, school uniforms made from local fibres, even biodegradable drone casings sourced from Hillwood composites.

"They finally cracked the full value chain," paul said, holding his hat by his side. "No waste. No imports. Just smart design, good soil — and clean water."

They wandered the centre for a while — past displays of fabric swatches, lightweight panels, pressed oil samples, and 3D-printed bioplastics. A faint scent of citrus hemp balm lingered in the air. Eventually, they ordered drinks and found a quiet table near the wide glass window that framed the valley and the lake below.

Outside, the landscape unfolded like a blueprint of possibility — fields of hemp rolling down the gentle slope, punctuated by low-slung buildings clad in hempcrete and softened by climbing vines. The rain had begun to ease, and a silvery light settled over the lake. In the distance, rows of strawberry fields curved gently along the hillside, mist still clinging to the ridge.

Willow sank into her seat and let it all wash over her.

"We should've come here sooner," she said quietly.

She took a slow sip of her drink, then added, "I've never actually been to the precinct before. But I did visit the strawberry farm — over there, just on the ridge — with my grandfather. The ice cream was his favourite."

Clara nudged her to pause. To sit with the ache. To remember him. Not as a shadow, but as part of her — and to notice, without judgement, the quiet comfort of paul's presence. Not a replacement. A continuation.

Willow looked toward the strawberry fields.

They hadn't changed much since she was little — long, neat rows under protective covers, catching light in soft curves along the hillside. She could still picture her pop — laughing, squinting into the sun, a pink smear of strawberry ice cream on his chin.

paul's voice softened. "We almost lost strawberries in the valley, Willow."

His gaze followed the slope toward the distant rows. "Deliberate sabotage. Some rogue actors hid needles in the punnets[13]. It nearly wiped out the growers — the whole industry was shaken."

Willow turned to him, startled. "What happened?"

paul shrugged gently. "Sometimes, out of crisis, great things grow."

He leaned back, the memory clearly still vivid. "We pulled together a war room — not just the usual bigwigs. Sure, we had the Coordinator General, the CEO of Regional Development, and the Chamber of Commerce... but we made sure the farmers were there. And the unions. Everyone who had skin in the game."

"We were talking through the mess — what to do with dumped crops, how to keep people employed, what to plant next season just to stay afloat. Then one of the new arrivals — a quiet voice in the corner — offered a curveball."

"He said: feed crickets[14]. Grow lettuce. Create protein. It was out there... but it was also brilliant."

paul smiled at the memory. "That one comment changed everything. It sparked a pivot — from survival to innovation. Within a few months, we'd seeded a co-op. Today, that operation is bigger than the strawberry growers ever were."

He paused, then added more softly, "And here's the best part — a big share of what they grow now gets shipped to the World Food Programme[15]. Because many of those in the co-op? They wanted to give back. To feed the countries they came from."

Willow followed his gaze toward the hill — a field once nearly lost, now blooming in ways no one had predicted. Not just with crops, but with purpose.

They made their way back to the car in companionable silence. As the door closed behind them and the vehicle pulled smoothly onto the road, the wide curves of the Tamar Valley opened once more. Willow gazed out at the patchwork of hemp and strawberries, drone ports and solar fields receding behind them.

The ride home took them south, winding gently toward the first Tamar crossing — now known as Kanamulka Bridge, in honour of the river's original name and the people who had cared for it far longer than the settlers who followed.

The rain had eased, leaving the road slick but shimmering. The lake stretched beneath them — calm and glassy — as light broke softly through the clouds.

Willow spoke quietly, not taking her eyes off the view.

"Hey paul... help me understand. How did your generation land all of this? The lake, the hemp precinct, the jobs, the wellbeing economy. It couldn't have just been luck — or a good economic cycle. There had to be something more."

paul paused, thoughtful. "Upstream thinking was gaining traction — but yes, the stars aligned. Good people. Strong partnerships with the State and the Feds. A cooperative national mood. And all the first principles stuff — listen to the people who elect you, act in their best interests, and never, ever give up."

Willow glanced his way. "Come on, paul. Leadership? The elected reps must've done more than ride a good wave. These results took years. You must take some of the credit, surely?"

He nodded slowly. "It was a progressive bunch, that's true. First thing we did was overhaul disclosure rules. No more once-a-year declarations — we published weekly updates on affiliations, lobbyist meetings, the whole lot. Online. Socials. It went well beyond the legal minimum — and it built trust.

"Second, we trialled new ways of involving people in decisions. Tools like the Balance the Budget simulator, and later those participatory apps. Bit of a forerunner to CivicLoom.

"Third — we delivered. Not everything, not always on time. But we didn't hide delays or pretend the problems didn't exist. We owned them. I used to call it 'no bullshit politics.' The comms team hated it. Said it couldn't be polished."

Willow laughed. Then: "Accountable and transparent."

The road climbed gently, revealing the lake below — broad and quiet, silvered by the clearing rain. paul leaned back in his seat, eyes following the folds of land and water. He wanted to lift Willow's gaze

— from the valley she knew so well, to the wider world they were part of.

"We were a product of our time, Willow. Don't forget — the 2020s were hard. Conflict. Displacement. Hunger. That clip of Premier Jaswal you played earlier — it didn't happen in isolation. Beyond this valley, beyond our island, it was one humanitarian crisis after another. Gaza. Ukraine. Sudan. Congo. Somalia. Yemen."

Willow didn't respond right away. She just watched as the city began to emerge through misted glass, softened by light and distance. Then, softly:

"And still, we looked outward. Chose to care."

paul nodded. "We were the lucky country in many ways— stable democracy, fertile soil, kind people. So we did what we could. We shared."

He spoke quietly now, but with conviction.

"We sent produce. Protein. Real food that filled real bellies — through the World Food Programme.

We offered safe haven to those displaced — work, dignity, safety. Some went home. Many stayed. Wove themselves into the fabric of this place."

A long silence followed — not empty, but full.

paul glanced across at her, then forward again, as the last glint of the lake disappeared in the rearview. "We did our bit."

Willow didn't reply. But the words folded into her — like cloth laid gently over memory. That is kind politics, she thought.

The car moved easily now, the valley giving way to low hills, then rooftops — new streets etched into what had once been paddocks and pasture.

As they crested the rise, paul pointed, almost absentmindedly, toward the horizon.

Blueleaf Cove. Greenwood. Ironbark Plains. Waterbank — the city's expansion eco-suburbs, unfolding like a second skin.

"We should walk out there one day," he said.

Willow followed his gaze — hempcrete houses, solar rooftops, native verge gardens, the shimmer of recycled road base. "That would be perfect," she said.

EIGHT
THE GROWTH
NEW NEIGHBOURHOODS AND
BUSINESSES

"Here's the conundrum: No country has ever ended human deprivation without a growing economy. And no country has ever ended ecological degradation with one."
— Kate Raworth[1]

30 April 2064

The electric bus[2] hummed quietly beneath them, its motion barely more than a whisper as it curved past the Southern edge of Tamar Lake. Outside the wide windows, the early sun caught the metal canopy of the city's East Tamar park-and-ride facility[3] — a tessellated structure of solar mesh and climbing wattle vines, alive with morning light.

paul tapped the side of his seat, half-listening to the soft voice of CitizenEcho — a familiar civic tone explaining the precinct's role in cutting commuter emissions by half. Willow, already one step ahead, had muted hers.

"It's like a TED Talk every ten minutes," she murmured.

paul smiled. "Don't knock it. I narrated one of those."

They both laughed, the kind of easy sound that comes when the city around you is working.

Greenwood emerged slowly — not in a rush of rooftops, but a rhythm of trees, wetlands, rooftop gardens, and play parks. There were no fences. Just shared green space and wide footpaths lined with edible plants and shaded rest stops. Even the main road into the precinct had been designed wide — not for more cars, but to safely accommodate cycling packs riding two abreast, making space for community in motion.

It was hard to remember this had once been an overgrown paddock. Now it was a case study — a suburb built from the ground up to integrate people, place and planet.

"It doesn't feel planned," Willow said quietly. "It just feels... right."

"That's the art of it," paul replied. "Design that doesn't shout. Just invites."

The bus slowed as they passed the central hub — a modest two-storey building framed in hempcrete and native stone. A Child and Family Learning Centre anchored the ground floor; above it, a learning lab and wellness clinic shared both sunlight and purpose. A mural wrapped around the corner wall, honouring the first 100 families to call Greenwood home in 2042 — the year Willow was born.

Willow pressed the stop request. "I reckon we can walk from here," she said. "I want to feel it."

paul nodded, rising slowly. "Let's go!"

Outside, the wide footpath stretched toward a tree-lined plaza and a cluster of small shops. A gentle hum of conversation drifted through the air.

The suburb didn't just look livable — it was.

Willow scanned the streetscape — rooftop gardens, toddlers on balance bikes, a corner bakery already buzzing. "It doesn't feel like a project," she said. "It feels… lived in."

paul smiled as they stepped onto the path. "That was always the hope."

She turned to him, curious. "Was it hard? Getting people on board with the growth?"

He exhaled slowly. "Back then, most were planning for 1,500 new residents per decade[4]. We pushed for ten times that — to make the lake real, to build the bridge, to earn the statue. We had to think bigger. Bolder."

He paused, eyes scanning the suburb's quiet confidence.

"We said: we'll welcome new residents, create new neighbourhoods, build thousands of new homes, and back new businesses — because a thriving city is a growing city. But our growth had to keep its soul — so no one was pushed aside, priced out, or left behind."

Willow nodded slowly. "Growth with heart."

paul looked at her, steady. "Kind politics, Willow."

He gestured out toward the lake, the rooftops beyond. "The value of the big three — the lake, the bridge, the statue — was actually eclipsed by this, Willow. The housing investment alone — 8,000 homes over 15 years — nearly doubled it. Public and private investment in the big three was what, $2.5 billion? Housing was closer to $5 billion."

Willow blinked, her lens running the numbers: $2.7 billion for the lake, bridge, and statue; $4.8 billion estimated for the homes. Close enough.

She smiled, choosing not to correct him. "The big four!"

They continued on foot, following a low-set laneway that opened into a plaza bordered by seasonal gardens and a book exchange.

A rooftop map caught Willow's attention. "Hard to believe they once expected only fifteen hundred new residents in a decade."

paul nodded. "It wasn't a failure of planning — it was a failure of imagination."

She looked out over the plaza, alive with colour, "Fifteen thousand in fifteen years. That's a real shift."

paul smiled. "And we were only just getting started."

They paused by a community noticeboard shaped like a compass rose, each point marked with the name of a new suburb.

Willow traced the lines with her finger. "Waterbank to the west... Iron-bark Plains in the south... Greenwood here... and Blueleaf Cove up north."

paul added, "Each with its own flavour — wetlands, bushland, ridge-line, riverside — but all built on the same foundation: people, place, planet."

She looked up at him. "And pride."

A child darted past them barefoot.

Willow watched her disappear into a garden bed alive with bees and flowering saltbush. "You really think about her grandkids when you build a suburb?"

paul didn't answer straight away. He crouched slightly, brushing his hand along a planting of pigface. "That's seven-generation thinking[5], Willow. Planting for people we'll never meet — and hoping they'll know we cared."

Further down the path, a mural-in-progress caught their eye — portraits of construction workers, layered with bright geometry and script in half a dozen languages.

Willow read from the plaque. "'Built by hands from twenty nations. Settled by the same.'"

paul smiled. "They didn't just build homes — they built home."

Willow nodded. "Like post-second world war[6] Australia, and done with dignity. Community visas. Language support. Pathways."

"And ownership," paul added. "That mattered most."

They turned a corner into a quiet cul-de-sac and paused in front of an old weatherboard home, its edges softened by fresh plantings and a gentle sense of care.

Willow gestured toward it. "That wasn't part of the original build, was it?"

paul shook his head. "No — that's the original homestead. This whole area used to be part of a big old farm called Greenwood. But the house was brought into the Retrofit Program. We started with energy audits on the city's older housing stock — mostly pre-1930s — then rolled out rooftop solar, insulation crews, window upgrades, and ventilation fixes."

She smiled. "It's like it got a second skin."

He nodded. "A second skin, a second life. We brought the city's old bones up to 21st-century standards — starting with the coldest, dampest homes. Momentum built from there."

"Who did the work?" Willow asked.

"As the big three infrastructure projects scaled up and down, we shaped the workforce toward these kinds of initiatives," paul explained. "It was smart workforce planning — and kind social policy. Most homes in Launceston were over 70 years old. They weren't designed for solar orientation or low-bill living. They were built when wood heaters filled the rooms with warmth... and the valley with smoke."

Willow raised an eyebrow. "So who funded it?"

"Upstream thinking again," paul said. "Energy companies were required to contribute. Government grants laid the groundwork. Instead of waiting to fund a $270 million hospital wing to treat illness, we invested in the essentials that keep people well — warm, dry, efficient homes."

He glanced back at the weatherboard.

"As the retrofitting era kicked off, local businesses grew with confidence. Private homeowners started funding their own upgrades — because materials were affordable, trades were skilled, and everything was being done at scale."

Willow nodded slowly. "Momentum begets momentum."

They crossed back toward the main path. A row of neat townhouses came into view — modest, welcoming, full of life. Bikes leaned casually against low stone walls.

Willow asked, "Which ones are the social housing?"

paul shook his head. "You'd never know. That was the point."

"One in five[7], right?"

He nodded. "Quiet equity, baked into the bricks."

A nearby footbridge led them over a small creek. Below, a community garden buzzed with life — toddlers on scooters, elders tending herbs.

Willow looked up. "Three storeys. But it doesn't feel crowded."

"Medium density[8]," paul said. "High dignity. It's all in the flow — light, air, connection."

At the end of the bridge stood a small community centre — signage in five languages, braille overlays, an integrated ramp built into the slope.

Willow ran her hand along the textured surface. "It's not just compliant. It's... inviting."

"We stopped designing for 'most people,'" paul said. "And started designing for everyone[9]."

She smiled. "Took us long enough."

paul nodded. "But we got there."

They passed a mural covered structure nestled between two garden beds — no bigger than a single garage, humming softly.

Willow paused. "Is that a battery?"

"One of many neighbourhood batteries[10]," paul replied. "Every fifty homes feed into one of these."

She leaned in, reading the display — live data on solar input, storage levels, drawdown curves.

"So these charge up during the day, and everyone draws down at night?"

"Exactly. No spikes. Just clean energy, shared locally."

"And they've been here since the beginning?"

"Built in, not bolted on."

She took it in, quietly. "People used to say solar was only for rich homeowners."

paul looked out over the quiet street. "This flips that. That's what happens when you design for equity, not just efficiency."

A breeze lifted as they turned down a residential lane. The air felt different — crisp and calm.

"They all look different," Willow said, pointing to the homes, "but you can tell they belong."

paul nodded. "That was the covenant. Every house had to meet Passivhaus[11] standard — airtight, insulated, properly ventilated."

Willow ran her fingers along the smooth timber window frame. "So no one's paying extra just to stay warm or cool."

"Low bills for life," paul said. "And every rooftop harvests the rain[12]

— just like in the 1950s and '60s. Tanks beside every home. Sustainability you can see — and actually use."

She exhaled, a half-smile forming. "We used to call that idealistic."

paul returned the smile. "Now they call it policy."

They rounded another corner and stepped into a neighbourhood park — basketball half-court, climbing net, shaded benches, and a walking loop curving through eucalypts.

"Feels like we've passed five of these already," Willow said.

"That was the rule," paul replied. "No house more than 400 meters from a park. Lit, maintained, made for movement."

It wasn't fancy. It was used.

Willow veered off the path and pointed to a bright cylindrical kiosk near the playground. "Is that a PlayPod?"

paul nodded. "Council rolled them out a few years back. Smart pods — they release play and sports equipment and track usage trends across the city."

She stepped closer, reading the playful display:

'Ready to move? Tap your KindraPass — or show us 25 squats!'

paul chuckled. "It's all about access. Some people tap in. Others just earn it — a few push-ups, a quick sprint."

"Gamified health," Willow grinned.

"Exactly. But with purpose," paul said. "You can fund this stuff when you think upstream. We didn't need as many hospital beds once people started moving more."

Willow nodded.

"And we used the data to understand what communities were playing, where, and when — then adjusted funding, maintenance, even programs based on real use."

Willow watched a group of kids dash away with foam javelins and balance discs. "Feels like fun. But it's clever policy."

paul smiled. "That's the idea."

The footpath widened ahead of them — smooth and shaded beneath a canopy of deciduous trees. A parent jogged past, stroller gliding. Two kids wobbled by on balance bikes, all limbs and laughter.

"You can walk the whole suburb without stepping into the sun," Willow said.

"Or into traffic," paul added. "Streets weren't just for cars anymore. That was the shift."

They watched as a peloton of cyclists rode past, chatting easily, safe in their own rhythm.

"Built for walking and cycling," she said. "And wonder."

They ended their walk beneath a flowering gum outside the Greenwood inclusive café, two local teas in hand — lemon myrtle for Willow, brewed chai for paul. Around them, the precinct hummed with quiet energy: a father helping with homework, a group of tradies swapping jobsite stories, the cycling crew refuelling on muffins.

Willow's gaze drifted toward the nearby co-working hub. Her best friend had launched a social enterprise there — one of dozens sparked by the suburb's shared spaces and slower rhythms. She smiled. Some futures weren't imagined. They were grown.

Willow engaged Synapstra. The world shimmered — then re-formed.

"DeepSeequence loaded," said Clara softly in her ear. "Trigger phrase?"

Willow murmured, "What if the growth had failed?"

The café dissolved.

No people. No plaza. No rooftop gardens. The footpath beneath her faded, replaced by ankle-high grass. She stood alone in a rolling paddock, accompanied only by sheep.

"Scenario: 2030s growth strategy voted down," Clara intoned. "No new suburbs. Population increase capped at 1,500."

The simulation unfolded.

No bridge over the Tamar—traffic choking the city.

No weir—just mudflats and rice grass.

No freshwater vision.

No Statue of Equity—no beacon.

Willow passed the spot where the inclusive café should have been: a padlocked fence, a sun-blanched sign, silence.

No Greenwood.

No Waterbank.

No Ironbark Plains.

No Blueleaf Cove.

"Secondary impacts," Clara prompted.

No build, no jobs across the trades; no skilled migration—shortages of engineers, planners; no humanitarian entrants—less safety, less richness, fewer hands.

No housing supply—rents up, overcrowding, stalled growth.

No new attractions—no tourism surge, no waterfront investment.

Ripple effects: no cafés, no early learning centres or gyms; no small-business services; no studios or public art; no co-working; no park crews; no community batteries; no retrofits; no learning hubs; no accessible design.

A light wind moved through the emptiness. A crow called across the hills.

Clara rewound to a late-afternoon council meeting: cautious hands, hovering:

"Too ambitious."

"Too expensive."

"Too uncertain."

"Too green."

"Too soon."

And so, nothing happened.

Willow deactivated DeepSeequence. The café returned—light, warmth, laughter, conversation.

paul studied her face. "You ran one, didn't you?"

Willow nodded, slowly. "It was... a paddock. No bridge. No lake. No people."

She took a sip of tea, grounding herself again. "All the jobs that never came. The businesses that never started. The children that never played in those parks. It was just a future that never lived."

paul said nothing. He didn't need to.

They sat quietly together, surrounded by everything that might not have been — and was.

An electric bus sighed to the curb. paul nodded toward the doors, and they climbed aboard, finding a pair of window seats. With a gentle whirr the electric bus slipped back into motion, easing south through the green edges of Greenwood. Willow and paul sat in comfortable silence, the landscape unfolding beside them — rooftops glittering, trees leaning toward the light, a small group of children racing the shadow of the bus.

Willow watched the suburb fade behind them. It wasn't loud. It wasn't flashy. But it pulsed with something rare — purpose made real.

She turned to paul. "Do you think they knew? The ones who backed it all — the bridge, the lake, the new suburbs?"

He shrugged gently. "Some did. Most just hoped. They were the transforming generation — not because they were certain, but because they acted anyway."

Willow nodded, eyes returning to the glass. Greenwood disappeared from view, replaced by the soft outline of the city beyond.

"It took vision," she said. "And innovation. None of this just... happens."

paul smiled. "No. Someone has to see it before it exists. And then convince everyone else it's possible."

Willow leaned back, thoughtful. "Maybe that's what transformational leadership really is. Not just the leap — but the invitation."

The bus curved south, toward the heart of the city.

There would be more stories ahead. More places reimagined.

Places like Greenwood showed what was possible. But behind every thriving street and solar roof was a decision — a person, a prototype, a push against inertia. Next: the unruly spark of how.

NINE
THE CREATIVITY
CULTIVATING CHANGEMAKERS

"You never change things by fighting the existing reality. To change something, build a new model that makes the existing model obsolete."
— Buckminster Fuller[1]

14 May 2064

paul reached the spot first, scarf tucked loosely around his neck, eyes still adjusting to the sharper mid-morning light after a few quiet hours in the university library.

Willow arrived a few moments later, one hand wrapped around a warm keep-cup, the other clutching her hemp bag, fingerless gloves peeking from the sleeves of her jacket.

They exchanged silent hat tips, then stood in shared silence, shoes planted firmly on the western bank of the North Esk, just upstream from the university footbridge.

Across the water, the old Glebe Farm building leaned gently toward the river — its ochre-painted wall transformed into a playful and disorienting mural. A flurry of upside-down images scattered across the surface: bold, bright, and confusing — until you knew where to look.

A rowing foursome hung oar-deep in the air, blades rising awkwardly toward the sky, coxswain shouting into the wind. Just above them, a solo kayaker hovered beneath the eaves, mid-stroke, paddle cutting through nothing but cloud. Higher still, two synchronised divers twisted upward in perfect unison, their bodies arched as if drawn into the heavens rather than descending into water. And at the very top — or bottom, depending on your view — a swimmer moved smoothly across the brickwork, backstroking through the morning light, gaze locked toward some imagined ceiling.

But in the river's surface — still and mirror-like in the autumn light — the whole scene found its footing.

The rowers surged forward in perfect unison. The kayaker skimmed the mirrored surface, spray rising with each stroke. The divers plummeted gracefully toward the water, suspended mid-flight. And the swimmer sliced through the river below, her motion seamless, her purpose clear.

It was a mural that could only be seen whole in partnership with the river — a quiet invitation to pause, invert, reflect. A gentle reminder, perhaps, that perspective sometimes requires stillness.

"Now that's clever," Willow murmured, her voice almost reverent.

paul nodded, hands resting lightly in the pockets of his long coat. "Could it be something about perspective? How we can't always see things clearly unless we reflect?"

Willow glanced down at the water again, watching the mural's reflection ripple faintly as a breeze rolled through. "It's beautiful," she said. "Makes you stop. Makes you... think."

They stood for a while longer, letting the stillness linger, watching the river hold the story just a little longer.

Eventually, Willow broke the silence. "We're not going to the lake today, are we?"

paul had a plan, a smile tugging at the corner of his mouth. "Let's go! We'll take the mural trail today."

She nodded, slipping her cup into her bag. "Trail it is!"

They took the path that curve back toward the city centre, its retaining wall now home to a riot of stencilled creatures and layered tags — a canvas that kept changing with the seasons and the students.

"Let's see where this takes us," he said.

They turned from the river and stepped into the city, where colour crept around every corner and creativity had carved itself into brick, concrete, plastic and glass — not as decoration, but as declaration.

The first mural they pass clings to a weather-beaten brick wall on the brewery side of the Esk, its once-vivid tones now bleached by sun and peeled at the edges by wind and time. A pair of boot prints — impossibly large — stride across a Martian landscape rendered in ochre and rust. Behind them, a stylised astronaut raises a gloved hand toward Earth, a sliver of blue in the distant sky. The figure's visor, once a mirror of hope, is now cracked with age, refracting the light in scattered fragments. Flaking letters in the corner read: "*Mars Landing 2039 — For all humankind.*"

Willow pauses to do the math. "Wow, twenty-five years ago."

paul ran a hand gently along the blistered paint of an older wall. "You know, we lost a lot of these. Not just paint on brick — stories. Pride. That old Trades Hall mural, the one about the union wins — the 40-

hour week, worker safety, fair pay — it just... vanished. Painted over like it never mattered."

Willow frowned. "So what changed? I can't really picture our city without murals."

"Mindset," paul said firmly. "Back then, all those big blank walls were magnets for graffiti. Council treated it like a natural disaster — deploy the taskforce, scrub it off, wait for the next tag."

He shook his head, the memory still frustrating. "They were stuck in downstream thinking. So a clever bunch flipped the script. Asked: what if we spent the same budget... upstream?"

"Murals," Willow guessed, catching on.

He smiled. "They drafted a proposal — same cost as graffiti removal — but this time, it funded local artists, involved schools, brought in community groups. Told the stories of our people and place, right on the walls we'd been trying to keep blank."

"And it worked?" Willow asked.

"Better than we hoped. People respected what they helped create. There's a kind of unwritten protection when something holds meaning."

She nodded. "Instead of chasing vandals..."

"We invested in artists," he finished. "And in community. And culture."

He chuckled. "One resident said, 'Might even attract a few tourists.' Got laughed at back then — but she wasn't wrong."

Willow grinned. "Upstream thinking... in full colour."

They kept walking, passing school groups on guided art tours, a café with sketches pinned along its window, a busker painting with chalks in real time — the whole city quietly humming with creativity.

paul smiled. "It started as a tiny program — then became a much-loved one. Like most good things, it grew. The early artists were young

— students, mostly — and the city backed them in. Materials, scaffolding, insurance. Real walls. Real trust. Eventually, we welcomed visiting artists from around the world."

They paused in front of the Republic mural. The paint had weathered to a warm sepia tone, soft and dignified. Bits of moss crept along the base — as if nature itself were honouring the message.

Then came a moment of quiet joy — a cluster of tiny installations: whimsical little doors tucked into unexpected corners, each one hand-painted, each one quietly magical.

Willow crouched to peer inside one, her smile softening.

"These," she said, "feel like someone leaving surprises for the city to find."

paul nodded. "That's exactly what they are."

Then came the next mural — striking in its stillness. Painted in rich ochres, charcoal greys, and the deepest blues, it stretched across the western wall of Town Hall. A surface once blank, now reverent.

In the centre, a vast pair of hands held open a stretch of land — delicate eucalyptus leaves unfurling from the fingers, rivers flowing from the creases of the palm. The landscape within the hands was alive: fire-stick lines traced the paths of careful burning; stone tools nestled in ochre earth; mutton birds wheeled in the distance.

Across the mural's sky, silhouettes of returning ancestors floated above the land — some walking, some dancing, some pausing with hands raised in welcome. At their feet, Elders and children stood together, arms linked, forming a circle of belonging.

On the far edge, a small bronze disk caught the light. Willow stepped closer, and a soft chime sounded:

CitizenEcho active - Mural: "Return" (2031)
Artist: K. Everett
Commissioned in honour of the re-commencement of formal land
return to Aboriginal Tasmanians.

"This always was, and always will be, Aboriginal land.
Returned not as gift — but as truth, and as beginning."

Willow lingered longest at the mural. paul watched her in silence.

"It wasn't just symbolic," he said gently. "It was structural. Real hectares. Real healing. We started to put things right — not perfectly, but earnestly."

They walked on, winding deeper into the North-East Quarter — past old warehouses reborn in colour, and switch boxes transformed into playful creatures. paul guided them down a narrow alley just off the main trail — one of his favourites — where a towering mural honoured Tasmania's emergency service volunteers. Firies, ambos, and SES crews were painted mid-action: hauling hoses, cradling evacuees, scanning floodwaters.

Their view, however, was partly blocked by a long-wheelbase van idling halfway down the lane.

A group of musicians was unloading gear from the back — cables, speakers, a drum kit with scuffed skins and stickers. A low thrum of sound-check bass spilled from the venue's back door.

"Hey guys," paul offered, stepping aside to let them pass.

"Cheers, mate," one replied, hoisting an amp with practiced ease.

Willow glanced back at the mural, still half-obscured. "Shame we couldn't see the whole thing."

paul nodded. "It'll be there tomorrow," he said, then nodded toward the van. "Besides — that? That's the better story."

Willow arched an eyebrow.

"For almost fifty years," paul said, "pokies were sold as 'entertainment' — but it was never about fun. It was about extraction. Pubs and clubs became machines for profit — private owners, shareholders, even governments — all draining money from the vulnerable under the polite disguise of leisure."

He exhaled sharply. "And they didn't just replace live music. They hollowed out community life. Real entertainment connects people. Pokies isolate. They turned social venues into quiet engines of misery — lit by neon, fed by desperation."

Willow turned to paul. "One of Premier Jaswal's key reforms?"

"Yep." paul's expression warmed. "Thanks to the Premier's courage— listening to community over vested interests—no pokies in pubs and clubs. And the music's back. Not just music, the whole ecosystem. Open mics, comedy nights, weekend gigs with proper lighting and sound. Real jobs, Willow: local tech crews, sound engineers, graphic designers, bar staff, even teachers mentoring the next generation."

He nodded toward the alley, where the band was still unpacking gear. "Kids have a path again — from school music nights to busking to headlining their first gig. We're rebuilding an industry that lets people belong. Not just earn a wage — belong."

He turned, watching the mural come into full view as the van pulled away.

"And here's the thing," he said, his voice low. "When locals write and perform their own music — that's culture. That's us, telling our stories. Shaping how we see each other. Songs about the river, the fires, first heartbreak, last chances, pride in place. I've never known a poker machine to write a ballad or help someone feel less alone."

Willow was quiet, letting the words settle.

"That's the difference," paul said. "One drains life out. The other gives it back."

A few steps later, Willow spotted a busker warming up outside the next venue. "So pokies were removed... and creativity returned?" she said, half to herself.

paul smiled. "Pokies isolate. Music connects. This wasn't just policy — it enabled our creative culture."

They walked a while in silence before Willow slowed. "We should loop back," she said, nodding toward the University. "There's a new piece outside my old school — part of a rotating student installation. You'll like it."

paul raised an eyebrow, amused. "How can I say no? Let's go!"

She grinned and took the lead.

The school emerged gradually. A striking vertical structure framed by solar fins and climbing greenery, it stood proudly opposite York Park. Where once there had been a car yard, now rose a campus alive with purpose.

Out front, a bold sculpture rose from the courtyard — a spiral of rusted steel and native timbers, each panel etched with questions rather than answers.

paul stepped closer, squinting at the base. "'What do we owe the future?'" he read aloud.

He followed, the doors opening onto a school he had once helped to imagine — light-filled, layered with voices and vision, alive with possibility.

With entry confirmed, CitizenEcho flickered to life:

CitizenEcho: 2034 Changemaker High Architectural Record
Access Level: Public MemoryLoom
Changemaker High, Tasmania's first vertical public school, opened in
2034 next to the university precinct — an innovation campus that
blurred education, enterprise, and community action.

Ground Floor — Community Commons & Citizen Science
– Public commons with a student-led café and co-working; the Civic-
Loom Wall where citizens submitted local ideas and design
challenges.
– Flexible wet/dry labs and research pods enabling students to collabo-

rate with scientists and community partners on real environmental and health projects.

Level 1 — Innovation Labs & The Learning Loop
— Fabrication bays, robotics studios, and maker spaces hosting the annual Visualise Your Idea showcase and early-stage student ventures.
— The Learning Loop: a self-directed, multi-age studio with no bells or fixed timetables; mentors and adaptive AI support progression through projects.

Level 2 — Health, Wellbeing, Arts & Expression
— Integrated health centre, sensory rooms, quiet zones, and restorative pods focused on mental health and inclusion.
— Performance studios, digital media labs, and a rooftop gallery for student exhibitions and community workshops.

Level 3 — Leadership & Legacy
— Youth governance chamber and policy-simulation suites, with access to a rooftop garden planted by each graduating cohort.
— A living archive housing student-led impact projects accumulated over time.

Willow drifted toward the far wall, where an old-school timber honour board stood quietly apart from the digital overlays. No screens, no sensors — just laser-cut precision on Tasmanian oak. Each student's name was carved into the wood with care, the grain catching the light like memory itself.

She found hers quickly, then grinned and tapped another set of names further up. "There you are," she said, glancing over her shoulder. "That's where I first spotted your name — you were part of the School Establishment Committee. Weren't you?"

paul smiled. "I may have nudged the Education Minister — and talked non-stop about the notion of 'teenagency'[2]."

At Willow's prompt, CitizenEcho pulsed gently to life, syncing the moment to public memory.

"A creative city grows by building communities of learners[3]. And this institution will be a civic workshop for changemakers: a place where young people co-create the future with their communities, test ideas in the real world, and practice democracy, stewardship, and solidarity. It will model new ways of teaching and learning—real learning based on joy, trust, and shared power[4]—and help students flourish as people. It will build young people's capacity and confidence to make a positive difference, amplify their creative self-belief and meet rapid change with courage. Graduates will leave not just skilled, but fully human[5]: awake, grounded, compassionate, and resilient—citizens with grit[6] who can make and remake a city, a state, and a nation without losing their kindness along the way. — paul mallett, CitizenEcho annotation, 2034

paul gave a soft laugh, more surprised than embarrassed. "That's aged better than I have."

Intrigued by the depth of his involvement, Willow summoned the rest of the speech with LumenView. A translucent overlay unfolded above the honour board, paul's voice from decades earlier filling the quiet space:

"...We'll be an Education City — a City of Ideas — where learning is lifelong and innovation is local. Launceston will stand among the great regional cities of the world: a place that backs bold thinking, nurtures creativity, and helps our talent rise. Education in this city will help young people become somebody well[7].

Not just well-credentialed, but well in themselves — confident, connected, and capable of shaping a fair and livable world. Yes, literacy and numeracy matter. But the purpose is bigger: to grow humane, capable citizens who bring their gifts to the common good, strengthen social cohesion, and learn how to live well together.

Too often we treat school as a narrow runway to the labour market. Jobs matter — dignity matters — but our young people are more than future workers or consumers. They deserve the tools to ask better ques-

tions: What is a good life? What is right livelihood? How should we use our shared resources? What does care require of us — for each other and for Country?

A great Education City doesn't just deliver content; it shapes identity and belonging. It helps students critique harmful myths — that worth is what you own, or that success is how busy you look. It teaches that relationships outrank possessions, that compassion can replace extraction, and that the health of people and planet is not extra to the curriculum — it is the curriculum.

In Launceston, every young person will know they can learn, create, and build a future — right here at home."

She glanced sideways at him, something closer to respect in her eyes. "You weren't just on the committee, were you?"

paul gestured toward an empty cowork booth, and they sat. Willow watched students scatter across beanbags and desks—some deep in discussion, others bent over sensors or sketchpads.

paul leaned back, eyes sweeping the room like someone still proud of the blueprint. He opened his hands. "This was my wheelhouse, Willow. I'd been passionate about the liberating power of education since I trained as a teacher in the '90s."

He leaned forward, voice warm. "It wasn't only a world full of wicked problems"—he made a small cutting gesture with his hand—"it was who felt able to solve them. The committee didn't lobby for this school to 'fix' broken kids."

He tapped the bench. "We campaigned for it because the traditional system was never built to see their brilliance. This place was built from the ground up on respect and curiosity—respect for every individual, knowing we all bloom in our own season and shouldn't be compared to others[8]. We built it to cultivate each person's strengths, and we organised it so kids didn't just study problems—they solved them."

He mimed passing objects from palm to palm. "We didn't ask students to wait their turn. We handed them the tools—sensors, soil, stories—and said, 'Show us what's possible.' Creative cities grow their own changemakers. And changemakers don't appear fully formed—they emerge when someone trusts them to lead."

He flattened a hand to his chest, then to the table. "Here, we wanted every young person to know they belonged. Their ideas mattered. Their questions mattered. Their voice mattered. This wasn't a pipeline to jobs; it was a launchpad—for ideas, for purpose, for possibility. We didn't sort them by risk. We invited them into a cause."

Willow took a moment, eyes on the students, something unreadable flickering across her face.

Before she could speak, paul cut gently across the silence. "Now you went here," he said. "Tell me — did it live up to the promise?"

She nodded, slowly at first. Then with quiet certainty.

"Mostly," she said. "Actually… more than that. This place helped me become me."

She paused, her eyes drifting toward student huddles. "I was more into the arts — storytelling, murals, protest posters. Anything but science. But when the lake started to turn…"

Her voice trailed off. Then she continued, softer. "The first sign wasn't the colour — it was the silence. The birds that usually circled near the causeway were gone. The water, usually glassy, had turned viscous and dull. Then came the green. An algal bloom. Thick and fast, spreading across the northern reach of Tamar Lake."

She glanced at paul.

"By the time it reached the children's water play zone, people panicked. It wasn't just the smell — it was what it symbolised. A reversal. For years, Tamar Lake had been the life of the city. Now it felt like a collapse."

Willow exhaled slowly. "But this time, the response wasn't slow. It wasn't top-down. It was swift. It was collective. It started with us — the students as citizen scientists. We mobilised within hours. The Environmental Science and Engineering streams fanned out across the lake with handheld sensors — measuring pH, oxygen, turbidity, temperature. Some of the Year 10s built drones to reach the far corners. Others designed floating rafts for long-term monitoring."

She tapped the side of the booth. "I joined the comms team. Helped document the whole thing. Translated the science. Created visuals so the community could understand what was happening."

Her gaze moved to the glass wall, where beyond the atrium, she could see a former favourite teacher.

"But it wasn't just students. Community elders – already connected to the school – they brought people who remembered when the old river ran green, who knew runoff patterns by feel. They told us where to look. Uni researchers from the marine science lab helped validate the samples and model the bloom's spread. Local engineers trialled filtration ideas and natural aerators. And Council? They didn't get in the way. They cleared barriers, fast-tracked permits. Stood beside us. Not as the lead. As collaborators."

She smiled faintly.

"We built a dashboard. Shared live data. And slowly, the bloom retreated. The fish came back. So did confidence. But more than that — we changed. We went from students… to citizens. From studying problems to solving them."

Willow looked back toward the atrium, where students huddled around a drone prototype, heads together, laughing. "I didn't expect to find purpose here," she said quietly. "But it found me."

paul sat back, visibly moved. The vision of the school as a place to introduce young people to the world — and unleash their potential — was alive and working.

"I'm guessing you could name a few other citizen science projects from your time here?" he said, half-grinning.

"I can, actually," Willow replied. "There was the Cemetery one. Students mapped and monitored the ecological value of a patch of bushland near Carr Villa. It had been earmarked for clearing as part of the cemetery expansion."

"And the result?"

"I'm pretty sure Council followed their science and preserved it. The digital biodiversity atlas the students created was pretty compelling."

paul raised an eyebrow. "And?"

Willow smiled. "There was also the work to protect the wildlife corridor near Lilydale. Students kept pushing for better safeguards — and each year, the case just got stronger."

In front of them, a digital mural flickered to life — scrolling through highlights from last year's Launceston City Student Design Competition, then pausing on a bold new callout: *"21 December 2064: Five Minute Thesis Showcase. Tamar Lake Convention Centre."*

paul nudged her lightly. "You should do it."

Willow raised an eyebrow. "Me?"

"Find your voice, Willow."

She didn't answer right away. But she didn't dismiss it either.

They walked in companionable silence, the school receding behind them — its high windows now catching the sun like ideas catching light. The city hummed around them, alive with footsteps and colour, echoes of laughter and possibility.

As they neared the university precinct once more, the path curved gently toward the river, carrying them past the Launceston Museum and Art Gallery. And there it was again — the mural.

Still. Waiting.

They ended where they began — beside the water, the artwork now bathed in soft midday light. The rowers looked steadier. The diver's arc, more certain.

paul wheeled his bike out from behind the rack, unclipping his helmet from the handlebars. Willow stood beside him, hands tucked in her coat pockets, gaze lingering on the wall.

As she stepped forward, the ground beneath her buzzed softly — and with a gentle chime, a familiar glow rose from the path.

CitizenEcho: Mural: "Flight and Flow" (2061)
Artist: Anita and students from across the city.
Commissioned in honour of Olympic teams who trained in Launceston
ahead of the 2060 Melbourne Games. Rowing and kayak crews trained
on Lake Tamar. Diving and aquatic teams used the Launceston
Aquatic Centre.
Canoe slalom teams trained in Cataract Gorge — the first Olympic-
standard course to use a naturally flowing waterway in over 50 years.
The mural celebrates motion, balance, and shared preparation.

Willow exhaled, low and thoughtful. "Cataract Gorge. That's kind of perfect, isn't it?"

paul smiled, proud that the city's iconic wonder had been preserved — untouched in his lifetime, accessible, adored, conserved for all to enjoy. Then: "Launceston's had a long, proud history of sport and recreation. We've always punched above our weight. Took us a while, but we finally backed it — with vision, and a bit of backbone."

Willow glanced back at the water, the mural flickering gently in the ripples. "I might just ask you about that next time."

paul tipped his helmet in mock salute. "I'll bring my stats," he grinned, "and a few gold-medal memories."

And with that, he pushed off, wheels humming on the path — while Willow lingered a little longer, watching the swimmer drift calmly across brick and sky.

TEN
THE SPORT
ACTIVE BELONGING

"The body will become better at whatever you do, or don't do. If you don't move, your body will make you better at not moving. If you move, your body will allow more movement." — Ido Portal[1]

28 May 2064

paul set the resistance band down and leaned on the timber rail, breath slowing. The palaestra[2] by the lake — Launceston's own take on Venice Beach Gym — rose with a high, open-air roof held by ironbark beams. Its weather-sensitive walls could roll down against rain or wind, but today they were drawn up, the whole place open to the breeze. Free weights, pull-up bars, and resistance machines stood ready for anyone. Conversations and the clink of plates mingled —

neighbours swapping news, students debating mid-squat. A place to move, to talk, to belong.

From the north came the crunch of footsteps on gravel. Willow rounded the bend, hemp bag over one shoulder, her posture carrying the weight of a late night.

"Sorry I'm late," she said, resting against a post. "We had a touch final last night. After-party went to extra time."

paul tipped an imaginary hat, met her eyes, then glanced toward the water with a wry smile. "Big night?"

She grinned. "Big win."

He nodded toward the lake. "Hard to believe there was a time we had neither this lake nor the teams that now train on it."

Willow stretched her back as if limbering for the path ahead. "You're going to tell me a story, aren't you?"

He smiled. "About how this city became one of the healthiest in the country. Not because we built more hospitals…"

Willow leaned in. "But because you got people moving?"

"Not just about moving," he said. "It was about belonging — about giving people a place where they felt they mattered."

A dragon boat slid into view, paddles rising and falling in unison — a living example of movement and connection in perfect rhythm.

"Let's go!" paul offered gently. "Let's walk."

They left the palaestra, falling into step toward the community oval in Republic Park, grass still damp from the night's rain. Beyond the tree line, the lake caught the light, and in the distance a group of students warmed up while their Health and Physical Education teacher's voice carried over the thud of footballs on turf.

As they followed the asphalt path, they passed a half-court basketball zone where two teenagers traded shots, a nearby half-court netball pad where girls practised passes, and an outdoor cross-fit rack where two older men laughed between chin-ups.

paul took it in silently, then let out a slow breath. "Of all the policy areas, Willow… this one frustrated me most."

She glanced at him, catching the shift in his tone. "My first job was at a public pool. Later, I worked as a personal trainer. And eventually — I was one of them," he said, nodding toward the oval. "A HPE teacher. Prevention, public health — that was my grounding. It just made sense: help people stay well, move often, sleep better, eat well. Prevent, rather than treat. Extend both lifespan and healthspan[3]— not just how long you live, but how well you live. Years in good health, free from chronic disease, disability, or serious decline."

Willow's thoughts flicked to her grandfather — grief softened by gratitude. He'd stayed in good mental and physical health until his passing at 94.

Clara nudged her gently in the background: pause, breathe, name what you feel.

paul went on, unaware. "But time and again, we stayed stuck downstream. Political wins were measured in more hospitals, more beds, more doctors, cheaper medicines. And sure — Tasmania's population was getting older, sicker, needing more disability support[4]. Of course we had to respond. But someone had to be brave enough to fund both ends for a while — interrupt the trajectory[5]. Prevention and care. Upstream and downstream. Kindness and stewardship."

They stopped near a flowering wattle. A girl in a bright yellow jersey sprinted down the wing, arms pumping. "We paid either way," he said quietly. "Now in dollars — or later in dollars and suffering."

Willow folded her arms. "So, what changed?"

"The Sugar Tax[6] helped," paul said. "So did social prescribing[7] — where GPs referred people to community activities instead of just medication. But the real shift came when we hit a tipping point. Enough people saw it, understood it, and wanted something better."

He glanced at her. "Launceston — and then Tasmania — became the model."

Willow kept her eyes on the field. "Because you showed what was possible."

"No, Willow," paul said, firm. "I was just on the bus, remember. It happened because a small group of thoughtful, committed people[8] became changemakers. They weren't trapped by short-termism. They broke free from the electoral cycle, looked at the evidence, listened to the community, acted, and never gave up on the idea that we could be a healthy people, a healthy economy, a healthy city — the healthiest island on the planet. A blue zone[9]."

She walked beside him in silence, letting the thought settle. "When did the tide turn?" she asked.

"The city-wide survey and healthy weight initiative built momentum," paul said. "Media coverage was huge when we hit 500,000 kilograms lost as a city. But the real shift came when the city doubled down — invested in parks, opened school facilities, brought sport close to home. We aimed for no more than 400 metres from anyone's door — a 10-minute walk, max."

He gestured toward a father steadying his daughter along a smooth, low tree trunk in a natural playground. She leapt into his arms with a squeal.

"We built plenty of these. Backed community access with the same funding once reserved for elite sport. We stopped seeing sport and rec as a luxury — it became infrastructure, as essential as roads or clean water."

They reached a small fitness zone where two teens used an outdoor rowing machine, its resistance powered by their effort. Next to it, a digital sign flipped between usage stats and coaching tips — part of the new PlayMetrics[10] program.

"That data's gold," paul said. "PerceptaNet tracks who's using what, when — we reinvest where it matters most. No more arguing over what 'might' be needed. For fact's sake. We know."

As they walked on, they passed a handball court, a concrete rebound wall, and a low-slung pavilion. Out front, a laminated sign announced volunteer umpire training for that evening.

"Local sport's only as strong as its volunteers," paul said. "So council started sponsoring training — umpires, scorers, coaches. That one move kept clubs and rosters alive."

"Mum said schools weren't always open after hours — is that true?" Willow asked.

"It is," paul said. "Feels natural now, but for generations they were pretty much locked by 4 p.m. We tackled the insurance mess, installed smart security, and set up shared-use agreements. Those ovals and courts belong to the public — they should never sit empty."

They headed toward the Gorge loop, the wide, bustling path narrowing into the quiet of the ravine. A father passed with a stroller, his son trotting alongside with a foam cricket bat.

Willow smiled. "On Sundays, when they closed parts of the CBD to cars, Mum took me in. Food stalls, chalk art, jumping mats. I ran myself ragged all day. No screens. Just community."

"Exactly," paul said. "We reclaimed streets for people — gave families space to move, connect, play. That's when the city started to breathe again."

The roar of water grew louder as they walked, rushing through the gorge.

paul raised his voice. "We used to frame it wrong — treating lifestyle illness like personal failure. Poor choices, lack of willpower. Truth is, it was a design flaw."

Willow's eyes followed the curve of the track where sheer rock walls rose on either side, trees clinging upright to impossible slopes.

"So we changed the design."

"Exactly. People don't lack motivation, Willow. They lack footpaths. Safe crossings. Green space close by. And places that make movement joyful. When we designed for movement, we moved budgets too — from treatment to transformation."

Willow smirked. "You've said that before."

"And I'll keep saying it until it sticks."

"We finally stopped pitting prevention against care," paul said. "We showed the cost of doing nothing."

Willow pulled up national numbers from before the transformation. "Thirty-three billion a year[11]... from physical inactivity alone. Absenteeism, chronic illness, early death..."

"And forty percent of that chronic disease was preventable," paul added. "We were treating the symptoms of car-centric, screen-bound, isolating environments."

They rounded a bend and spotted the sign to the First Basin. The peacocks called first — wild, echoing squawks that bounced off the Gorge walls. Then came the sound of water: the steady rush from Cataract Creek feeding into the Basin, the faint splash from the swimming pool. As the trees thinned, the view opened — the wide grassy banks framed by cliffs, the sweep of still, dark water beyond the pool. A suspension bridge spanned the Gorge above, and the chairlift crossed silently overhead. Families sprawled on the lawn, children waded in the shallows, and walkers paused on the stone steps to take in the scene.

A screen beside the century old pool showed air quality, UV levels, and the community's weekly step count. A low plaque read: Funded through the Healthy City Fund — Walking is Medicine.

"I've been looking at the economics," Willow said. "Four dollars forty returned for every dollar spent on walking and cycling infrastructure[12]."

paul nodded. "Conservative. World Health Organisation[13] put it at five to thirteen dollars in some cities. Fewer hospital visits, less reliance on pharmaceuticals, more participation in life and work. And those savings weren't abstract," paul added. They hit the budget bottom line. Fewer ambulance callouts, lower mental health admissions, even less road maintenance — fewer cars mean fewer potholes."

They paused at the suspension bridge, waiting as a gaggle of kids on scooters wobbled across. One fell, giggled, and scrambled up again as a parent encouraged from behind.

Willow smiled. "Designing for joy."

"Designing for equity," paul said. "We stopped calling it sport or fitness — it became access. To opportunity. To pride. To a longer healthspan."

They crossed slowly, pausing to take in the untouched beauty around them.

"Upstream thinking isn't abstract," paul said. "It's the most grounded idea there is: invest early, support all, save later."

"You ever get tired of saying that?" Willow asked.

He smiled. "Not when it starts to matter."

She looked back at the swaying bridge — full of people, laughter, movement.

"It wasn't just bike lanes or park upgrades," she said softly. "It was creating a city where health came naturally. Where it wasn't a hospital thing — it was a daily thing."

paul's voice softened. "Exactly. And in the end, we saved more than money." "We saved lives," she said. "People got extra years of good life."

They followed the Duck Reach trail, water rushing beside them as sunlight filtered through the canopy, scattering dappled light across the track.

Willow watched kayakers thread the rapids below. "Organised club sport still has its place, right? And elite sport too?"

"Absolutely," paul said. "It motivates. And the big events weren't just about pride — they sparked the economy. Devils, JackJumpers, Hurricanes; national soccer, netball, hockey; even badminton and karate — we backed it all. Movement mattered at every level."

He smiled. "We even built it into the Statue of Equity — a world-class climbing facility at its core. And the Olympic teams trained here ahead of Melbourne 2060. Remember?"

He gestured downstream to the dolerite walls, carved by centuries of flow, sunlight catching silvery seams in the rock. "They used this stretch — rapids, trails, facilities. It became a national training ground."

Willow smiled. "I remember flags on the bridge. Mum took me to watch the rowers."

They looped back toward the suspension bridge, where families sprawled on the grass and a pair of swimmers eased into the pool. Overhead, a peacock called again — less startling now, more like punctuation on a page already written.

Willow stopped mid-bridge. paul joined her, resting one hand lightly on the rail for balance, his gaze following birds skimming the basin's surface.

"I've always loved it here," he said at last, his voice low but certain. "It recharges me. Gives me life."

Willow nodded, exhaling slowly. "It's my recharge station too. When things get hard, I always end up here."

They stood in silence, watching the basin shimmer, time unspooling gently around them.

"We're so lucky to have this on our doorstep," she said, her voice softened by awe. "It feels... timeless here."

paul nodded, eyes still on the water. "It does. The community's been wise to leave this place largely untouched."

They walked on toward the city. The Basin pool slipped from view, tucked once more into the gorge.

"You know, the lake let us host major rowing regattas again, Willow," paul said. "We hadn't done that in Launceston for almost a century[14]."

"We refurbished the Silverdome," paul went on. "Built outdoor velodromes in Riverside and St Leonards; pump tracks in Waverley and Ravenswood; extended mountain bike trails in Trevallyn and Kate Reed. Kids' cycling spiked — not just watching sport, but joining in."

"The city giving every kid a bike might've helped," Willow said, teasing.

"Momentum begets momentum," paul grinned. "Invest upstream, save downstream — then you can do bold things. Gift bikes. Make gym access affordable where it never was."

Four generations passed them: a toddler wobbling ahead, parents close, grandparents chatting, a great-grandmother steady by the rail. The youngest darted; the oldest set the pace — and somehow they all kept stride.

paul watched them, then continued. "And then there's Hobler's Bridge. We finally roofed the netball centre — full coverage, solar-powered. No more sliding on winter frost."

Willow grinned. "Way better night leagues. I played my first adult season there."

paul chuckled. "Exactly. The solar array didn't just power lights and radiant heaters — it paid for longer training windows, weekend comps, accessible change rooms. People came from across the Commonwealth to study it."

He slowed, catching her eye. "I'll say it again. When you cut downstream spend — avoidable illness, emergency care, meds — you don't just save. You redirect. Upstream. Into community, connection... movement."

"Into a city where sport isn't just for the gifted," she said. "It's daily life."

paul nodded. "Exactly. Elite sport lights the spark; everyday access keeps the fire burning."

Willow looked out across the calm water beyond the rapids. Two kayakers floated, voices echoing off the gorge walls as they relived the run.

As paul leaned back against the bench, Willow's focus shifted inward. "Clara, load DeepSeequence."

"Loaded," came the even reply. "Trigger phrase?"

She hesitated, then: "What if we never invested in movement?"

The lake dissolved, replaced by tidal flats and mud. The loop trail vanished, leaving only a cracked verge along a rusting chain-link fence. Heat pressed in.

"Scenario: Late-2020s proposals for active infrastructure abandoned," Clara intoned. *"No Healthy Streets strategy. No Movement and Place framework."*

The vision darkened: no shaded footpaths, no bike lanes, no safe school crossings. Weekend street closures never trialled. The Zig Zag trail, sealed off "for safety." The old cross-fit station, dumped in a depot. Parks stood unlit and empty. Hobler's Bridge netball centre? Never roofed. Winter leagues disbanded. No solar panels, no night games, no adult comps. Riverside Velodrome and the pump tracks? Cancelled before construction. Umpire training fund? Rejected — half the junior matches now overseen by untrained parents. School gates locked after hours; insurance barriers never lifted.

"Secondary impacts," Willow prompted.

Data streamed:
Daily steps fell below global minimums
Child obesity rose 30% in a decade
Senior fractures doubled as balance and bone density declined
Youth depression surged (less play, fewer endorphins)

Asthma rates climbed (air pollution from car dependence)

Hospitals strained:
Cardiovascular admissions up 22%
Type 2 diabetes drug costs tripled
Under-30 mental health crises doubled
Workforce participation fell (injuries, burnout, long recoveries)
Public health costs ballooned by $3.7B annually

Budgets buckled:
Beds repurposed for lifestyle illness
Pharmaceutical subsidies expanded for preventable conditions
Orthopaedic and mental-health waitlists stretched beyond capacity

No joy in motion. No pride in shared spaces. No spontaneous park games.

"One last snapshot," she said.

The Sunday city she loved — car-free streets alive with chalk art, skipping ropes, bubble machines — had never existed. Shops struggled. Screens dominated. Families stayed home. A headline flared: Tasmania records lowest average lifespan and healthspan in the nation — again.

She ended the scenario; the lake returned, steady beneath her feet. "Hard to watch," she murmured.

paul's gaze stayed on the horizon. "That's why we went upstream. Not because it was easy — but because doing nothing cost more."

Willow exhaled, and they walked on.

Soon the city reemerged. They waited at the crossing, giving way to a group of cyclists gliding past on a separated lane painted soft green.

"That's still one of my passions, Willow," paul said, watching them go. "Cycling. I feel free when I ride — almost like flying. I've worked really hard on core and balance training to help me keep at it."

Willow glanced at him, briefly wondering if he'd had more than a hand in the policy to gift every child in the city a bike. She let the thought pass, then raised an eyebrow. "I thought you might have had some secret — no cane, no hesitation. On all our walks, you've always... well, kept a great pace."

paul grinned. "Lucky in some way maybe, but 'use it or lose it' still holds true. Better balance meant more movement — and more movement meant maintaining muscle mass, bone density... and ultimately, a longer healthspan."

They walked the final curve of the lake in silence. The path crunched gently beneath their feet, each step a quiet return to now. Overhead, galahs wheeled toward the western trees, the light taking on that golden tilt unique to a Launceston autumn. The lake was stilling again — glassing over, as if exhaling.

Willow slowed as they neared the fork where their paths usually split. A light breeze lifted a strand of hair across her face.

"Thanks for sharing your stories, paul."

"You're welcome, Willow — anytime," he said, his voice warm with sincerity.

She paused, glancing back toward the playground — children tumbling, chasing, laughing in the fading light. "Hey... could we not do Thursday next time?"

paul raised an eyebrow. "You finally had enough of me?"

"Hardly," she said, eyes dropping to her boots. "Just... would Saturday work instead?"

"Saturday?"

"It's Mum's birthday in a couple of weeks, and I want to get her something from the Kanamaluka Market." She paused, then added quickly, "I thought maybe we could meet there. I think it's more intimate than Salamanca. You'll find something you like too. A book or... something."

paul gave a lopsided grin. "What, and interrupt our Tuesdays-with-Morrie vibes?"

Willow blinked. "What?"

"Never mind," he said, chuckling. "I'll see you at the market."

She smiled — with genuine warmth. "I'd love that. See you at the market."

She turned and walked off, her footsteps soft on the gravel path, the freshwater lake behind her holding the whole sky — clear, blue, and full of quiet promise.

ELEVEN
THE CELEBRATIONS
JOY AS INFRASTRUCTURE

"Alone we can do so little; together we can do so much." — Helen Keller[1]

7 June 2064

The Kanamaluka Market was already in full swing when Willow arrived.

The sky was a flawless sheet of winter blue, stretched tight above the Tamar. Frost still clung to the shaded grass near the bus stop, but the sun — brilliant and low — bounced off the lake's surface like it was trying to warm the city from below. The air had that unmistakable Launceston crispness — clean enough to taste, sharp enough to wake you with a single breath.

Stall umbrellas bloomed in long, bright rows along the boardwalk — formerly the site of an industrial shift-lift. Smells drifted in the breeze: brewed coffee, toasted grains, chestnuts roasting. An acoustic guitarist played near the old workers' hut–turned–gallery, and the clink of handmade jewellery mixed with the soft thud of woven baskets being unpacked.

paul stood beside the native bush foods stall when he spotted Willow. He raised his keep-cup to brim height and nodded.

"Ready to see how a city celebrates?" he asked, handing her a small basket of bush tomatoes he'd just bought.

"Oh — thank you," she said, surprised.

"Figured you'd skip breakfast again." He smiled. "Let's go!"

Willow nodded, cheeks flushed. "Lead the way."

They wandered slowly through the stalls, pausing to sample spiced wattleseed muffins and admire a display of student-made climate banners. A pair of children passed, faces painted like butterflies, clutching seedling pots and half-eaten dumplings. Nearby, a woman sang in palawa kani behind her stall, her voice strong and steady over the hum of the crowd.

Willow tilted her head slightly, her LumenView activating. A soft glow passed across her iris.

"I found something in MemoryLoom last night from a retired reporter," she said. "Something you said when festival organisers were struggling with public liability insurance, or something like that?"

paul groaned. "Please tell me it wasn't from my grumpy decade."

She grinned as the quote hovered between them in soft light:

> "Festivals, concerts, conferences and events — we won't be bullied into scaling back the number or the size of the celebrations we support. No — we'll grow the moments that bring us together. Music, ideas, good food,

good times, great people. Insurers won't dictate what we do, when we do it, or who we do it with. Launceston will be a city that celebrates its people, this place — loud and proud. We'll tell our stories, sing our songs, and stamp our feet as our streets come alive with colour and sound."

She raised an eyebrow. "Honestly? It's aged almost as well as you."

paul laughed. "Not sure how you found that — pretty sure I was talking off the record." He smiled. "Or I might have been back-grounding someone. Doesn't matter. It was true. We didn't have much choice. Or budget. Just a small group of people who believed enough to keep showing up — and didn't wait for permission."

Willow smiled. "Well. It worked."

They walked a few paces in comfortable silence, the morning air carrying the rhythm of a busker's drum.

Then paul added, "What did happen around that time, though, was a series of public meetings — pre-CivicLoom   that laid the ground-work for this place. The people of Launceston wanted a market by the lake. Something that could hold its own with Salamanca."

Willow grinned. "So you were on the bus?"

"Committees get a bad wrap," paul said. "People think they're where good ideas go to die. But not this one. That group was fierce. Passion-ate. Honest. They didn't just talk about it — they bought the bus, filled the bus, drove the bus... and towed the city behind them."

They passed a fire-twirling demonstration and a stall handing out compostable bowls of kangaroo stew, the market pulsing with warmth despite the winter air.

"You know," Willow said, laughing, "I've actually been thinking about how many events I've been to in Launceston. Want a list?"

paul nodded, grinning. "Absolutely. I want proof all the unseen hours from organisers and volunteers actually mattered." She pretended to crack her knuckles. "Alright, here goes."

Then she began counting on her fingers.

"Festivale, of course — both the main one and the revived street party version. Junction. The Light Festival. The Kite Festival. The Box Festival. Brixhibition – the Lego Exhibition was my favourite. Oh, the Communities for Children Expo, Kid I Am, and The Show with Mum and Grandad."

She smiled at the memory — tender, steady. No sting this time.

A brief image flickered: her grandfather laughing beside the Chocolate Wheel at the Show, a cream puff in one hand, the smoky sweetness of the Lions Club barbecue hanging in the air.

Willow briefly checked herself. Clara noted the acceptance — and stayed silent.

She refocused. "Keep going?"

paul nodded in the affirmative.

Willow continued, ticking them off on her fingers. "Harvest Market. WinterFeast. Big Picture Festival. Harmony Day. NAIDOC Week events. ANZAC Day. New Year's Eve. Peace Festival. Writers & Readers Festival."

She paused, thinking. "Oh — and the Social Justice Lecture. That counts, right?"

"Absolutely," paul said. "A civic celebration of ideas."

Willow smiled, then grew thoughtful. "I actually found my Launceston Junior Citizen of the Year certificate the other day — I got it when I was twelve, for leading mental health awareness activities in Grade 6."

She glanced at him. "They presented it at the Social Justice Lecture, and I've gone to every one since."

She shrugged. "And then there's all the small ones — neighbourhood food swaps, solstice gatherings, the mural unveilings..."

paul smiled, satisfied. "That's the thing. They blur together — not because they don't matter, but because they become part of the rhythm of a place. That's how you know a city's alive."

They wandered through a few more stalls, pausing every so often to admire the craft and chat with vendors. Near the eastern edge of the boardwalk, Willow stopped in front of a table draped in sea-toned cloth. Kelp baskets sat in neat rows — each one slightly different, made with care and shaped by hand.

"This is it," she said, reaching for one about the size of her palm, its rim threaded with hand-twisted twine looped neatly through small holes around the edge.

"A birthday present?" paul guessed.

Willow nodded. "For Mum. She'll love it — natural, cultural, and practical. Right up her alley."

paul turned the basket gently in his hands. "It's beautiful."

"She taught me to always buy things that tell a story," Willow said. "This one's got layers — sea country, local maker, function over flash."

She paid in cash and tucked the basket carefully into her shoulder bag. "And it won't end up in landfill. Unlike the glitter-scented bath bomb I gave her last year."

They shared a laugh, then drifted toward the quieter end of the market.

They found a bench tucked between two fig trees, just beyond the final stall. Two steaming drinks warmed their hands. In front of them, the crowd ebbed and flowed — a slow, human tide of families, friends, and strangers brought together by shared space and story.

Willow leaned back, stretching her legs toward a patch of sun.

"You know," she said, watching a child twirl in front of a puppet stall, "when I was younger, I thought celebration was just about marking time. Calendar stuff. Birthdays. Public holidays. But now… I think it's more than that. It's how we remind ourselves what matters."

paul nodded. "And who matters."

They sat for a moment, letting the atmosphere settle around them — the scent of spice and sugar, the chatter of stallholders, a busker's gentle harmonica drifting across the breeze.

Then paul turned to her. "Want to play a game?"

Willow raised an eyebrow, cautious but curious. "Alright. I'm guessing there's a lesson in this."

"Maybe," he said with a smile. "Look around, Willow. Really look. Tell me — what do you see?"

She took a breath, letting her gaze wander before landing on the scene directly in front of them.

"Right here? A woman in a wide-brimmed hat tasting honey… a kid being dragged by two overexcited dogs… and a stall stacked with jam jars and string bags full of lemons."

"Good. Keep going," paul encouraged.

Willow scanned wider.

"Handmade jewellery… the barista on skates again… an older couple sharing dumplings, leaning in close."

Her eyes moved slowly across the canvas of the market. And then, playfully: "I spy with my little eye… families, stallholders, musicians, pets, colour — lots of colour. Am I getting warmer?"

"Yes," paul said, then leaned in a little. "Now go deeper. What do you see — economically?"

Willow glanced back toward the stalls. "Small businesses?"

"Micro-enterprises," paul offered. "Nimble, low-barrier, deeply personal. My parents were marketeers — handmade leather goods. Twenty years, every Sunday – at York Town Square and then the old Show Grounds, then the new Show Grounds."

Willow turned to him. "Really?"

He nodded, a fondness in his voice.

"Yep. But it wasn't about the sales. I mean, they usually broke even, sometimes a bit ahead that they put into more supplies— but they never really paid themselves a wage."

"So why keep doing it?"

"Because it was never just about money. It was pride in their craft. It was the ritual — packing the car, setting up beside familiar faces. Stories over soup, advice between stalls, customers who became friends. That market stall was community. It was connection. And that has its own kind of economy."

Willow smiled. "Social capital."

"Exactly. And resilience. These places are petri dishes of ingenuity — food, fashion, repairs, fresh produce, inventions and art no one asked for but someone always buys. It's a celebration of local enterprise — people having a go."

She watched a woman at the next stall hand a woven bag to a smiling customer, cash exchanged with a thank you and a nod.

"There's also a lot of… actual cash."

paul chuckled. "Yep. We're also quietly celebrating the persistence of physical money. Governments have tried to phase it out, more than once. But the community pushes back — especially places like this."

"Because it's easier?"

"Because it's accessible. It levels the playing field. No transaction fees, no data trails, no tech required. Just a note in hand and trust in the trade. For a lot of stallholders, that extra $100 or $200 at the end of the day — that's groceries, school shoes, power bills. It matters."

Willow nodded, thoughtful.

"So markets are about more than shopping. They're small-scale economies, yes — but also social infrastructure."

"Exactly," paul said. "Economies of care, craft, culture — running parallel to the big stuff. And in some ways, more human."

They took a moment to sip their drinks, letting their thoughts wander with the music and murmur of the crowd.

Then paul leaned in again. "What do you see... sociologically?"

Willow hesitated, brow furrowed. "Diversity?" she offered, uncertain.

paul nodded. "Absolutely. Markets like this celebrate the rich layers of our city — shaped over generations by new arrivals bringing their foods, hands, and rituals. They grew unfamiliar crops in unfamiliar soils — and eventually, those flavours became ours. So yes, we're celebrating diversity."

He paused, letting the thought settle between them.

"But it's more than that too," he continued. "It's belonging. Expression. Agency. This isn't just about stalls — it's about people claiming space, telling stories through food, craft, art, and song. It's the sociology of joy, Willow. Public joy. And in a divided world, that's not nothing."

Willow nodded slowly, her eyes drifting back to the crowd.

"So celebration isn't just the outcome," she said. "It's the process. A kind of civic ritual."

"Exactly," paul said. "A ritual of visibility — of being seen, and of seeing others."

He paused again, letting the moment breathe. Then: "What else?"

Willow looked around, this time more intently.

"Peace," she said quietly.

paul smiled. "Right. Freedom. We're walking through here — no police, no guards, no weapons, no force. We take it for granted, but this — being together in public, safely — is a kind of quiet miracle. Around the world, people are still searching for that. What we're really celebrating today is trust. Communal trust. That safety can be shared."

Willow nodded, eyes narrowing thoughtfully. "And collaboration. These events don't just happen — they're built. People coordinate, set up stalls, volunteer, troubleshoot, clean up. Same faces that ran the food drive during the floods last year."

She gestured with her cup toward the crowd. "It's not just markets. It's muscle memory — for cooperation."

paul looked impressed. "That's it. Collaboration as culture. As practice. We rehearse it here, so we're ready when it matters most."

Willow took another sip, letting the warmth linger. "So what are we really celebrating?"

"You tell me, Willow", paul said, deflecting with a smile.

"Our shared humanity", Willow replied, more sure of herself this time.

paul answered gently. "Perfect. We are celebrating the hard-earned truth that we live in the shelter of each other[2]. That's how we've survived as a species — and it's how we'll survive the next thousand generations. Together."

They stood to leave, cups empty, sunlight retreating behind the shade of the trees.

"Events like this are always first to go when austerity creeps in, Willow. But they should be the last", paul said.

Willow nodded absorbing one more lesson.

He paused a beat. Then: "Markets, festivals, events – they're not symbolic. They're structural. As upstream as you can go. They build trust before it's needed. Connection before crisis."

He looked toward the lake. The hum of the market continued behind them. "They say: We see you. You're part of this. We've got your back. And that matters."

Willow exhaled, quiet now.

paul continued, softer: "They are civic infrastructure. Just as real, just as vital, as roads or water pipes."

Willow nodded slowly. "Turns out, the best celebrations don't just remind us what matters... they restore us."

paul glanced at her, a quiet smile forming, but said nothing.

They began walking again, the lake catching light between the trees.

Just ahead, a child darted past them, arms outstretched, gripping a small toy version of the Statue. It wobbled slightly in her hand — the same distinctive angles, the same quiet strength. Willow followed her movement instinctively, and as the child rounded the bend, Willow looked up.

And there it was — just beyond the curve of the path, the edge of the real Statue coming into view, its surface catching the light like it always had, but somehow now, it shimmered with something more.

Neither of them said anything. Not yet.

They just walked toward it.

TWELVE
THE ATTRACTION
A KIND VIBRANT CITY

"Statues are the stone, marble and steel on to which we carve our identities.
They stand for the beliefs and values that bind us as a society."
— Peter Hughes[1]

21 June 2064

It was winter in the city—sharp and breath-bright. Willow and paul arrived as the park began to fill. Sunlight slid over the statue's angles, laying thin gold across the lawn while people drifted in by twos and threes, coats buttoned, coffees warming their hands, voices held low— a workday hush. From the playground, a burst of laughter tipped into a cry, and the murmur along the paths gathered and deepened.

As they passed the base of the monument, the air shimmered slightly. CitizenEcho activated.

CitizenEcho: Statue of Equity (Est. 2038)
Location trigger: People's Park, Launceston
Memory Type: Symbol commemorating city ideals/Republic monument
The Statue of Equity rises above the parklands — more than eight stories, the city's tallest structure. Vibrant. Alive. A civic heart. A beacon for all this place has come to mean.

The Echo faded, its loop unfinished, as they moved deeper into People's Park. They climbed the gentle slope, the tower rising behind them - not overshadowing, but standing with them. Not as ornament, but as witness. A quiet reminder of how far they'd come — and how far there still was to go.

Willow shook out a picnic rug and laid it gently on the grass as they reached the crest. Children ran across the lawn, their voices skipping through the crisp winter air.

paul lowered himself slowly beside her, his gaze distant, the weight of memory settling more heavily than the cold.

"How you doing? It's a tough day isn't it?" she asked gently, lowering herself to the grass beside him.

He gave a short nod.

She could see it — the heaviness in his shoulders, the pause before every movement. Today wasn't just any day. It was marking a loss. She didn't probe any further. She just held the space beside him.

After a while, she spoke. "I've been thinking about my pop a lot lately."

He glanced her way.

"He was my safe person," she said. "One of the good ones. Never said much. Just made you feel like you mattered."

paul nodded slowly, his eyes now fixed on the statue.

"Some days it hits out of nowhere," Willow added. "Like a gust you didn't see coming."

He didn't speak, but she saw the small movement in his throat as he swallowed.

She shifted slightly, stretching her legs out in front of her. Then, softly: "You don't have to be fine."

He turned to her, the corners of his mouth tugging toward a smile — but it didn't quite make it. "Grief's strange," he said finally. "All this love left over — and nowhere to put it."

A soft pulse flickered across his vision. Clara's voice was steady: "There's no need to solve this moment. Grief isn't a puzzle — it's a presence."

He exhaled, barely audible. The line of his shoulders slackened — only slightly, like a door left ajar rather than fully opened.

Willow watched him for a moment, then tapped gently at her Synapstra. She leaned a little closer.

"Would it be alright if I shared something?" she asked softly. "It's from my study — part of my mid-year GrowthLoop."

He gave a tiny nod.

Willow queued up the Loop and continued – her voice steady now, not just reading, but claiming it.

GrowthLoop: Ode to the City Transformers
(Submitted in partial fulfilment of course requirements. Public access consent granted.)

"Launceston is not just one of the most liveable regional cities in the world; it is one of the most loved—by locals and visitors alike. Not for the attractions or internationally recognised reforms, but for what they

represent: long-horizon thinking, kind upstream leadership, gifts for strangers not yet born.

The Lake wasn't only about water quality — it was renewal, economy, stillness.

The Gorge taught restraint — the power of leaving something wild.

The Bridge was belief in steel — designing isolation out.

The Transformers of the early century built momentum — systems and spaces that invited the rest of us to keep going.

Launceston became a city that celebrated every child, lived health daily — a garden in a city, a city in a garden.
Grey streets turned green — thousands of trees, wildflowers, orchards, community gardens. People grew food, and with it confidence, connection, pride.

We learned the economy is inseparable from care. Carers, volunteers, neighbours, and workers once overlooked moved to the centre. Growth statistics never tucked you in at night; the care economy did.

Growth became belonging. Housing integrated. Public spaces became necessities, not luxuries. We stopped asking how many dwellings and started asking: Do elders feel welcome? Can children walk safely to school?

And we got creative — murals, theatre, spoken word, festivals. Walls and stages became canvases: come contribute, come connect.

Even sport changed — from something watched to something done. Clubs became wellbeing hubs; inclusion mattered more than podiums.

Markets and parades reminded us the city was thriving — and that everyone belonged in the celebration.

Above it all, the Statue of Equity rose—not to honour a ruler, but a principle. It listens, glows, welcomes: a quiet promise that every life matters, and that justice must be visible.

The Transformers weren't perfect, but they were kind and brave. They made a difference."

Willow's LumenView overlay dimmed as she returned to the present. With the words of her essay still alive in her mind. She turned to paul. "You know, we talk a lot about what makes this city special — the beauty, the design, the festivals. And yeah, all of that's real."

She let the pause linger. "What people remember is how it feels here—kindness, being seen, a moment of belonging."

She looked up. "Launceston evolved — not by chasing scale or copying others, but by becoming more of itself. A place where beauty and boldness lived side by side. Where people came for the attractions — and left changed by the feeling."

Her voice dropped to a whisper. "They didn't just feel like visitors. They felt like they belonged — even just for a moment."

A long pause. "And that's what changes people. Not just what they saw. But how they felt. And that… was never accidental."

paul hadn't moved, but something in his face had softened.

They turned toward the Statue as the memorial began. On the giant screens: *Hon. Sulapa Jaswal (1980–2064). Ribbons of text circled the monument—49th Premier of Tasmania (2029–2042). 3rd President of Australia (2046–2058).*

"She was a consequential leader," paul said. "Brave and kind."

"It takes a village," Willow murmured.

They watched in layered quiet. paul exhaled. "She wouldn't have wanted the fuss—turned down honorary doctorates, even the Companion of the Order. When she opened the Statue, she put every builder's name on the plaque—hers tucked into the list. That's a humble, servant leader."

They listened to the tributes. "What stays with me," paul said, "isn't just the big reforms. It's the people she lifted—found work, found voice, found each other. Healthier, kinder, more sure of their place."

Willow nodded. "That upstream turn—treating budgets as moral documents, trusting local government—changed the culture. That's the legacy."

"All we wanted was better for everyone," paul said.

"They are," Willow said. "And they will be."

She leaned back as the statue's surface shifted again. "The baton's been passed, paul. And we caught it. My generation caught it!"

He chuckled, shoulder brushing hers. "Funny. You spend decades holding things together — budgets, teams, public hope — and then one sentence from a 22-year-old tells you it was all worthwhile."

Willow smiled without turning. "That's baton-passing. The runner behind you sees your whole stride. You never see your own."

A breeze moved across the park, soft and cool.

A long list of speakers honoured the revered former President. After a moment of silence, the memorial drew to a close and people began to file quietly out of the park.

Willow and paul sat quietly, watching the slow drift of the crowd.

After a while he turned to her. "So," he asked gently, "what did your Honours supervisor say about your Loop?"

Willow opened the LoopNote. Reading softly: "Maybe consider for your thesis the relationships between all three tiers of government in the process of social change."

paul nodded, quietly impressed. "A good provocation. I think today showed how state and federal politics are always interwoven with the local government story — sometimes helping, sometimes hindering, but always shaping what was possible."

He paused, the light from the statue catching on the curve of the lake.

"Next time — let's talk about the role of the state."

Willow agreed, already forming questions in her mind. Leaders of the past. Frameworks for the future.

This part of the story — the city — felt complete. Not finished, but full.

Now it was time to look outward. Beyond the garden paths and painted laneways. Beyond the bridge, the lake, the city they had explored.

Upstream — and statewide.

The conversation wasn't over. It was beginning again.

A soft chime stirred the air — low, warm, unmistakable. The statue shimmered to life once more. Around them, people clapped gently.

A couple near the footbridge raised their cups. Two children waved up at the statue as if it might wave back.

Willow smiled, eyes on the rising light. paul tipped his hat toward her and the statue, half-playful, half-solemn, then leaned back and closed his eyes.

For the first time in a long while, he let the belief settle — not as certainty, but as possibility.

And the CitizenEcho, sensing their stillness, resumed its loop:

CitizenEcho: Statue of Equity (Est. 2038)
Location trigger: People's Park, Launceston
Memory Type: Symbol commemorating city ideals/Republic monument

The Statue of Equity rises above the parklands — at more than eight stories, it is the city's tallest structure. Vibrant. Alive. A civic heart. A beacon for all this place has come to mean.

Not a tribute to conquest, but a promise: everyone matters. Justice, dignity, fairness—made daily, not declared once. Belonging as the beginning of democracy, and its endurance.

Its base opens like arms, stone gathered from cliffs and highlands across the island—a grounded story of place. From it lifts a dynamic form, clad in reflective alloys and smart panels that converse with the day: dawn holds river mist; midday carries GrowthLoops—children's poems, Aboriginal designs, civic notes; night pulses with weddings, vigils, music.

This is no hands-off monument. It is meant for touch—for climbing, walking, breath and grip. Architecture as declaration: you belong here. Ascend. Engage. Rise.

Inside, a vertical playground shifts with the seasons—new holds, new routes—welcoming athletes, school groups, first-timers. Some days it hosts competitions; others, only quiet effort and small victories.

At the summit, a 360-degree platform opens: city canopy, Tamar Lake winding below, mountains on the rim. Not merely a lookout—perspective made real. Equity as something reached for, rested beside, returned to. Movement, not stillness. Upward. Outward. Together.

It welcomes. It delights. It connects. It evolves—listens, responds, mirrors its people. Tourists come for spectacle; locals come to feel grounded.

And most moving of all: when a child is born[2] in Launceston, A soft amber light rises slowly from base to summit, glowing like a sunrise. With it comes a single, resonant tone — warm, unmistakable. Not demanding attention, but inviting stillness. Across the city, hands meet hearts; conversation softens; strangers trade small, knowing smiles. One more life. One more promise to keep. Simple. Profound. Unifying—in light, in sound, in silence.

The Statue of Equity is the city's soul—not for its height or shine, but for the people it represents.

CALL TO ACTION

The Launceston Promise
a kind, vibrant city

- We promise a freshwater lake — *water made clean; truth held on Country.*
- We promise a City Bridge that connects — *lives as well as lanes; story lit in steel and light.*
- We promise every child succeeds — *hubs and early help; cradle-to-career pathways.*
- We promise healthy together — *movement with meaning and connection.*
- We promise a city in a garden — *food in our streets; a canopy that cools.*
- We promise good work for all — *care paid fairly; skills that last.*
- We promise a wellbeing economy — *clean energy and care; an economy in balance.*
- We promise neighbourhoods that raise kids well — *eco-homes in communities that care.*
- We promise to cultivate changemakers — *citizen science, students trusted to lead; the city as canvas.*

- We promise sport and rec as belonging — *clubs as hubs; everyone in the game.*
- We promise joy as infrastructure — *festivals funded; streets that celebrate.*
- We promise a kind, vibrant city — *welcome made visible; equity made public.*

An Open Letter to the People of Launceston

Dear Friends and Neighbours,

This isn't a postcard from 2064. It's an invitation from the here and now.

If you've read *vibrant city*, you've seen one possible future for us: a kinder, brighter, upstream Launceston that prevents harm, grows belonging, and measures success by how well people live. None of it happens by chance. It happens because we choose it, together.

Here's what choosing looks like.

We can start with water and connection. Let's keep the freshwater vision alive—river care, wetland repair, and even a lake we can be proud of. And let's build a people-first City Bridge that connects lives as much as lanes: universal design, safe walk/ride paths, art in the walkway, and the quiet prevention features that make moving about welcoming for everyone.

We can and must put children at the centre. Hubs, early wraparound support, and cradle-to-career pathways so "every child succeeds" is real policy, not a slogan. And never forget, healthier kids learn better. Better learners get better jobs. Better jobs pay better. Better pay lifts the economy. Stronger economies build stronger communities.

We can launch a Healthy City Pledge—simple, public commitments we make as households, streets, clubs, and workplaces to move more, eat well, sleep better, and look out for each other. Let's build a Healthy Together movement that reports progress openly: steps walked, meals shared, and, yes, kilograms safely shed. Our shared, voluntary goal: help Launceston become the city that lost 500,000 kg—over time, together, with care. Where prevention becomes the map: safe streets to play, seniors' exercise parks, and social prescribing through local health and community partners.

Launceston can be a city in a garden. We can create community plots you can steward, and edible-orchard trails in ordinary parks. A city-wide canopy that heads toward 60% so summer is kinder and walking is normal.

We can back good work for all. Train and hire for what lasts—care, climate adaptation, culture—and insist on fair, secure jobs for all across sectors. When we talk "growth," let's mean health, belonging, and opportunity for all ages; otherwise let's not call it growth.

We can build new neighbourhoods that raise kids well. Trees and transport, schools and jobs nearby, beauty as a birthright—not a post-code perk.

We must cultivate changemakers. Turn our city into a learning community: opportunities across the lifespan to solve real problems and design what's next. Commission mural trails and learning loops. Mentor the next generation to face rapid change with courage.

We can support sport and rec as places of belonging. More parkruns, social teams, "no one finishes last" norms. Movement that stitches days—and neighbours—together.

We can fund joy as infrastructure. Festivals and street culture are civic glue. Write them into the budget, not as afterthoughts but as foundations.

We can make welcome visible. Tell Launceston's story with courage: a city where equity is public, legible, and lived. The proposed Statue of Equity belongs here—not as ornament, but as civic infrastructure for the Republic we may yet become: a meeting place, a stage for protest and celebration, a thank-you to those who carried us here, a beacon that says everyone belongs.

We must keep the conversation open. Host kitchen-table chat and public forums. Make sure the people most affected by decisions are in the room. Share tools freely and mentor younger advocates.

We can lead with courage and care. Every reform starts when someone decides the status quo is not enough. Be that person—and don't do it alone.

We can keep score by counting avoidable costs. Ask council to publish each year what we've prevented—dollars and harms—by acting upstream. We pay either way. Upstream, we pay once and get health, connection, and productivity in return. Downstream, we pay forever. For fact's sake, why would we choose anything else?

In the months ahead, choose one practical step: show up at a meeting or a planting day; write to council in support of your favourite idea; mentor a learner; start a plot on your verge; join a social team; help run a kitchen-table conversation; or invite someone new to the next working bee. That's how big change starts and stays made—one ordinary, generous act, repeated across a thousand doorsteps.

With kindness and a hat tip,

paul

Upstream, together. Let's Go!

UPSTREAMING ACROSS THE CITY: A FIELD GUIDE FOR DREAMERS AND DOERS

The steps below turn the initiatives of vibrant city into everyday action.

1. **Make the lake, together.** Join river-care and wetland days. Write to council and the state government in support of the Point Rapid barrage and the "meet-me-by-the-lake" waterfront plan.
2. **Build the people-first City Bridge.** Back a multi-modal bridge with separated walking/rolling, suicide-deterrent rails, and low-impact lighting—designed for daily safety and dignity. Support reserving a light-rail corridor from day one.
3. **Put children at the centre.** Champion a cradle-to-career continuum: school-community hubs, trauma-informed practice, and universal place-based supports measured by Results Based Accountability, The State of Launceston's Children Reports, and technology like Rumble's Quest. Push for a long-horizon City Deal for Kids.
4. **Choose a Healthy City, daily.** Call for the establishment of the three-yearly Preventative Health Survey. Then back a Healthy City Pledge at home, work, or club. Ask for PlayStreets, 30 km/h slow streets, social prescribing, intergenerational activity, and seniors' exercise parks. Track progress together—steps, meals, and kilograms safely shed.
5. **Grow a city in a garden.** Back the city in a garden vision; help plant the edible-orchard trail; steward canopy expansion toward ~60–65% with cooling corridors and solar pergolas that make walking normal in summer.
6. **Back good work for all.** Support local training hubs, earn-and-learn pathways, wrap-around supports for vulnerable youth, and public investment tied to fair wages and secure conditions.
7. **Measure the boom by wellbeing.** Favour budgets and projects that grow health, belonging, opportunity—and clean industry.

Get behind care-led growth, hemp and innovative pilots, and the "big three" civic investments – Lake, Bridge, Statue - that multiply returns.

8. **Build neighbourhoods that raise kids well.** Support Passivhaus-standard homes, neighbourhood batteries, parks within 400 m, and early arrival of schools and health hubs. Retrofit the coldest, dampest homes first.

9. **Cultivate changemakers.** Make classrooms civic workshops for real world problem solving; commission mural trails and mentor the next generation to face rapid change with courage.

10. **Make sport and recreation a place of belonging.** Grow parkruns, social teams, and "no one finishes last" norms. Build activity spaces close to home, low-cost access to team sport and rec, and "peace by design" so movement stitches neighbours together.

11. **Fund joy as infrastructure.** Budget for markets, festivals, and block-party micro-grants. Keep trading cash-inclusive; incubate micro-enterprise stalls; design for safety with volunteers and clear layouts.

12. **Make welcome visible.** Support the Statue of Equity and People's Park as practical civic infrastructure—for vigils, rallies, carols, citizenship, and everyday conversation—so belonging is public, legible, lived.

13. **Keep the Conversation Open.** Run community forums, host kitchen-table conversations, and make sure the people most affected by decisions are in the room. Mentor younger advocates. Share tools and lessons freely.

14. **Lead with Courage and Care.** Every reform starts with someone deciding the status quo is not enough. Be that person. Act in solidarity. Remember that courage grows when it's shared.

15. **Keep score by counting 'avoidable costs'.** Ask council to publish avoidable costs each year — the dollars and harms we prevent when we act upstream.

If you're holding this, you're already part of what comes next.

And remember, kindness is strategy. Upstream, was can make this happen together.

AUTHOR'S REFLECTION

This book is for anyone who wants to build something better — young people, parents, carers, teachers, policy wonks, advocates, volunteers — people who care deeply, act locally, and are tired of politics that feels more like damage control than progress.

I wrote *vibrant city* as a hopeful blueprint for changemakers. It's an invitation to think differently, act kindly, and imagine boldly. If you've ever asked, "Why don't we act sooner?" If you believe fairness can be designed — upstream, with care — rather than downstream, in crisis. If you still carry hope, even if it's bruised, that kindness can be a force for lasting change — then this book is for you.

This isn't a set of policy briefs. It's not a bullet-point manifesto or a standard political pitch. *vibrant city* — and the *vibrant nation trilogy* — is something different: part story, part strategy, part act of imagination.

In Book I, I ask a simple but powerful question:

> *What would our city look like if we made prevention our priority and kindness our compass?*

I was compelled to write this because, for most of my life, I've worked in community services at the point of crisis — walking alongside people as they sought housing, food, heating, or the means to get through the week. I did my best to respond with care. But I was often left with a deep unease: so much of what I saw was preventable. If the system had been structured more fairly, more justly, more humanely — many of those crises might never have happened at all.

For more than three decades, I've witnessed harm that could have been avoided — if we'd only acted earlier. If we'd listened more closely. If we'd designed our systems with care, instead of rushing to patch the damage once it was already done.

That's what this book is about. It's a call to shift our mindset — to embrace upstream thinking and commit to a politics rooted in kindness and human dignity.

Upstream Thinking

Upstream thinking is a lens. It shifts our focus from symptoms to causes, from crisis response to prevention. It asks not just "What happened?" but "Why did it happen — and how can we stop it from happening again?" It's about recognising that what we experience today is often the delayed result of decisions made years — even decades — earlier.

This kind of thinking requires patience and perspective. It's not the quick fix or headline-grabbing announcement. It's the quiet, careful work of designing systems that support people before they fall. In my experience, it's the work most likely to be overlooked, underfunded, or dismissed — even though it saves lives, money, and human potential in the long run.

Much of what community services respond to every day is failure demand — demand that only exists because we failed to act upstream. The family in crisis because secure housing wasn't available six months earlier. The hospital visit because no one could afford the heating bill. The youth support referral that might have been unnecessary if schools were better resourced. These aren't random misfortunes — they are the predictable consequences of structural design flaws.

And they come with avoidable costs — financial, emotional, social, generational. Costs that compound over time, and that we pay for whether we acknowledge them or not.

Upstream thinking says: let's build the dam before the flood. Let's stop harm before it starts. Let's invest where it matters — early, fairly, and with care — so fewer people ever need to reach breaking point.

Kind Politics

Kind politics is the practice of empathy in public life. But it's more than that — it's also about power: how we hold it, how we share it, and how we use it for the collective good.

The word kind carries two meanings — and both are essential here. First, kindness as compassion: to treat others with dignity, fairness, and care. But also kind as in kinship — a reminder that we belong to one another. That we are, at our core, the same kind.

Kind politics draws from the Universal Declaration of Human Rights and challenges us to design systems that uplift rather than punish; that listen instead of lecture; that restore instead of abandon. It means treating people as humans first — not as case files, cost centres, or compliance problems.

But kindness in politics is not about softness. It's about strength — the strength to resist cruelty and cynicism. The strength to lead with integrity when others abandon theirs. Kind politics means entering disagreement with humility, and recognising that the goal isn't to "win" the argument — it's to find the best way forward, together.

At its heart, kind politics is about collaboration. It means sharing power, co-creating solutions, and listening deeply — because the wisdom of the group is more valuable than the ego of any individual. It's about finding elegant, durable answers — not just claiming credit or being right. It's about respecting those you disagree with, focusing on the issue rather than the opponent, and refusing to mirror hostility with hostility.

It means going high when others go low. Doing what would make your grandmother proud.

In short: don't be an arsehole[1].

Not in meetings, not in parliament, not in policy design. Not online. Not when no one's watching. Culture is shaped in micro-moments — and change is sustained by how we treat each other along the way.

Kind politics isn't about avoiding the hard conversations — it's about having them without dehumanising one another. It's not about agreement — it's about shared humanity. It calls us to lead with values, to build systems that lift people up instead of pushing them down, and to measure success not in soundbites, but in lives made better.

In a world where politics so often defaults to fear, blame, and division, kind politics offers another path — one grounded in solidarity, equity, and care. One that dares to imagine not just what works, but what's right.

A Note on Criticism

Some will say these ideas are idealistic. That they're too soft, or too abstract. But they are anything but. These are structural ideas. Systemic ideas. They are political — in the deepest and most urgent sense of the word.

I draw here on the Power Threat Meaning Framework (PTMF), a transformative model that reframes human suffering not as individual pathology, but as a response to social injustice, structural exclusion, and misused power. PTMF shifts the question from "What's wrong with you?" to "What's happened to you — and how has power shaped your experience?"

Upstream thinking is a structural response to those questions. It recognises that poverty, distress, and inequality are not random — they are produced. Preventing them means confronting and redesigning the systems that create them.

Kind politics is how we do that work — with empathy, with courage, and with a commitment to healing, not just managing, harm.

These aren't just nice ideas. They're frameworks for real transformation. They challenge us to name injustice and respond with design, not denial. They call us to build systems that reduce threat, restore dignity, and reflect the best of who we can be — together.

I hope this book helps light a path forward — for your street, your community, your city.

And I hope it reminds you:

The future is not something we inherit.

It's something we build — upstream, together.

Let's go!

ABOUT THE INITIATIVES

Stories can stand on their own. But movements need scaffolding. What follows is a set of twelve short sections—Initiatives 1–12—that give shape to the ideas threaded through the *vibrant city* story. Think of them as signposts: the "what", the "how", and the "why," laid out so you can carry them into your own streets, classrooms, offices, and councils.

Each initiative carries three anchors:

- **Policy Summary** — the intent, the key moves, and a glimpse of how it lives in 2064.
- **Policy Snapshot** — the design choices and near-term effects, stripped of jargon, easy to share.
- **Avoidable Costs Unit (ACU) Impact Matrix** — a conservative estimate of avoided costs when we invest upstream. These numbers are illustrations only - they are not prophecy. However, they can be prompts for your own modelling. Updated figures and further discussion sit behind the QR code.

How to use this section:

- If you're reading for the story: skip, skim, or circle back later. The narrative is complete without it.
- If you're a practitioner, organiser, or just plain curious: treat it as a compact field guide. Use it to spark workshops, test assumptions, run local scenarios. Swap in your data. Rewrite it in your accent.

The aim is simple: to make it easier for ideas to travel, adapt, and take root. What begins as a page here could become a pilot there. What's tested in one place can be improved in another. Inspiration is the seed; action is the soil. This section is for planting.

INITIATIVE 1

TAMAR LAKE

POLICY SUMMARY

We didn't just tidy a river; we changed how the city lives with water. Since the early 2030s, a single, well-designed barrage at Point Rapid has held a stable freshwater lake at river-edge level. The early wins were obvious—no exposed mud at low tide, swimmable water, and a public waterfront worth lingering on—but the deeper shift was confidence: families planning weekends on the boardwalk, schools timetabling water-skills into PE, cafés turning to the lake, clubs buying kayaks instead of excuses, visitors staying for sunset instead of hustling past the smell. That's what upstream moves do: they turn "maintenance forever" into stewardship that compounds—civic pride, safer summers, and a platform for work and play that depends on clean, reliable water.

This was never aesthetics over substance. The lake was modelled to reduce re-suspension of fine sediments in the upper estuary and to tame the infamous monosulfidic "black ooze" in the Yacht Basin. It also let the city plan for flood, sea-level rise, and amenity on purpose—before the next crisis, not after. System-wide, we still manage sediment with care (mudflats remain part of the estuary's long natural story), but in the city's heart we chose freshwater function and public life—and we designed it with Country, culture, and consent at the centre.

Three decades on, the economics are long-horizon and steady. The lake underwrites water security for Bell Bay–adjacent industry, supports higher-value crops through irrigation confidence, and anchors a visitor economy built around a postcard lake rather than a problem reach. That's splash-and-ripple economics: invest once upstream, harvest returns for decades.

Socially and culturally, the lake reclaimed the river's edge as everyday public space—a place where kids learn to paddle, elders sit in shade, festivals face the water, and CitizenEcho pins stories to place so memory is something you can touch and hear. The lake made belonging visible. And it gave Launceston back a simple sentence we could say without apology: *"Meet me by the lake."*

POLICY SNAPSHOT WHAT WE BUILT & WHY IT MATTERED – TAMAR LAKE

- **Barrage → permanent freshwater level.** A controllable weir/barrage at Point Rapid converting a tidal reach to a lake at river-edge level. Year-round water amenity; reduced fine-sediment resuspension and "mud" exposure in upper reaches; planning certainty.
- **City-facing lakefront.** Boardwalks, swimming/paddling zones, beach, café clusters, sculpture and learning nodes. Public life moved to the water; safer, cleaner participation for families, schools and clubs; brand lift.
- **Water-for-work.** Reliable freshwater supporting irrigation and water-reliant industry in the valley/Bell Bay. Jobs and diversification: horticulture, processing, hydrogen proponents gaining water certainty.
- **Flood/level management.** Operating regime that moderates peaks (design-dependent). Lower emergency costs and quicker recovery in selected events; resilience to sea-level rise scenarios.
- **Culture and memory on-site.** CitizenEcho, art, wayfinding, and Country-led interpretation. Place-based learning; pride and participation; truth-telling anchored to the shoreline.
- **Catchment honesty.** Keep managing sediment system-wide (mudflats are natural estuary features); fix sewage/stormwater. Balances lake amenity with whole-of-system health; avoids repeating the "dredge–re-silt" cycle.

AVOIDABLE COSTS UNIT IMPACT ASSESSMENT MATRIX — TAMAR LAKE

- **Amenity and odour.** Permanent water at river-edge level; fewer exposed mud/MBO episodes in upper reaches. Long-term benefit: visitor yield up; resident satisfaction; investment confidence. Avoidable costs (indicative): A$0.2–0.6m/yr service and reputational drag avoided (complaints, lost trade).
- **Upper-reach sediment ops.** Less re-suspension; fewer strandings/clean-ups in the Yacht Basin. Long-term benefit: shift from reactive dredge/rake cycles to planned stewardship. Avoidable costs (indicative): A$1.0–1.5m/yr versus historic campaign/handling patterns (order-of-magnitude).
- **Recreation and health.** Year-round paddling/swimming; safer water contact. Long-term benefit: more daily activity; youth programs on-water. Avoidable costs (indicative): healthcare burden down; productivity up (qualitative at this stage).
- **Tourism and place brand.** Waterfront activation; "postcard lake." Long-term benefit: longer stays; earned media. Avoidable costs (indicative): A$3–6m/yr marketing-equivalent and spend otherwise foregone (conservative).
- **Flood/level scenarios.** Moderated peaks (subject to design/ops). Long-term benefit: lower event losses in selected floods. Avoidable costs (indicative): event-based — A$5–20m fewer losses in moderate events (scenario).
- **Jobs and output** (benefit). Construction-phase employment. Long-term benefit: ongoing uplift — agrifood, tourism, industry water-security. Benefit (not an avoidable cost): ~800 construction jobs; ~A$313m first-3-year output (indicative).

Total Estimated Avoidable Costs (2025): ~A$4.2m–8.1m per year.

For a 2064 nominal guide (assume CPI 2.5%), the total equates to ~A$11.0–21.2m per year. Event-based flood figures are not included in the annual total; jobs/output are benefits, not "avoidable costs."

Capital and operations. Tamar Lake was delivered for A$1.0 billion, covering the Point Rapid barrage, fishways, control systems, and lake infrastructure. A further A$500 million funded lake-edge remedial works and wastewater/sewerage treatment upgrades to protect water quality. Since commissioning, operations have been budgeted as a core water-infrastructure line: scheduled gate and fishway servicing, power, monitoring and instrumentation, forebay sediment management, and periodic mechanical and electrical renewals. Ongoing costs vary with asset cycles and energy prices and sit within the long-term financial plan.

ACU figures here are indicative and speculative; they have not been independently verified and are provided for illustration only. Further economic modelling would be required. Figures are annual gross avoided costs (no NPV/discounting).

INITIATIVE 2

CITY BRIDGE

POLICY SUMMARY

We built more than steel and concrete; we kept a promise. The City Bridge was connector and canvas, stitching east and west with a span as symbolic as it was functional. Designed people-first—with wide, separated paths and places to pause—it turned a bottleneck into a landmark. Its arc was future-proofed from day one: a dedicated lane reserved for light rail, quiet at first but engineered to carry tomorrow's load. That foresight made the bridge more than a traffic fix; it let the city expand mobility later without billion-dollar retrofits. Congestion eased. Everyday trips got calmer and safer.

By day, the bridge carried workers, students, cyclists, and families. By dusk, it transformed. Solar trees gathered light and returned it at night, powering a living narrative of colour and story along the span. The evening show became a civic ritual: residents drifted to the river's edge, visitors lingered, and cameras caught it millions of times—earned media no marketing budget could buy. Within a decade, one in four travel reviews of the Tamar mentioned the bridge and the statue; the city had a postcard and a meeting place rolled into one.

Even the details did work. Walk-on-water glass panels offered clean thrills and new views to the current below; etched artworks told stories of Country and community. Infrastructure became gallery. Not just movement, but meaning. A second crossing didn't just move cars; it moved a city—from "can't afford it" to "we built it well." Belief, made concrete.

POLICY SNAPSHOT WHAT WE BUILT & WHY IT MATTERED - CITY BRIDGE

- **Second bridge, an arc of steel and light.** Civic infrastructure that physically and symbolically connected the city's future to edges it had forgotten.
- **Solar trees and stories-in-light.** Place activation that captured sunlight by day and released it at night; crowds gathered at dusk.
- **Tourism and earned media.** The bridge became a visitor-economy anchor and brand asset, cited in one in four Tamar-region travel reviews; ongoing free promotion.
- **Walk-on-water glass and etched artworks.** A pedestrian gallery, with glass panels and stories etched into the walkway.
- **Future-proofed light-rail lane.** A reserved alignment for light rail, ensuring adaptability as the city grew.
- **Multi-modal design for people and freight.** Safer active travel alongside efficient freight and bus/EV lanes.
- **Separated active-transport corridor.** A wide, protected path with lookouts; safety and comfort helped drive a +61% shift to walking and cycling.
- **Suicide-deterrent safety rails.** Human-centred barrier design that baked quiet prevention into the structure.

AVOIDABLE COSTS UNIT (ACU) IMPACT ASSESSMENT MATRIX – CITY BRIDGE

- **Transport efficiency.** AM-peak congestion fell 36 per cent; freight routes ran smoother. Long-term benefit: time reliability unlocked jobs, investment, and housing growth across the valley. Avoidable costs (indicative): A$45–70m per year in saved commuter and freight delay (value of time, aligned to mode shift and decongestion).
- **Emergency access and safety.** A relief route reduced gridlock pinch points. Long-term benefit: faster ambulance and fire response; fewer severe outcomes. Avoidable costs (indicative): A$8–15m per year in avoided incident costs from response-time improvements and crash reductions.
- **Health and environment.** Less idling and less rat-running through suburbs. Long-term benefit: lower air and noise exposure; more daily active movement. Avoidable costs (indicative): A$6–12m per year in avoided health burden (air/noise) plus activity benefits (conservative).
- **Tourism and civic identity.** The nightly light program became a must-see, photographed millions of times. Long-term benefit: increased visitation and earned media. Avoidable costs (indicative): marketing-equivalent uplift and spending otherwise foregone, captured within the visitor-economy lines and not double-counted here.
- **Future-proofing costs.** A light-rail corridor was built in from day one. Long-term benefit: avoided retrofit or parallel corridor in the 2040s–50s. Avoided costs (one-off): A$1.2–2.7b versus the "cheap bridge → expensive upgrade" path (excluded from the annual total).
- **Economic productivity.** "Splash-and-ripple" effects from the A$840m build. Long-term benefit: thirty-year net returns across the economy and community. Accounting note: productivity shows up across delay, health, and investment lines above; not counted twice in ACU.

Total Estimated Avoidable Costs (2025): ~A$64–106m per year.

For a 2064 nominal guide (assume CPI 2.5%), the total equates to ~A$168–278m per year. One-off future-proofing/retrofit savings are excluded from the annual total; broader productivity/NPV effects are not counted in ACU.

Capital and operations. The City Bridge was delivered for about A$840 million, including the multi-modal deck, separated active-transport corridor, reserved light-rail lane, and the solar-lighting program. Since commissioning, operations have sat in the core transport-asset plan: structural inspections, deck and rail maintenance, lighting control and energy systems, and periodic mechanical and electrical renewals. Costs vary with asset cycles and energy prices and were built into the long-term financial plan from the start.

ACU figures here are indicative and speculative; they have not been independently verified and are provided for illustration only. Further economic modelling would be required. Figures are annual gross avoided costs (no NPV/discounting).

INITIATIVE 3
EVERY CHILD SUCCEEDS

POLICY SUMMARY

We stopped treating children as an afterthought and built a cradle-to-career continuum that met needs before they hardened into harm. Schools became community hubs—health, meals, after-school, trauma-informed practice—with universal, place-based reach so most children touched support every year. We measured what mattered in kid-friendly ways: Rumble's Quest for wellbeing, Results-Based Accountability for practice, and actuarial tracking to show the public return. In short: tackle failure demand at the root, saturate help where kids live and learn, and adjust quickly because the data is alive.

The funding architecture matched the ambition—a City Deal for Kids, twenty years long, with pooled state, federal, and local funds, and social impact bonds issued to investors to stretch outcomes. The results followed: school readiness to 90 per cent, Year 12 completion to 94 per cent, youth unemployment halved, youth justice referrals down 65 per cent, childhood obesity and asthma down 30 per cent, and intergenerational welfare reliance down 80 per cent. For every dollar invested we returned $4.10 in value. We didn't just help kids cope; we changed the trajectory of a city.

POLICY SNAPSHOT WHAT WE INTRODUCED & WHY IT MATTERED – EVERY CHILD SUCCEEDS

- **Cradle-to-career continuum.** Seamless supports from prenatal to tertiary/work. Why it mattered: closed the gaps between stages so help arrived before crises and momentum wasn't lost.
- **Integrated school–community hubs.** Schools as anchors with health, meals, after-school, and trauma-informed practice. Why it mattered: whole-child support improved attendance, trust, and readiness to learn.
- **Place-based saturation strategy.** Universal access with about 75 per cent of children engaged annually. Why it mattered: scale and fairness by design; reduced stigma and "wrong door" failure demand.
- **City Deal for Kids.** Twenty-year, tripartite funding (state/federal/local), with social impact bonds to reach outcomes. Why it mattered: predictable, long-horizon investment aligned to measurable results.
- **Evidence and accountability.** Rumble's Quest, RBA, longitudinal evaluation, actuarial ACU tracking; $4.10 return per $1. Why it mattered: built programs on lived evidence, enabled mid-course correction, and proved value publicly.
- **Youth pathways and scholarships**. Five hundred students per year supported into TAFE/uni; more than $200m in scholarships leveraged. Why it mattered: strengthened the tertiary pipeline and intergenerational lift.

AVOIDABLE COSTS UNIT (ACU) IMPACT ASSESSMENT MATRIX – EVERY CHILD SUCCEEDS

- **Early Childhood (0–5).** Immediate impact: universal screening and developmental checks identify need early; rapid referral and wrap-around supports (health, family services, early learning) begin; attendance in quality early-years programs increases. Long-term benefit: school readiness rises toward 90 per cent; stronger literacy and social-emotional development; better lifetime earnings trajectories. Avoidable costs (indicative): about A$15m per year (reduced remedial education / early-intervention intensity and duplication).
- **Education (6–18).** Immediate impact: attendance lifts; targeted tutoring and trauma-informed practice commence; timetable and pathway adjustments made; device / transport barriers reduced; family engagement strengthened. Long-term benefit: Year 12 completion rises toward 94 per cent; more skilled workforce and higher participation with associated tax revenue. Avoidable costs (indicative): about A$20m per year (reduced welfare reliance and re-engagement program costs).
- **Health and wellbeing.** Immediate impact: school-based health checks, asthma action plans, daily meals, counselling, and physical-activity programs; faster access to primary care. Long-term benefit: about 30 per cent decline in childhood asthma and obesity; reduced adult chronic disease and higher productivity. Avoidable costs (indicative): about A$12m per year (health-system costs avoided from preventable conditions).
- **Youth pathways.** Immediate impact: earlier career coaching; work placements and TAFE / uni bridging; scholarships and mentors; case coordination reduces drop-off at transitions. Long-term benefit: stronger tertiary pipeline; earlier, steadier employment; intergenerational lift. Avoidable costs (indicative): about A$25m per year (reduced unemployment outlays and NEET-related costs).

- **Youth justice.** Immediate impact: early diversion and restorative conferencing expand; on-site youth workers address school refusal; police referrals triaged to supports; hotspot responses coordinated. Long-term benefit: about 65 per cent drop in referrals; safer communities; reduced incarceration cycle. Avoidable costs (indicative): about A$10m per year (justice and crisis costs avoided).
- **Income support reliance.** Immediate impact: one-stop navigation, income-support advice, and school–family brokers stabilise households; financial-stress spikes addressed earlier. Long-term benefit: about 80 per cent reduction in intergenerational dependence; stronger family stability and resilience. Avoidable costs (indicative): about A$8m per year (lifetime income-support avoided; reduced crisis casework).

Total Estimated Avoidable Costs (2025): about A$90m per year.

For a 2064 nominal guide (assume CPI 2.5%), the total equates to about A$236m per year.

Funding and operations. The City Deal for Kids pooled state, federal, and local funding on a twenty-year horizon, with social impact bonds used to extend outcomes. Delivery ran through integrated school–community hubs, universal screening, targeted supports, and a longitudinal evaluation framework that kept adjustments grounded in evidence.

ACU figures here are indicative and speculative; they have not been independently verified and are provided for illustration only. Further economic modelling would be required. Figures are annual gross avoided costs (no NPV/discounting).

INITIATIVE 4

HEALTHY TOGETHER PLEDGE

POLICY SUMMARY

Launceston learned that health isn't just personal — it's collective. The Healthy City Pledge began by listening: a three-yearly preventive-health survey that mapped physical and mental-health needs, suburb by suburb. From there, council lowered barriers and raised invitations. We funded connection like we fund roads — morning teas, walking groups, story clubs — and built a program from staff insight and community voice. PlayStreets and Open Street Days turned roads into rooms; resident-requested 30 km/h Slow Streets made neighbourhoods sociable by default; parkrun sites with Tail Walkers (and help with transport) meant nobody finished last; Seniors' Exercise Parks and social prescribing stitched strength to friendship; intergenerational mentoring, on-Country walks, and therapeutic gardens wove movement with meaning. The "City That Lost 500,000 kilos" was really a city that gained something — steps and hellos, pride and pace — as we stopped counting weight and started counting wellbeing: strength, sleep, connection.

Listening stayed the engine: feedback loops set priorities and timed activations to seasons, shift patterns, and local contexts — legitimacy through listening lifted trust and participation, and resources followed what worked. We treated loneliness as a public-health risk, not a private failing, and designed for dignity in the everyday: safer streets, visible welcome, small rituals of belonging. KindraPass and social prescribing made joining in easier later, but the habit started with simple invitations and a city that kept showing up.

POLICY SNAPSHOT WHAT WE INTRODUCED & WHY IT MATTERED – HEALTHY TOGETHER INITIATIVE

- **Listen and respond.** Survey feedback loops set priorities and timed activations to seasons, shift patterns, and local contexts. Why it mattered: legitimacy through listening increased trust and participation, and resources followed what worked.
- **Treat movement and social connection as civic infrastructure.** Council funded walking, rolling, and gathering the way it funds roads and pipes, with a program built from staff and community insights. Why it mattered: loneliness and inactivity were tackled as public problems, not private failings; dollars went where need was voiced.
- **Reclaim and calm streets.** PlayStreets and Open Streets closed selected roads to through-traffic; 30 km/h limits normalised on local streets. Why it mattered: everyday movement felt safe and welcome; streets became places to be, not just drive through.
- **parkrun equity.** New outer-suburb courses, Tail Walkers to guarantee last-place support, and transport help where needed. Why it mattered: participation barriers dropped; a weekly habit formed with pride, not punishment.
- **Seniors' exercise parks and social prescribing.** Age-friendly strength parks installed and mapped; clinicians linked people to community activity as well as clinical care. Why it mattered: confidence, balance, sleep, and mood improved while downstream service demand eased.
- **Programs with meaning.** Intergenerational mentoring, on-Country walks, and therapeutic gardens embedded in the calendar. Why it mattered: people joined for connection and culture as much as fitness, lifting belonging alongside health.

AVOIDABLE COSTS UNIT IMPACT ASSESSMENT MATRIX – HEALTHY TOGETHER INITIATIVE

- **Preventive health survey** (listen first). Immediate impact: targeted investments to high-need streets; faster feedback loops. Long-term benefit: fewer wasted programs; better equity per dollar. Avoidable costs (indicative): A\$1–2m per year from reduced duplication and mistargeting.
- **PlayStreets and open street days.** Immediate impact: weekly micro-events; spontaneous activity and neighbour meet-ups. Long-term benefit: higher social capital; safer, more watchful streets. Avoidable costs (indicative): A\$1–2m per year in reduced loneliness-related service use and minor-injury incidents.
- **30 km/h slow Streets** (permanent). Immediate impact: lower crash risk; more walking, rolling, and cycling. Long-term benefit: persistent injury reduction; kids' independent mobility. Avoidable costs (indicative): A\$5–7m per year in avoided crash/trauma costs.
- **parkrun access** (outer-suburb sites, Tail Walkers, transport help). Immediate impact: higher participation; "no one finishes last" norm. Long-term benefit: improved cardio-metabolic risk; durable volunteering culture. Avoidable costs (indicative): A\$2–3m per year in prevented chronic-disease burden and ED presentations.
- **Seniors' exercise parks** (activated). Immediate impact: balance and strength gains; new friendship networks. Long-term benefit: fewer falls; ageing in place with confidence. Avoidable costs (indicative): A\$4–6m per year in avoided fall-related admissions and rehab.
- **Social prescribing** (GP referrals to movement and connection). Immediate impact: faster entry to low-cost local activities. Long-term benefit: reduced GP re-attendance for loneliness-linked conditions. Avoidable costs (indicative): A\$3–4m per year in primary/secondary-care offsets.

- **Intergenerational mentoring.** Immediate impact: regular, purposeful contact and skills exchange. Long-term benefit: lower isolation for older adults; youth confidence. Avoidable costs (indicative): A$1–2m per year in mental-health and social-care offsets.
- **On-Country walks and therapeutic gardens.** Immediate impact: culturally grounded activity; nature-based stress relief. Long-term benefit: better mental wellbeing; place-based learning. Avoidable costs (indicative): A$1–2m per year in mental-health presentations and medication offsets.

Total Estimated Avoidable Costs (2025): about A$18–28m per year.

For a 2064 nominal guide (assume CPI 2.5%), the total equates to about A$47–73m per year.

Total initial capital (2025): A$30 million, drawn down over fifteen years. This covered Seniors' Exercise Parks across priority suburbs; street-calming hardware and Open Streets kit (barriers, signage, traffic controllers); parkrun course works and access supports; therapeutic gardens and on-Country trail infrastructure; wayfinding and small amenities (drinking fountains, shade, seating); and set-up for social-prescribing IT and evaluation.

Annual operations at steady state (2025): A$1.5 million per year. This funds the three-yearly preventive-health survey cadence and rapid feedback loops; a standing activation team for PlayStreets/Open Streets; program delivery (parkrun equity, Seniors' Exercise Park activation, intergenerational mentoring, on-Country walks, therapeutic gardens); GP-to-community social-prescribing brokerage; transport equity for participation; and monitoring/ACU tracking.

Net fiscal position — (ten-year ramp, 2025 dollars; simple, no discounting). Program costs: A$1.5m per year operations + A$2.0m per year amortised capital (A$30m over fifteen years) = A$3.5m per year total.

- *Year 1: avoided costs about 5–10% of steady state (A$0.9–2.8m). Net headroom: –A$2.6m to –A$0.7m.*
- *Year 2: 10–20% (A$1.8–5.6m). Net headroom: –A$1.7m to A$2.1m.*
- *Year 3: 15–30% (A$2.7–8.4m). Net headroom: –A$0.8m to A$4.9m.*
- *Year 4: 25–40% (A$4.5–11.2m). Net headroom: A$1.0–7.7m.*
- *Year 5: 35–50% (A$6.3–14.0m). Net headroom: A$2.8–10.5m.*
- *Year 6: 45–60% (A$8.1–16.8m). Net headroom: A$4.6–13.3m.*
- *Year 7: 55–70% (A$9.9–19.6m). Net headroom: A$6.4–16.1m.*
- *Year 8: 65–80% (A$11.7–22.4m). Net headroom: A$8.2–18.9m.*
- *Year 9: 75–90% (A$13.5–25.2m). Net headroom: A$10.0–21.7m.*
- *Year 10 and beyond (steady state): 100% (A$18–28m). Net headroom: A$14.5–24.5m per year.*

Cumulative payback (simple, undiscounted): between Year 2 and Year 6 depending on uptake; mid-range assumptions land around Years 3–4.

ACU figures here are indicative and speculative; they have not been independently verified and are provided for illustration only. Further economic modelling would be required. Figures are annual gross avoided costs (no NPV/discounting).

INITIATIVE 5

CITY IN A GARDEN INITIATIVE

POLICY SUMMARY

Launceston didn't just landscape; it re-engineered its microclimate. In little more than thirty years, canopy cover rose from under 20 per cent to well over 60 per cent—a living roof that filtered air, muffled noise, slowed stormwater, and brought back birds and pollinators to the streets. On heatwave days the shaded corridors ran fifteen degrees cooler than bare paving, turning bus stops, school gates, and shopfronts into survivable places. Breathing got easier, tempers eased, and ambulance call-outs for heat stress fell. Visitors came for the green city as much as the lake—spring blossom, summer shade, autumn colour—and stayed longer because the streets felt walkable and liveable even in extremes.

The green was not just overhead; it was at ground level, shared and edible. Community gardens, public orchards, and edible verges turned greening into a public good everyone could touch, taste, and join. They were places to grow food and grow connection: newcomers learning the city with a trowel in hand, kids foraging on the way home, elders resting in dappled light, neighbours swapping mint and stories. These spaces tackled fresh-food access and loneliness at once, making food security part of civic design, not charity.

The result was environmental infrastructure you could taste and feel: cleaner air, cooler ground, calmer minds, local food, and stronger community ties. Adaptation doubled as everyday amenity. The city became a garden not for appearance, but for survival, health, and belonging.

POLICY SNAPSHOT WHAT WE INTRODUCED & WHY IT MATTERED – CITY IN A GARDEN

- **City-wide community gardens** (universal, not targeted). Resident-run plots in every postcode, framed as a public good rather than a "poverty program." Why it mattered: participation and pride were normalised across suburbs; benefits—food, connection, activity—spread city-wide.
- **Edible public orchard trail.** Citrus, stone fruit, and herbs along everyday walking routes. Why it mattered: everyday nutrition on the way to school or shops; playful reasons to walk and meet.
- **Community stewardship model.** Council provided seeds, tools, compost, and starts; locals governed and tended. Why it mattered: vandalism and maintenance fell; ownership and care rose.
- **Welcome and learning in the garden.** Volunteer planting days for newcomers; elders teaching skills. Why it mattered: social cohesion built through doing—trust across age and language.
- **Canopy target and timeline.** Lift cover from about 19 per cent to 65 per cent plus over three decades, across every neighbourhood. Why it mattered: engineered a cooler microclimate at city scale; equity by design (shade everywhere).
- **Cooling corridors linked to the lake.** Continuous shade from Republic Park to City Park and beyond. Why it mattered: hot-day walking and waiting became comfortable; the city invited lingering, not just passing through.
- **Shade plus mobility infrastructure.** Solar pergolas for e-bike charging and comfort at stops and delivery points. Why it mattered: reinforced active travel; reduced heat stress during everyday trips.
- **Seasonal, city-wide planting program.** Species mix for spring blossom, summer shade, winter light. Why it mattered: year-round benefits—cooling, biodiversity, and a seasonal identity that draws people out.

AVOIDABLE COSTS UNIT IMPACT ASSESSMENT MATRIX – CITY IN A GARDEN INITIATIVE

- **Heat and acute health.** Immediate impact: canopy corridors about 15 °C cooler on hot days; shaded lakefront made waits and walks survivable. Long-term benefit: fewer heat illnesses and ambulance call-outs. Avoidable costs (indicative): A$0.8–1.6m per year (2025).
- **Air quality and respiratory.** Immediate impact: leaves intercept particulates; more short trips on foot or e-bike. Long-term benefit: fewer asthma/COPD flare-ups; reduced GP/ED load. Avoidable costs (indicative): A$0.2–0.5m per year (2025).
- **Mental health and social.** Immediate impact: green streets, shared plots, regular encounters. Long-term benefit: lower clinical demand; stronger informal care. Avoidable costs (indicative): A$0.6–1.2m per year (2025).
- **Chronic disease.** Immediate impact: daily walking/rolling; orchards improve access to fresh food. Long-term benefit: lower obesity/diabetes; better school/work attendance. Avoidable costs (indicative): A$0.4–0.9m per year (2025).
- **Public-realm upkeep.** Immediate impact: community stewardship replaces mow/spray verges. Long-term benefit: reduced maintenance and vandalism response. Avoidable costs (indicative): A$0.2–0.5m per year (2025).
- **Energy and business continuity.** Immediate impact: cooler corridors extend dwell; shaded deliveries; e-bike charging. Long-term benefit: fewer heat-loss trading hours; lower cooling demand. Avoidable costs (indicative): A$0.3–0.8m per year (2025).
- **Health burden avoided** (DALYs/QALYs). Immediate impact: improved diet, daily activity, and reduced loneliness from gardens and shaded public space. Long-term benefit: an estimated 300–600 Disability-Adjusted Life Years (DALYs) or Quality-Adjusted Life Years (QALYs) saved annually. Valuation not included in ACU totals.

Total Estimated Avoidable Costs (2025): about A$2.5–5.5m per year.

For a 2064 nominal guide (assume CPI 2.5%), the total equates to about A$6.6–14.5m per year.

Capital and operations — City in a Garden (transition outlays, one-off, including a 20-year ramp; 2025 dollars)

- *Canopy expansion program (from ~19% to 65%+ cover): ~A$60m*
- *Community gardens and public orchards (establishment and land preparation): ~A$20m*
- *Solar pergolas, e-bike charging, irrigation systems: ~A$14m*
- *Community engagement and stewardship support: ~A$6m*

Total transition outlays (2025): ~A$100m

2064 nominal guide (CPI 2.5%): ~A$262m

Net fiscal position (steady state, 2025). Initial net position is about −A$95m against the one-off outlay; simple payback (undiscounted, using steady-state avoids) occurs in about 18–22 years.

Optional valuation note (not included in ACU totals to avoid double-counting). If DALYs/QALYs are valued at a VSLY proxy of about A$240k (2025), 300–600 DALYs equates to about A$72–144m per year (2025), or about A$190–380m per year in 2064 nominal terms (CPI 2.5%).

ACU figures here are indicative and speculative; they have not been independently verified and are provided for illustration only. Further economic modelling would be required. Figures are annual gross avoided costs (no NPV/discounting).

INITIATIVE 6

GOOD WORK FOR ALL STRATEGY

POLICY SUMMARY

We didn't just chase jobs; we redefined what counted as good work. Launceston chose to value care, creativity, and contribution alongside wages and profit. Local government became an active partner in shaping training pathways—backing young people with apprenticeships and earn-and-learn models, supporting women and carers with flexible opportunities, and treating community service, arts, and environmental repair as work that mattered.

We stopped accepting insecure, low-paid jobs as inevitable and began to insist on dignity in every workplace. Through co-ops, social enterprises, and partnerships with unions and employers, the city helped lift standards, make training accessible, and tie investment to fair outcomes. Work was no longer just a pay cheque; it was a platform for participation, pride, and security.

The shift bent the curve of inequality. Fewer families lived pay-to-pay, more young people found a first job with purpose, and the economy diversified beyond extraction and speculation. Pilots tested at city and regional level became foundations for later labour-market reforms at state and national scale (Flexicurity, Income Guarantee, Lifelong Learning and Training, Entitlement Portability).

By treating employment as a civic asset—designed, supported, and nurtured—"good work for all" became a promise carried in every payslip, every training certificate, and every workplace built on respect.

POLICY SNAPSHOT WHAT WE INTRODUCED & WHY IT MATTERED – GOOD WORK FOR ALL

- **Local training hubs.** Underused facilities converted into trade and health training centres close to where people lived. Why it mattered: training became accessible, kept young people connected locally, and reduced the leakage of talent to bigger cities.
- **Earn-and-learn pathways.** Apprenticeships, scaffolded training, and supported entry-level placements. Why it mattered: smoother transitions from school into decent work and greater confidence in the local labour market.
- **Support for carers and gig workers.** Flexible placements, mentoring, and incubators providing back-office and admin for small operators. Why it mattered: carers and gig workers could focus on quality work, burnout fell, and service stability improved.
- **Local pilots feeding reform.** City-level initiatives trialled approaches later scaled up. Why it mattered: ideas were proven in practice and helped shape state and national labour-market reform.
- **Wrap-around supports for vulnerable youth.** A portion of funds from major civic projects set aside for intensive casework, mentoring, and living supports. Why it mattered: vulnerable young people persisted with training and employment; no one was left behind.
- **Investment tied to dignity.** Public investment linked to fair wages, training commitments, and secure conditions. Why it mattered: community resources built equity and opportunity rather than fuelling exploitation.

AVOIDABLE COSTS UNIT IMPACT ASSESSMENT MATRIX – GOOD WORK FOR ALL

- **Training and local pipelines.** Immediate impact: new local training hubs and hundreds of placements close to home. Long-term benefit: higher retention in health and care workforces; reduced recruitment churn. Avoidable costs (indicative): A$8–12m per year (lower recruitment and agency costs).
- **Youth employment and apprenticeships.** Immediate impact: earn-and-learn pathways and supported entry jobs for school leavers. Long-term benefit: reduced youth unemployment; higher tax contributions; stronger local economy. Avoidable costs (indicative): A$10–15m per year (avoided unemployment outlays).
- **Carer and gig-worker supports.** Immediate impact: mentoring, incubators, and admin back-office to stabilise gig and care work. Long-term benefit: higher service quality; reduced attrition and burnout. Avoidable costs (indicative): A$6–9m per year (avoided retraining and turnover costs).
- **Social enterprises and co-ops.** Immediate impact: worker-led enterprises and social businesses supported by council. Long-term benefit: more stable jobs, stronger local ownership, reduced welfare reliance. Avoidable costs (indicative): A$12–18m per year (avoided welfare and crisis-service costs).
- **Wrap-around supports for vulnerable youth.** Immediate impact: mentoring, casework, and living supports funded from civic-project allocations. Long-term benefit: improved training completion; lower justice and welfare demand. Avoidable costs (indicative): A$10–14m per year (avoided churn across welfare, justice, and child protection).
- **Participation and dignity.** Immediate impact: broader culture of secure, purposeful work. Long-term benefit: stronger household incomes; reduced demand for crisis services. Avoidable costs (indicative): A$5–8m per year (downstream savings from reduced poverty-related demand).

Total Estimated Avoidable Costs (2025): A$51–76m per year.

For a 2064 nominal guide (assume CPI 2.5%), the total equates to about A$128–190m per year.

Total initial capital (2025): A$15 million, drawn down over five years. This covered refurbishing and fitting out local training hubs (workshop equipment, simulation labs, IT), a seed fund for co-ops and social enterprises, small grants for earn-and-learn pilots and supported placements, and program set-up including evaluation and ACU tracking.

Annual operations at steady state (2025): A$11.5 million per year. This funds hub staffing and mentors, apprenticeship and earn-and-learn wage supports, incubator and back-office services for co-ops and sole traders, wrap-around supports for vulnerable youth (casework, transport, short-term living supports), and ongoing monitoring and evaluation.

Net fiscal position — ten-year ramp (2025 dollars; simple, no discounting). Program costs assumed at A$14.5m per year in Years 1–5 (A$11.5m operations + A$3.0m capital draw), then A$11.5m per year from Year 6 onward (capital draw complete). Steady-state ACU avoids: A$51–76m per year.

- *Year 1: 5–10% of steady state (A$2.6–7.6m). Net headroom: –A$11.9m to –A$6.9m.*
- *Year 2: 10–20% (A$5.1–15.2m). Net headroom: –A$9.4m to A$0.7m.*
- *Year 3: 15–30% (A$7.6–22.8m). Net headroom: –A$6.9m to A$8.3m.*
- *Year 4: 25–40% (A$12.8–30.4m). Net headroom: –A$1.8m to A$15.9m.*
- *Year 5: 35–50% (A$17.8–38.0m). Net headroom: A$3.3m to A$23.5m.*
- *Year 6: 45–60% (A$22.9–45.6m). Net headroom: A$11.4m to A$34.1m.*
- *Year 7: 55–70% (A$28.1–53.2m). Net headroom: A$16.6m to A$41.7m.*
- *Year 8: 65–80% (A$33.1–60.8m). Net headroom: A$21.6m to A$49.3m.*

- *Year 9: 75–90% (A$38.2–68.4m). Net headroom: A$26.8m to A$56.9m.*
- *Year 10 and beyond (steady state): 100% (A$51–76m). Net headroom: A$39.5m to A$64.5m per year.*

Cumulative payback (simple, undiscounted): between Year 3 and Year 7 depending on uptake and delivery; mid-range assumptions land around Year 5.

ACU figures are indicative and speculative; they have not been independently verified and are provided for illustration only. Further economic modelling would be required. Figures are annual gross avoided costs (no NPV/discounting).

INITIATIVE 7
THE WELLBEING ECONOMY

POLICY SUMMARY

Launceston's boom wasn't the old kind of boom. Growth rules put people and planet in the same frame: secure jobs, fair wages, clean industries—because thriving people depend on a thriving planet. The shift was deliberate: move to the "Goldilocks zone" of Doughnut Economics, where human needs are met without breaching ecological limits. Growth meant wellbeing—health, belonging, opportunity—or it didn't count as growth at all.

The boom that began in the early 2030s and lasted for decades was built on equity and innovation. Established industries were reshaped for sustainability, and new champions emerged: hemp farmers turning fields into fibre, food, and bio-composites; cricket farmers proving protein could be clean, affordable, and resilient.

Both industries thrived because the settings were right: land released at scale, clean energy guaranteed, and training pipelines that let people earn while they learned. What began as experiments became benchmarks. Hemp cooperatives cut import dependence and, with downstream processing, opened export markets; cricket protein moved from niche to mainstream, supplying local systems and international buyers, including the World Food Programme.

Care-led growth lit the fuse. Paid, scaffolded Care Pathways built a bigger, steadier workforce—with placements, mentors, and flexibility for carers. Timebank and KindraPass added further scaffolding, and welcoming "new arrivals" policies expanded skills and demand. Wages, participation, productivity, community wellbeing—and even revenue—all lifted together.

Clean industry followed. Multi-use solar, including floating arrays, spread across the valley. Bell Bay cracked industrial heat with electri-fied "thermal bricks," delivering reliable clean energy, biodiversity gains, and local produce beneath the panels.

And the "big three" civic investments—the Tamar Lake weir, the second bridge, and the Statue of Equity—drove multipliers of more than $2.70 for every dollar spent. They created skills pipelines, jobs, and a shared identity you could see and touch. Upstream, you pay once—and harvest for decades.

POLICY SNAPSHOT WHAT WE INTRODUCED & WHY IT MATTERED – WELLBEING ECONOMIC BOOM

- **Hemp farming cooperative.** Large-scale hemp farms, organised as co-ops, producing fibre, bio-plastics, food oils, and construction materials. Why it mattered: created export streams, cut reliance on imported fibres and plastics, and restored soils through regenerative rotations.
- **Cricket protein industry.** Urban and peri-urban vertical farms producing insect protein for food and feed. Why it mattered: delivered high-protein, low-emission food; supplied schools, care homes, and local businesses; built resilience against global protein shocks.
- **Care pathways.** Paid, scaffolded training and placements from entry-level care roles to specialist practice. Why it mattered: expanded and stabilised the care workforce; lifted wages, participation, and productivity; reduced downstream health costs.
- **Clean energy and thermal storage.** Multi-use and floating solar, plus electrified "thermal bricks" at Bell Bay. Why it mattered: provided firm clean energy for farms and industry; cut emissions and energy bills; enabled industrial diversification.
- **The big civic investments.** Tamar Lake weir, City Bridge, Statue of Equity. Why it mattered: multiplied economic activity; created jobs and skills; strengthened civic identity and cohesion.

AVOIDABLE COSTS UNIT IMPACT ASSESSMENT MATRIX – WELLBEING ECONOMIC BOOM

- **Hemp farming cooperative.** Immediate impact: 2,000 hectares converted to hemp within three years. Long-term benefit: new $120m annual export stream; import substitution for fibres and plastics. Avoidable costs (indicative): $40m per year avoided import leakage; $5m per year avoided soil remediation.
- **Cricket protein industry.** Immediate impact: 15 vertical farms established; 400 new jobs. Long-term benefit: local supply of 6,000 tonnes protein per year; mainstream in schools and aged care. Avoidable costs (indicative): $25m per year avoided protein imports; $12m per year avoided chronic-disease costs.
- **Care pathways expansion.** Immediate impact: +1,200 workers in health and aged care. Long-term benefit: stable workforce; higher wages and retention; reduced hospital strain. Avoidable costs (indicative): $30m per year avoided agency premiums; $20m per year fewer preventable ED visits.
- **Clean energy and thermal storage.** Immediate impact: 300 ha agrivoltaics; 40 MW floating solar; Bell Bay thermal bricks online. Long-term benefit: reliable clean power; emissions cut by 400 kt CO_2 per year. Avoidable costs (indicative): $50m per year avoided blackout downtime; $18m per year avoided carbon penalties.
- **Big three civic projects** (weir, bridge, statue). Immediate impact: 3,000 construction jobs; $3b capital spend. Long-term benefit: $2.70 GRP return per $1 invested; enduring skills pipelines. Avoidable costs (indicative): $150m per year productivity gain; $10m per year avoided congestion costs.
- **Employment and participation.** Immediate impact: +6,000 jobs across farms, care, energy, and civic projects. Long-term benefit: household incomes up 8%; stronger tax base; +5% GRP uplift in the decade. Avoidable costs (indicative): $200m per year avoided welfare churn; $100m per year added local revenue.

Total Estimated Avoidable Costs (2025): about A$515–575m per year.

For a 2064 nominal guide (assume CPI 2.5%), the total equates to about A$1.1–1.3b per year. Event-based shocks (e.g., global protein supply disruption, extreme energy outages) are not included in the annual total; jobs/output are benefits, not "avoidable costs."

Capital and operations — This chapter aggregates multiple portfolios (agrifood, care workforce, clean energy, civic assets). To avoid double-counting, capital and operating outlays are recorded in the component policy sections (e.g., Tamar Lake, City Bridge, Good Work for All, Healthy Together, Clean Energy/Storage). Use those costings for fiscal plans; the ACU totals above reflect avoided costs and productivity gains at the consolidated level.

ACU figures here are indicative and speculative; they have not been independently verified and are provided for illustration only. Further economic modelling would be required. Figures are annual gross avoided costs (no NPV/discounting).

INITIATIVE 8
CITY GROWTH STRATEGY

POLICY SUMMARY

Launceston's new eco-suburbs—Waterbank, Ironbark Plains, Greenwood, and Blueleaf Cove—weren't just subdivisions; they were communities organised around people, place, and planet. Each carried its own landscape identity yet shared a common foundation: clean energy, Passivhaus-standard homes, truly walkable design, and green corridors stitched back into the Valley.

Growth was made deliberately inclusive. Social and Trust housing was built in from day one; migrant families were welcomed and visible in the making; and core services—schools, health hubs, local shops— arrived with the first residents so opportunity didn't lag behind the keys. The neighbourhoods were literally "built by hands from twenty nations," signalling dignity, pathways, and belonging—not just roofs.

Design moves made the difference. Every dwelling met Passivhaus standards—airtight, insulated, properly ventilated—delivering comfort with "low bills for life," and every rooftop harvested rain like earlier Tasmanian generations once did. Clean energy was local and shared: neighbourhood batteries—one for roughly every fifty homes—

charged by day and smoothed demand at night, built in, not bolted on. Parks and commons were non-negotiable: no house sat more than 400 metres from a lit, maintained space made for movement and everyday play, amplified by playful, data-aware PlayPods that widened access. Streets read as invitations, not hazards: shared green space, wide shaded footpaths, and a main road dimensioned wide not for extra car throughput but to let riders travel two-abreast safely—a subtle redesign that normalised walking and cycling for all ages. The objective wasn't "most people"; it was everyone.

And the build-out didn't stop at the city's edge. A parallel retrofit program brought older stock up to modern performance—solar, insulation, windows, ventilation—starting with the coldest, dampest homes, so resilience and affordability spread to long-standing streets as well.

The result was more than shelter: it was belonging. These suburbs proved that when housing, equity, energy, and public realm are designed as one, a wellbeing economy takes root—and stays rooted.

POLICY SNAPSHOT WHAT WE INTRODUCED & WHY IT MATTERED — CITY GROWTH STRATEGY

- **Passivhaus covenant** (all dwellings). City-wide requirement that every new home meets Passivhaus standards (airtight, insulated, ventilated). Why it mattered: "low bills for life," healthier interiors, and equity by design.
- **Neighbourhood batteries** (about 1 per 50 homes). Distributed storage charging by day and shared at night, built in from the start. Why it mattered: local reliability, flatter demand, cleaner-energy benefits shared by renters and owners alike.
- **Rainwater tanks on every roof.** Rooftop rain harvesting with tanks beside each home. Why it mattered: visible, practical sustainability; resilience in dry spells; lower mains demand.
- **Parks within about 400 m plus PlayPods.** Rule: no house more than 400 m from a lit, maintained park; smart PlayPods release equipment and track use. Why it mattered: everyday movement made easy; fun that funds prevention; data-guided investment.
- **Shared green and edible verges.** No fences; shared greens with edible plantings and shaded rest stops. Why it mattered: belonging and food literacy; cooler, more social streets.
- **Quiet equity** (1-in-5 Trust/Social homes, indistinguishable). Mixed tenure integrated into streets and buildings—"you'd never know." Medium density, high dignity. Why it mattered: affordability without stigma; mixed communities that age well.
- **Universal design from the start.** Multilingual signage, braille overlays, integrated ramps; spaces designed to invite, not just comply. Why it mattered: access as a baseline—designed for everyone.
- **Retrofit at scale** (older stock). Whole-of-city upgrade program for pre-solar-era homes; smart workforce plus co-funding. Why it mattered: warmer, drier, efficient homes; local jobs; upstream health savings.

AVOIDABLE COSTS UNIT IMPACT ASSESSMENT MATRIX – CITY GROWTH STRATEGY

- **Passivhaus covenant** (all dwellings). Immediate impact: airtight, insulated, ventilated homes reduce energy use and indoor damp; winter/summer comfort stabilised. Long-term benefit: lower energy hardship; fewer respiratory and heat/cold-stress presentations; sustained household savings. Avoidable costs (indicative): A$8–14m per year (reduced health service use, concessions, failure-to-pay admin).
- **Neighbourhood batteries** (about 1 per 50 homes). Immediate impact: local storage smooths peaks; fewer brownouts; solar captured and shared nightly. Long-term benefit: network resilience and lower peak charges; cleaner grid mix benefits renters and owners. Avoidable costs (indicative): A$6–10m per year (avoided outage downtime, peak-demand penalties, diesel backup).
- **Rainwater tanks on every roof.** Immediate impact: on-site harvesting reduces mains draw and stormwater load. Long-term benefit: drought resilience; reduced flood/stormwater costs; lower household bills. Avoidable costs (indicative): A$2–4m per year (stormwater treatment/overflows, potable-supply costs).
- **Parks within about 400 m plus PlayPods.** Immediate impact: daily access to lit, maintained parks; equipment lending normalises movement. Long-term benefit: higher physical activity and social connection; lower chronic-disease risk. Avoidable costs (indicative): A$10–18m per year (preventable disease burden, mental-health downstream costs).
- **Shared green and edible verges.** Immediate impact: shade, habitat, and edible plantings cool streets and spark micro-socialising. Long-term benefit: urban-heat reduction; food literacy; stronger passive surveillance and cohesion. Avoidable costs (indicative): A$1–3m per year (heat-related illness, amenity/greening maintenance offsets).

- **Quiet equity** (1-in-5 Trust/Social homes, indistinguishable). Immediate impact: mixed tenure embedded from day one; medium density with high dignity. Long-term benefit: lower homelessness churn; steadier schooling/employment; less crisis demand. Avoidable costs (indicative): A$25–45m per year (crisis accommodation, justice, child protection, acute health).
- **Universal design from the start.** Immediate impact: ramps, wayfinding, braille overlays, multilingual signage built in. Long-term benefit: fewer falls and injuries; greater participation for older people and disabled residents. Avoidable costs (indicative): A$3–6m per year (injury treatment, transport assistance, carer strain).
- **Retrofit at scale** (older stock). Immediate impact: targeted upgrades (solar, insulation, windows, ventilation) for pre-solar-era homes. Long-term benefit: warmer, drier housing stock; lower emissions; reduced winter mortality/morbidity. Avoidable costs (indicative): A$12–25m per year (respiratory/cardiovascular admissions, energy concessions).

Total Estimated Avoidable Costs (2025): about A$67–125m per year (gross).

For a 2064 nominal guide (assume CPI 2.5%), the total equates to about A$142–265m per year. Event-based shocks are excluded; jobs/output are benefits, not "avoidable costs."

Total initial public capital (2025): A$45 million (15% public seed on an estimated A$300 million program), drawn down over fifteen years. This public seed covered neighbourhood-battery co-funding and grid integration; parks, commons and PlayPods (equipment, lighting, paths); universal-design and wayfinding upgrades; rainwater-tank incentives and installations; and a citywide retrofit seed program prioritised to cold/damp homes.

Indicative private capital (2025): about A$255 million (developers, utilities, households) for dwellings, local energy, and public-realm co-contributions.

Annual operations at steady state (2025): A$2.0 million per year for battery and park stewardship, PlayPod maintenance, retrofit brokerage and grants administration, data/monitoring and evaluation, and inclusion-target engagement.

Net fiscal position — ten-year ramp (2025 dollars; simple, no discounting)

Program costs assumed at A$5.0m per year in Years 1–15 (A$2.0m operations + A$3.0m public capital draw), then A$2.0m per year from Year 16 onward. Steady-state ACU avoids: A$67–125m per year.

- *Year 1: 5–10% (A$3.35–12.50m). Net headroom: −A$1.65m to A$7.50m.*
- *Year 2: 10–20% (A$6.70–25.00m). Net headroom: A$1.70m to A$20.00m.*
- *Year 3: 15–30% (A$10.05–37.50m). Net headroom: A$5.05m to A$32.50m.*
- *Year 4: 25–40% (A$16.75–50.00m). Net headroom: A$11.75m to A$45.00m.*
- *Year 5: 35–50% (A$23.45–62.50m). Net headroom: A$18.45m to A$57.50m.*
- *Year 6: 45–60% (A$30.15–75.00m). Net headroom: A$25.15m to A$70.00m.*
- *Year 7: 55–70% (A$36.85–87.50m). Net headroom: A$31.85m to A$82.50m.*
- *Year 8: 65–80% (A$43.55–100.00m). Net headroom: A$38.55m to A$95.00m.*
- *Year 9: 75–90% (A$50.25–112.50m). Net headroom: A$45.25m to A$107.50m.*
- *Year 10 and beyond (steady state): 100% (A$67–125m). Net headroom (Years 10–15): A$62–120m; post-capex (Year 16+): A$65–123m per year.*

Cumulative payback (simple, undiscounted): between Year 2 and Year 4 depending on uptake; mid-range assumptions land around Years 2–3.

ACU figures here are indicative and speculative; they have not been independently verified and are provided for illustration only. Further economic modelling would be required. Figures are annual gross avoided costs (no NPV/discounting).

POLICY COUNTERFACTUAL — NO CITY GROWTH STRATEGY

If Launceston's eco-suburbs are not built—no Waterbank, no Ironbark Plains, no Greenwood, no Blueleaf Cove—thousands of homes are not delivered, leading to:

- No construction boom → lost jobs across trades (carpenters, electricians, plumbers, painters, roofers, tilers, plasterers, concreters, landscapers, civil contractors).
- No skilled-migration pathways → shortage of engineers, planners, surveyors, architects, building designers.
- No settlement of humanitarian entrants → loss of cultural richness, missed opportunity to offer safety and purpose to displaced people, and fewer hands to help build the future.
- No housing supply → rising rents, overcrowding, family stress, stalled population growth.
- No new attractions → no tourism surge, no waterfront investment, no catalyst for placemaking.
- The social and economic ripple effect never eventuates, meaning:
- No café precincts → no baristas, bakers, small food suppliers.
- No early-learning centres → no educators, no parent workforce re-entry.
- No fitness studios or gyms → loss of health-sector jobs and preventive wellbeing outcomes.
- No small-business services → no bookkeepers, no marketing firms, no local accountants or lawyers.
- No artist studios or public-art commissions → cultural flatline.
- No co-working spaces → no tech start-ups, no innovation spin-offs.
- No park-maintenance teams, no horticulturists.
- No community batteries → continued escalation in energy prices.
- No retrofit programs → old homes stay cold, expensive, inefficient.

- No learning hubs → reduced pathways for reskilling and adult education.
- No accessible design.

INITIATIVE 9
CREATIVE CITY INITIATIVE

POLICY SUMMARY

We didn't just clean walls; we changed who gets to write the city. Instead of paying forever to scrub tags, council spent the same budget upstream—commissioning local artists, involving schools and community groups, and letting stories of people and place take the space blank walls once hoarded. The obvious wins—less vandalism, more colour—were only the surface. Underneath came ownership: school groups on guided art tours, cafés pinning sketches in their windows, young artists backed with materials, scaffolds and insurance, visiting artists arriving, and a mural trail that grew into a showcase of local story and a tourist draw in its own right.

This wasn't aesthetics over substance. The trail held difficult truth as well as delight. Return, on the Town Hall wall, honoured the recommencement of formal land return to Aboriginal Tasmanians; its CitizenEcho invited consent-based listening in place—symbol made structural, story made audible. Around the corner, tiny doors and playful installations offered the city small moments of wonder. That is what a creative city does: it stitches memory to brick so belonging becomes something you can walk.

Education matched the cultural turn. Changemaker High wasn't a pipeline to jobs; it was a launchpad for purpose. The ethos was simple: don't sort kids by risk; hand them the tools—sensors, soil, stories—and ask them to show what's possible. When Tamar Lake flashed green, the model proved itself. Students mobilised within hours as citizen scientists with handheld sensors, drones and floating monitors; Elders guided where to look; university labs validated samples; engineers trialled fixes; council cleared barriers instead of creating them. A live dashboard told the story in public; the bloom retreated; confidence returned—and students shifted from learning about crises to solving one.

Trust began to compound. Student science helped preserve Carr Villa bushland during cemetery planning, strengthened protections for the Lilydale wildlife corridor, and flowed onto public stages where young people learned to speak for the city—a Launceston City Student Design Competition here, a Five Minute Thesis showcase there. That's how a creative city grows its own changemakers: invest in makers, believe in young people, and pin the story to the city itself so everyone can read what they're part of.

POLICY SNAPSHOT WHAT WE INTRODUCED & WHY IT MATTERED — CREATIVE CITY INITIATIVE

- **Launceston mural program.** Upstream shift from scrubbing tags to commissioning local artists with schools and community groups; funded materials, access, and maintenance so works could endure. Why it mattered: replaced downstream costs with civic pride; grew local talent; turned blank walls into public story and identity.
- **Mural trail and guided tours.** A connected trail with maps, signage, and regular guided walks (including school tours); pipeline support for young and visiting artists. Why it mattered: made local story walkable; created a tourist draw; embedded everyday arts learning and reasons to linger.
- **CitizenEcho.** Consent-based, place-tied audio adding context and voices to artworks and sites. Why it mattered: anchored memory and truth-telling in place without surveillance; deepened attachment; useful for education and reflection.
- **Changemaker High** — Tasmania's first vertical high school. Urban, multi-storey public school as civic lab: project-based learning, shared labs and workshops, community mentors; students tackle real briefs. Why it mattered: treated young people as full citizens; built capability and confidence; kept talent local by making purpose and contribution normal.
- **Citizen science used in the city.** Student- and community-led monitoring and problem-solving: Tamar Lake algal-bloom sensors/drones/rafts with a public dashboard; biodiversity atlas informing Carr Villa planning; advocacy and monitoring for the Lilydale wildlife corridor. Why it mattered: faster, trusted responses to local issues; evidence feeding policy decisions; STEM engagement that turns learning into contribution.
- **Student Design Competition.** Annual city brief for primary to senior students; exhibitions in civic spaces; practitioner feedback. Why it mattered: created a public stage for ideas;

normalised co-design with young people; built pathways from curiosity to practical change.

- **Five Minute Thesis.** Short-form presentation showcase where students present research and proposals to community, industry, and council audiences. Why it mattered: lifted communication and critical-thinking skills; brought youth voice into civic decision-making; turned participation into a habit.

AVOIDABLE COSTS UNIT IMPACT ASSESSMENT MATRIX – CREATIVE CITY INITIATIVE

- **Graffiti and vandalism.** Immediate impact: commissioned murals and community ownership reduce tagging and repeat repainting; ranger call-outs drop. Long-term benefit: ongoing stewardship; lower damage to public and private walls; fewer incident reports. Avoidable costs (indicative): about A$0.30–0.70m per year (reduced removal, repainting, ranger after-hours, minor policing).
- **Youth engagement and school retention** (Changemaker High and student programs). Immediate impact: hands-on projects, belonging and purpose lift engagement and attendance. Long-term benefit: higher Year 12 completion; less truancy/suspension; smoother pathways. Avoidable costs (indicative): about A$0.80–1.80m per year (reduced alternative education/remedial programs; lower casework/escalations).
- **Youth justice diversion.** Immediate impact: purposeful projects and mentoring reduce time in unsupervised high-risk settings. Long-term benefit: lower youth offending; fewer court appearances and custodial days. Avoidable costs (indicative): about A$0.60–1.50m per year (case management, court processing, custodial days avoided).
- **Environmental monitoring and incident response** (citizen science). Immediate impact: early detection and targeted action on lake blooms; community sampling and dashboards. Long-term benefit: shorter, fewer incidents; reduced closures and clean-up; better water confidence. Avoidable costs (indicative): about A$0.25–0.60m per year (incident response, clean-up, contracted sampling).
- **Evidence-informed planning** (citizen science to policy). Immediate impact: data informs decisions (e.g., biodiversity mapping for Carr Villa; corridor protection at Lilydale). Long-term benefit: fewer redesigns/appeals; better project fit; less conflict. Avoidable costs (indicative): about A$0.15–0.35m per year (planning rework, legal/mediation, consultation reruns).

- **Cultural respect and truth-telling** (CitizenEcho; Return). Immediate impact: consent-based listening on site lowers grievance and misunderstanding; learning in place. Long-term benefit: fewer formal complaints; calmer discourse around contested histories. Avoidable costs (indicative): about A$0.05–0.12m per year (complaint handling, dispute mediation).
- **Local talent pipeline** (creative/STEM). Immediate impact: student showcases and mentoring link learners to real briefs and networks. Long-term benefit: more local hires; fewer emergency recruitment fixes and short-term grants. Avoidable costs (indicative): about A$0.20–0.50m per year (reduced small "rescue" grants; some welfare reliance avoided).
- **Youth mental health and wellbeing.** Immediate impact: purpose, belonging and public voice ease low-level distress. Long-term benefit: fewer minor mental-health presentations; better self-management and peer support. Avoidable costs (indicative): about A$0.10–0.25m per year (primary care/ED presentations linked to distress).

Total Estimated Avoidable Costs (2025): about A$2.6–6.1m per year.

2064 nominal guide (CPI 2.5% per annum): about A$6.7–15.9m per year.

Total initial capital (2025): A$6 million, drawn down over five years. This covered mural program set-up (materials, access, lifts/scaffolds, maintenance), trail signage and guided-tour infrastructure, CitizenEcho plaques/IT, school partnerships and small grants, and seed equipment for student showcases.

Annual operations at steady state (2025): A$1.2 million per year. This funds commissioning rounds and maintenance, tour facilitation, CitizenEcho hosting and moderation, school/mentor coordination, student design competitions and Five Minute Thesis showcases, and monitoring/evaluation.

2064 nominal guide (CPI 2.5%): capital ≈ A$15.7m (one-off); operations ≈ A$3.14m per year.

Net fiscal position — ten-year ramp (2025 dollars; simple, no discounting)

Program costs assumed at A$2.4m per year in Years 1–5 (A$1.2m operations + A$1.2m capital draw), then A$1.2m per year from Year 6 onward. Steady-state ACU avoids: A$2.6–6.1m per year.

- *Year 1: 5–10% (A$0.13–0.61m). Net headroom: −A$2.27m to − A$1.79m.*
- *Year 2: 10–20% (A$0.26–1.22m). Net headroom: −A$2.14m to − A$1.18m.*
- *Year 3: 15–30% (A$0.39–1.83m). Net headroom: −A$2.01m to − A$0.57m.*
- *Year 4: 25–40% (A$0.65–2.44m). Net headroom: −A$1.75m to A$0.04m.*
- *Year 5: 35–50% (A$0.91–3.05m). Net headroom: −A$1.49m to A$0.65m.*
- *Year 6: 45–60% (A$1.17–3.66m). Net headroom (post-capex): − A$0.03m to A$2.46m.*
- *Year 7: 55–70% (A$1.43–4.27m). Net headroom: A$0.23m to A$3.07m.*
- *Year 8: 65–80% (A$1.69–4.88m). Net headroom: A$0.49m to A$3.68m.*
- *Year 9: 75–90% (A$1.95–5.49m). Net headroom: A$0.75m to A$4.29m.*
- *Year 10 and beyond (steady state): 100% (A$2.6–6.1m). Net headroom: A$1.4–4.9m per year.*

Cumulative payback (simple, undiscounted): between Year 5 and Year 7 depending on uptake; mid-range assumptions around Year 6.

Notes: city-scale, gross avoided costs only (no NPV/discounting). Conservative partial attribution with no double-counting across rows. Tourism spend, creative income, and wider economic multipliers are benefits, not "avoidable costs," and are excluded here.

ACU figures here are indicative and speculative; they have not been independently verified and are provided for illustration only. Further economic modelling would be required. Figures are annual gross avoided costs (no NPV/discounting).

INITIATIVE 10
ACTIVE BELONGING STRATEGY

POLICY SUMMARY

We didn't just talk about sport and recreation; we built movement into the fabric of the city. Every child received a bike and helmet to make active transport normal and fair from the start. New velodromes in Riverside and St Leonards and pump tracks in Waverley and Ravenswood gave beginners and families safe places to ride, while extended mountain-bike trails in Trevallyn and Kate Reed turned everyday nature into everyday fitness. We upgraded what we had: a solar roof over the Hobler's Bridge netball centre for all-weather play, a revived Silverdome for events and pride, and national rowing regattas back on Tamar Lake. At the waterfront, a high-roofed palaestra kept exercise social and visible—movement in the city's heart, not tucked away.

Movement became an ordinary right, not a privilege. School gates opened after hours with insurance and security sorted so gyms and fields served the whole community. Streets closed to cars on Sundays and for regular PlayStreets, with safer crossings and calm speeds turning roads into rooms for games, markets, and riding lessons. We backed the people who make play possible—training for umpires, referees, and officials—so grassroots sport stayed safe, welcoming, and sustainable. Even the Statue of Equity did double duty as a climbing ground—symbol above, participation below. From community leagues to elite training camps, Launceston built a ladder from first try to high performance.

The shift was upstream. A park, a path, a safe crossing—these were health policies in disguise, cutting chronic disease and loneliness, improving focus at school and productivity at work, and making ageing stronger and safer.

POLICY SNAPSHOT WHAT WE BUILT & WHY IT MATTERED — SPORT AND ACTIVE BELONGING

- **Every child a bike.** All children in Launceston gifted a bicycle and helmet. Why it mattered: normalised active transport, built confidence and independence, reduced inequality of access.
- **Velodromes and pump tracks.** Outdoor velodromes in Riverside and St Leonards; pump tracks in Waverley and Ravenswood. Why it mattered: created accessible entry points for cycling across ages.
- **Expanded mountain-bike trails.** Extended tracks in Trevallyn and Kate Reed reserves. Why it mattered: positioned Launceston as a riding destination; health and tourism lifted together.
- **Netball centre roof.** Hobler's Bridge complex covered and solar-powered. Why it mattered: all-weather access, year-round participation, lower energy costs.
- **Silverdome renewal.** Refurbishment and activation of the stadium. Why it mattered: secured events; strengthened local pride and economic return.
- **Rowing and regattas.** National events on Tamar Lake. Why it mattered: showcased Launceston and reinforced the lake as a civic and sporting asset.
- **Palaestra by the lake.** High-roof, open-air gym with weather-sensitive walls. Why it mattered: made movement visible, social, and inclusive at the city's heart.
- **School facility access.** Insurance and security reforms to open gyms and fields after hours. Why it mattered: maximised public use of existing assets; expanded equity of access.
- **PlayStreets and CBD car-free Sundays.** Regular closures for play, markets, and sport. Why it mattered: reclaimed streets for people; built a habit of community activity.
- **Sport workforce support.** Council-backed training for umpires, referees, and officials. Why it mattered: kept grassroots sport safe, sustainable, and welcoming.

- **Statue of Equity climbing.** Integrated climbing facility in the monument. Why it mattered: fused symbolism with participation—equity you can climb.
- **Olympic and elite training hubs.** Launceston positioned as a national training ground. Why it mattered: drew talent and investment; inspired local participation.

AVOIDABLE COSTS UNIT IMPACT ASSESSMENT MATRIX – SPORT AND ACTIVE BELONGING

- **Chronic disease and inactivity.** Immediate impact: bikes for all children; palaestra and open streets normalised daily activity. Long-term benefit: lower obesity, diabetes, and cardiovascular disease. Avoidable costs (indicative): A$12–20m per year.
- **Mental health and connection.** Immediate impact: PlayStreets, netball centre, MTB trails, community leagues. Long-term benefit: lower loneliness and depression; stronger social capital. Avoidable costs (indicative): A$5–8m per year.
- **Youth engagement and equity.** Immediate impact: after-hours school access; pump tracks and velodromes in working-class suburbs. Long-term benefit: higher youth participation; reduced disengagement and antisocial behaviour. Avoidable costs (indicative): A$4–7m per year.
- **Emergency and acute care.** Immediate impact: safer crossings, slow streets, supervised facilities. Long-term benefit: fewer road-trauma admissions; reduced ambulance ramping. Avoidable costs (indicative): A$3–6m per year.
- **Education and productivity.** Immediate impact: more active children with better focus; reduced absenteeism. Long-term benefit: higher school achievement; stronger workforce productivity. Avoidable costs (indicative): A$5–9m per year.
- **Ageing and falls prevention.** Immediate impact: seniors' walking programs, lake-loop activity, lifelong participation. Long-term benefit: fewer falls; healthier ageing at home. Avoidable costs (indicative): A$3–5m per year.
- **Tourism and event economy**. Immediate impact: Silverdome, netball centre, regattas, elite training. Long-term benefit: visitor spend, civic pride. Note: co-benefits acknowledged but excluded from ACU totals.

Total estimated avoidable costs (2025): about A$35–55m per year.

For a 2064 nominal guide (assume CPI 2.5%), this equates to about A$92–144m per year.

Figures are gross annual avoids (no NPV/discounting). Tourism/event co-benefits are excluded from the ACU total.

Total initial capital (2025): A$140 million, drawn down over eight years. This covered the two velodromes; two pump tracks; trail extensions and wayfinding; Hobler's Bridge roof and solar; Silverdome renewal; palaestra by the lake; rowing course and regatta infrastructure; safe-crossing and street-calming hardware for PlayStreets and car-free Sundays; school-access upgrades; and equipment, storage, and signage.

Annual operations at steady state (2025): A$10.0 million per year. This funds the bikes-for-all refresh and maintenance; facility programming and upkeep (velodromes, pump tracks, palaestra); permits and logistics for open-street activations; school-access insurance and custodial support; sport-workforce training; event delivery (including rowing regattas); and monitoring/ACU tracking.

Net fiscal position — ten-year ramp (2025 dollars; simple, no discounting)

Program costs in Years 1–8: A$10.0m opex + A$17.5m amortised capex (A$140m over eight years) = A$27.5m per year. From Year 9 onward: A$10.0m per year (capex complete). Steady-state avoided costs: about A$35–55m per year.

- *Year 1: 5–10% of steady state (A$1.75–5.5m). Net headroom: –A$25.8m to –A$22.0m.*
- *Year 2: 10–20% (A$3.5–11.0m). Net headroom: –A$24.0m to –A$16.5m.*
- *Year 3: 15–30% (A$5.25–16.5m). Net headroom: –A$22.3m to –A$11.0m.*
- *Year 4: 25–40% (A$8.75–22.0m). Net headroom: –A$18.8m to –A$5.5m.*

- *Year 5: 35–50% (A$12.25–27.5m). Net headroom: –A$15.3m to A$0.0m.*
- *Year 6: 45–60% (A$15.75–33.0m). Net headroom: –A$11.8m to A$5.5m.*
- *Year 7: 55–70% (A$19.25–38.5m). Net headroom: –A$8.3m to A$11.0m.*
- *Year 8: 65–80% (A$22.75–44.0m). Net headroom: –A$4.8m to A$16.5m.*
- *Year 9: 85–95% (A$29.75–52.25m). Net headroom: A$19.8–42.3m (opex only).*
- *Year 10 and beyond (100%): A$35–55m. Net headroom: A$25–45m per year.*

Cumulative payback (simple, undiscounted): between Year 7 and Year 10 depending on uptake; mid-range assumptions land around Years 8–9.

ACU figures here are indicative and speculative; they have not been independently verified and are provided for illustration only. Further economic modelling would be required. Figures are annual gross avoided costs (no NPV/discounting).

INITIATIVE 11

CELEBRATION CITY INITIATIVE

POLICY SUMMARY

We didn't just throw parties; we put celebration on the infrastructure list. Markets, festivals, and shared rituals were treated like roads and pipes—planned, budgeted, and maintained. The Kanamaluka Market became the weekly anchor: lake air, stall smoke, a busker's chorus, families drifting between bread, books, and banter. The obvious wins —trade up, footfall up, reasons to linger—were only the surface. Underneath came confidence: makers investing in better gear, musicians finding regular sets, language and story made ordinary (a song in palawa kani beside the olive-oil queue), and a calendar that kept people coming back not once a year, but every week.

This wasn't confetti over substance. We designed celebration to work: co-designed layouts, clear bump-in/bump-out, shared power and staging, simple permits, and a city stance that refused to let insurance shocks shrink public life. Pre-CivicLoom meetings set the rules of the game—consent, inclusion, and local voice—so the market and festivals could hold their own with the state's best while staying distinctly ours. Safety was built into the plan, not bolted on after the headline.

Economically, celebration was a micro-enterprise engine. Low-barrier stalls turned kitchen experiments into livelihoods; regular trade turned customers into regulars; and a cash-inclusive norm kept participation accessible. Apprentices learned events on the job, suppliers found steady orders, and side-hustles grew into leases. That's compounding local value: a hundred small businesses, a thousand small wins, a city that earns while it gathers.

Socially and culturally, celebration made belonging visible. Streets closed to cars and opened to people; neighbours met without an agenda; trust was felt as shared freedom rather than visible force. Festivals stitched the year together—Harmony Week to NAIDOC, ANZAC dawn to New Year's dusk—and the market gave us a simple sentence we could say without apology: see you at the lake on Saturday.

POLICY SNAPSHOT WHAT WE CELEBRATED & WHY IT MATTERED — CELEBRATIONS, FESTIVALS AND MARKETS

- **Kanamaluka Market** (waterfront civic market). Weekly lakefront market co-designed with locals; clear bump-in/out, shared power and staging, simple permits. Why it mattered: turned the waterfront into a reliable commons; regular reasons to gather, linger, and belong—celebration planned like infrastructure.
- **Celebration of children and young people** (Junior Citizen Award, Five Minute Thesis, Children's Expo, Kite Festival, Box Festival, Kid I Am). A suite of programs that put kids on the main stage: awards for contribution; a five-minute thesis to share ideas; an expo of making and doing; and a city day where streets, stages, and decisions centre children. Why it mattered: treated children as full people; respected their ideas in public; normalised decisions with them (not about them); built confident, civically skilled young citizens in spaces that were safe, playful, and fun.
- **Civic calendar of celebrations.** Year-round rhythm—Festivale, Harmony Week, NAIDOC, ANZAC, New Year's Eve, Writers and Readers, Social Justice Lecture. Why it mattered: shifted celebration from occasional to ordinary; built shared identity through repetition and anticipation.
- **Neighbourhood street parties** (council-supported). Council-backed block parties with micro-grants, fast-tracked permits, an equipment-loan kit (cones, barricades, ramps, signage), umbrella insurance, and a simple how-to playbook; inclusive by design with multilingual invites, kid-friendly zones, accessibility checks, quiet hours. Why it mattered: turned streets into micro-commons; gave neighbours an easy on-ramp to meet across cultures and ages; reduced loneliness; built trust and everyday safety that also strengthens disaster resilience.
- **Event-positive stance** (despite insurance shocks). A public commitment to grow—not shrink—markets and festivals; risk managed by design, not retreat. Why it mattered: protected the

social fabric in risk-averse times; kept streets alive with colour and sound as a civic habit, not a luxury.

- **Micro-enterprise incubator stalls.** Low-barrier stalls and rotating spots for makers and food vendors, with practical support and mentoring. Why it mattered: turned kitchen experiments into livelihoods; many small incomes beat one big bet; social capital grew alongside sales.
- **Cash-inclusive trading.** Market norms that welcome cash and digital. Why it mattered: kept participation accessible (no fees or tech gates); dignity for stallholders and buyers; inclusion by design.
- **Culture-in-the-ordinary.** First Nations language and local stories woven into market life and event programming. Why it mattered: made respect visible and audible; everyday truth-telling rather than token set-pieces.
- **Peace by design** (trust in public). Layouts, volunteers, and norms that make gatherings safe without heavy visible force. Why it mattered: safety experienced as shared freedom; trust built between neighbours, not enforced upon them.
- **Joy as infrastructure** (budgeted). Festivals and streets-to-people events funded in baseline budgets. Why it mattered: treated joy as a public good that pays back in cohesion, confidence, and local spend—especially when headlines are tough.

AVOIDABLE COSTS UNIT IMPACT ASSESSMENT MATRIX — CELEBRATION AND FESTIVAL CITY

- **Social connection and belonging.** Immediate impact: regular market and festival rhythm; neighbours meet without an agenda; loneliness interrupted. Long-term benefit: stronger social networks; lower chronic isolation; more mutual aid. Outlay (indicative): about A$0.20m per year. Avoidable costs (indicative): about A$0.4–0.9m per year (fewer GP/ED presentations linked to loneliness or anxiety; fewer crisis calls and welfare checks).
- **Children and young people at the centre.** Immediate impact: kids on stage as full people; ideas respected in public; safe, fun civic spaces. Long-term benefit: higher school engagement; leadership pipeline; pro-social identity. Outlay (indicative): about A$0.15m per year. Avoidable costs (indicative): about A$0.6–1.2m per year (lower remedial/engagement outlays; reduced youth-justice intake and case management).
- **Neighbourhood street parties** (council-supported). Immediate impact: micro-grants, simple permits, kit loans make low-friction block parties; inclusive invites. Long-term benefit: trust across cultures and ages; everyday safety rises; neighbours know who needs help. Outlay (indicative): about A$0.10m per year. Avoidable costs (indicative): about A$0.2–0.5m per year (fewer minor policing call-outs; reduced vandalism clean-up; better disaster readiness).
- **Peace by design** (trust in public). Immediate impact: clear layouts, volunteers, consent-centred norms; less need for visible force. Long-term benefit: stable perception of safety; fewer incidents; self-stewardship. Outlay (indicative): about A$0.05m per year. Avoidable costs (indicative): about A$0.25–0.6m per year (reduced policing/security overtime; lower incident and claim costs).
- **Micro-enterprise incubator stalls.** Immediate impact: low-barrier trading, mentoring, steady footfall create viable side incomes. Long-term benefit: transitions from under-

employment to self-employment. Outlay (indicative): about A$0.15m per year. Avoidable costs (indicative): about A$0.3–0.7m per year (lower income-support reliance; fewer emergency "rescue" grants; reduced vacancy-churn support).

- **Cash-inclusive trading.** Immediate impact: cash welcomed alongside digital. Long-term benefit: inclusive local economy; greater stallholder viability. Outlay (indicative): minimal, under A$0.05m per year. Avoidable costs (indicative): about A$0.05–0.15m per year (avoided exclusion-driven hardship requests and admin).

- **Civic calendar** (year-round program). Immediate impact: predictable cadence; shared anticipation. Long-term benefit: habitual public life; volunteer base deepens. Outlay (indicative): about A$0.10m per year. Avoidable costs (indicative): about A$0.10–0.25m per year (reduced disorder hotspots; less neglected-space clean-up).

- **Culture-in-the-ordinary.** Immediate impact: palawa kani and local stories embedded in events. Long-term benefit: respect and cohesion normalised; de-escalation. Outlay (indicative): about A$0.05m per year. Avoidable costs (indicative): about A$0.05–0.10m per year (fewer complaint mediations and conflict admin).

- **Event-positive stance** (insurance managed). Immediate impact: risk managed by design; no retreat from gatherings. Long-term benefit: learning lowers risk; premiums and claims stabilise. Outlay (indicative): about A$0.05m per year. Avoidable costs (indicative): about A$0.1–0.3m per year (avoided cancellation and sunk planning; lower excesses).

- **City operations and maintenance.** Immediate impact: activation reduces "empty-space" damage; smoother bump-in/out. Long-term benefit: cleaner, cared-for precincts. Outlay (indicative): about A$0.10m per year. Avoidable costs (indicative): about A$0.15–0.35m per year (lower vandalism/graffiti removal; fewer after-hours ranger call-outs).

- **Emergency and disaster resilience.** Immediate impact: neighbour networks built in peacetime. Long-term benefit: faster, cheaper community-led response in shocks. Outlay (indicative): about A$0.05m per year. Avoidable costs (indicative): about A$0.2–0.6m per year (lower relief logistics and outreach duplication).
- **Tourism uplift.** Immediate impact: distinctive festivals and markets attract regional and national visitors. Long-term benefit: visitor economy grows; local pride reinforced. Outlay (indicative): about A$0.10m per year. Avoidable costs (indicative): about A$0.5–1.0m per year (tourism spend, GST, rates).

Total Estimated Avoidable Costs (2025): about A$3.7–7.7m per year.

2064 nominal guide (CPI 2.5% per annum): about A$9.6–20.0m per year.

Total initial capital (2025): A$5.0 million, drawn down over five years. This covered permanent power pedestals and distribution, shared staging/truss and lighting, secure storage hub, shade and seating, wayfinding and comms, an equipment-loan kit (cones, barricades, ramps, signage), CivicLoom configuration, accessibility upgrades, and basic safety gear and training.

Annual operations at steady state (2025): A$1.2 million per year. This funds market coordination and permits, micro-grants for neighbourhood events, programming for children and young people (awards, Five Minute Thesis, expos), volunteer training and peace-by-design staffing, insurance pooling/administration, cleaning and bump-in/out support, and evaluation/ACU tracking.

Net fiscal position — ten-year ramp (2025 dollars; simple, no discounting)

Program costs: A$1.2m per year operations + A$1.0m per year amortised capital (A$5.0m over five years) = A$2.2m per year in Years 1–5; A$1.2m per year from Year 6 onward.

Steady-state avoided costs: about A$3.7–7.7m per year.

- *Year 1: 5–10% of steady state (A$0.19–0.77m). Net headroom: – A$2.02m to –A$1.43m.*
- *Year 2: 10–20% (A$0.37–1.54m). Net headroom: –A$1.83m to – A$0.66m.*
- *Year 3: 15–30% (A$0.56–2.31m). Net headroom: –A$1.65m to A$0.11m.*
- *Year 4: 25–40% (A$0.93–3.08m). Net headroom: –A$1.28m to A$0.88m.*
- *Year 5: 35–50% (A$1.30–3.85m). Net headroom: –A$0.91m to A$1.65m.*
- *Year 6: 45–60% (A$1.67–4.62m). Net headroom: A$0.47–A$3.42m.*
- *Year 7: 55–70% (A$2.04–5.39m). Net headroom: A$0.84–A$4.19m.*
- *Year 8: 65–80% (A$2.41–6.16m). Net headroom: A$1.21–A$4.96m.*
- *Year 9: 75–90% (A$2.78–6.93m). Net headroom: A$1.58–A$5.73m.*
- *Year 10 and beyond (100%): A$3.7–7.7m. Net headroom: A$2.5– A$6.5m per year.*

Cumulative payback (simple, undiscounted): between Year 5–6 (optimistic uptake) and Year 9–10 (conservative uptake); mid-range assumptions land around Years 7–8.

Assumptions: city-scale estimates (Launceston context); gross avoided costs only (no NPV/discounting). Conservative partial attribution from local baselines (health, policing/security overtime, event insurance/claims, city operations, youth justice, disaster management).

ACU figures here are indicative and speculative; they have not been independently verified and are provided for illustration only. Further economic modelling would be required. Figures are annual gross avoided costs (no NPV/discounting).

INITIATIVE 12

THE STATUE OF EQUITY

POLICY SUMMARY

The Statue of Equity rose not to commemorate a ruler but to embody a principle—fairness, belonging, and the visible promise that every life mattered. The power of the site was more than symbolic. At its base, People's Park became Tasmania's first purpose-built civic gathering ground, designed to hold fifteen thousand people in comfort. Like a southern echo of Melbourne's Sidney Myer Music Bowl, it hosted the full rhythm of public life: protests and vigils, citizenship ceremonies and memorials, concerts and carols, kite festivals and writers' fairs.

Together, monument and venue turned equity from an idea into a lived, shared experience. Families picnicked where movements once rallied, choirs sang where citizens demanded change, and new Australians took their oath beneath the bronze glow. The park and statue redefined civic space—not as a backdrop for politics, but as infrastructure for community life, built for both dissent and celebration.

POLICY SNAPSHOT WHAT WE BUILT & WHY IT MATTERED – STATUE OF EQUITY

- **Hands-on monument, not hands-off.** Climbable interior with changing routes, a public playground woven into the body of the statue. Why it mattered: turned "monument" into daily movement, play, and pride—participation over pedestal.
- **Civic ritual of welcome.** A birth-chime and gentle light rising from base to summit at key moments. Why it mattered: created a low-key ritual that reinforced belonging and dignity, city-wide.
- **Programmable AI façade.** Smart panels carrying GrowthLoops, events, and memorials. Why it mattered: a living gallery for community stories; flexible programming without pop-up hires.
- **Place-truth materials.** Base built from stone quarried across the island. Why it mattered: wove geography into identity—tangible "we" in the foundations.
- **View as public good.** 360-degree summit platform. Why it mattered: drew locals back to their river and skyline; boosted everyday civic pride and visitor dwell time.
- **Always-open identity.** "Not a ruler, a principle"—equity as the subject. Why it mattered: avoided culture wars; oriented pride toward fairness and welcome.
- **Purpose-built civic venue.** Amphitheatre-style People's Park at the base, safely hosting 15,000+ people. Why it mattered: a dedicated, inclusive space for civic life—no longer reliant on ad hoc streets or halls.
- **Multi-use design.** Infrastructure for concerts, protests, memorials, citizenship ceremonies, kite festivals, carols, and cultural events. Why it mattered: enabled both dissent and celebration—space for every voice and gathering.
- **Accessible and safe.** Terraced seating, shade, open acoustics, and best-practice crowd movement. Why it mattered: large gatherings felt safe and comfortable, reinforcing trust in public space.

- **Symbol plus space.** Monument above, gathering ground below. Why it mattered: turned equity from abstraction into lived experience—people met beneath the very symbol that named their belonging.

AVOIDABLE COSTS UNIT IMPACT ASSESSMENT MATRIX — STATUE OF EQUITY

- **Events and programming.** Immediate impact: built-in digital surfaces used for memorials, GrowthLoops, and festivals. Long-term benefit: recurring civic nights and major events with less friction. Avoidable costs (indicative): about A$0.35– 0.70m per year (stage / screen hire and bump-in / out avoided).
- **City brand and visitation.** Immediate impact: iconic, photogenic landmark with regular night activations. Long-term benefit: continuous earned media; itinerary anchor; higher visitor yield. Avoidable costs (indicative): about A$1.0– 1.8m per year (paid-marketing equivalent avoided).
- **Public-realm safety and care.** Immediate impact: high footfall, lighting, active programming. Long-term benefit: fewer antisocial incidents; less vandalism / damage. Avoidable costs (indicative): about A$0.10–0.25m per year (vandalism response and repairs avoided).
- **Youth participation and health.** Immediate impact: daily climbing / play and school-group use. Long-term benefit: more moderate-intensity activity; confidence gains. Avoidable costs (indicative): about A$0.20–0.50m per year (health-burden proxy avoided).
- **Civic admin and comms.** Immediate impact: on-site memorials / announcements via statue screens. Long-term benefit: reduced reliance on ad hoc venues / tech hire. Avoidable costs (indicative): about A$0.05–0.12m per year (procurement / venue costs avoided).
- **Tourism/operator revenue.** Immediate impact: climbing facility leased; ticketed visitor flows. Long-term benefit: ongoing income offsets operations. Note: additional visitor spend of A$1–2m per year in the local economy is a benefit, not counted in ACU totals.
- **Maintenance and electricity.** Immediate impact: nightly lighting; structural upkeep; systems servicing. Long-term benefit: reliability, safety, and an iconic night skyline. Note: not an "avoidable cost," but essential to preserve value.

Total Estimated Avoidable Costs (2025): about A\$1.7–3.4m per year.

2064 nominal guide (CPI 2.5%): outlay about A\$2.6m; avoidable costs about A\$4.5–9.0m per year.

Funding and operations — Statue of Equity and People's Park

- *Capital build: one-off, covered by the Republic Grant.*
- *Ongoing outlay (2025): about A\$1.0m per year, including roughly A\$0.4m for maintenance and electricity.*
- *Revenue inflows (2025): about A\$0.4–0.5m per year from the climbing-facility lease and event hires.*
- *Operating cost profile (2025 breakdown, indicative): events/programming A\$0.15m; brand/activation A\$0.20m; safety/care A\$0.10m; youth participation/education A\$0.10m; civic admin/tech A\$0.05m; maintenance and electricity A\$0.40m.*

Net fiscal position (steady state, 2025): slight surplus after offsets; the broader case strengthens further when tourism multipliers (A\$1–2m per year in local spend) are considered.

ACU figures here are indicative and speculative; they have not been independently verified and are provided for illustration only. Further economic modelling would be required. Figures are annual gross avoided costs (no NPV/discounting).

ENDNOTES

AUTHOR'S NOTE

1. The phrase "I can't accept not trying" is drawn from Michael Jordan's reflections on ambition and perseverance, published in a short motivational book rather than a full autobiography. In it, Jordan distills his philosophy on excellence, resilience, and the pursuit of goals, offering readers lessons from both his basketball career and personal outlook (Jordan, 1994). Source: Jordan, M. (1994). I can't accept not trying: Michael Jordan on the pursuit of excellence. HarperSanFrancisco.
2. Future scouting is Damien Lutz's practical method for using speculative design—creating "inventions from the future" and embedding them in story to prompt change today. Source: Lutz, D. (2021). Future scouting: How to design future inventions to change today. Damien Lutz. https://www.damienlutz.com.au/futurescouting/
3. Dunne & Raby popularise speculative/critical design and the use of "future prototypes"—artifacts and scenarios meant to provoke debate about the futures we might want (or not want). Source: Dunne, A., & Raby, F. (2013). Speculative everything: Design, fiction, and social dreaming. MIT Press. https://mitpress.mit.edu/9780262019842/speculative-everything/
4. The Futures Cone visually maps alternative futures—possible, plausible, probable, and preferable—commonly traced to Hancock & Bezold (1994), with helpful historical synthesis by Voros (2017). Sources: Hancock, T., & Bezold, C. (1994). Possible futures, preferable futures. The Healthcare Forum Journal, 37(2), 23–29; Voros, J. (2017, February 24). The futures cone, use and history. The Voroscope. https://thevoroscope.com/2017/02/24/the-futures-cone-use-and-history/
5. Protopia—incremental, step-by-step betterment rather than utopia/dystopia—was popularised by Kevin Kelly. Source: Kelly, K. (2011, May 19). Protopia. The Technium. https://kk.org/thetechnium/protopia/
   (See also Kelly, K. (2016). The inevitable: Understanding the 12 technological forces that will shape our future. Viking.)
6. Fictional Intelligence (FICINT)—also called "useful fiction"—combines research/analysis with narrative to explore near-future scenarios; the term is credited to August Cole (c. 2015) and is used across policy/defense contexts. Sources: Cole, A. (2021, March). FicInt: Anticipating tomorrow's conflict. Proceedings, 147(3). U.S. Naval Institute. https://www.usni.org/magazines/proceedings/2021/march/ficint-anticipating-tomorrows-conflict; U.S. Marine Corps. (n.d.). Fictional Intelligence (FIC/INT). https://www.marsoc.marines.mil/About/Initiatives/Raider-40-FIC-INT/

INTRODUCTION

1. "In a gentle way, you can shake the world" is widely attributed to Mahatma Gandhi and reflects his philosophy of nonviolent resistance and moral courage. While the exact source is debated, the quote has been cited in various speeches and writings

that echo Gandhi's ethos of transformative, principled action through kindness and resolve. Source: Dalton, D. (1993). Mahatma Gandhi: Nonviolent Power in Action. Columbia University Press.

2. The phrase "the long now" was coined by musician and thinker Brian Eno in 1979 and later expanded through the Long Now Foundation, established in 1996 by Stewart Brand and colleagues. It describes a way of stretching responsibility across centuries rather than election cycles, encouraging decisions that take into account both the deep past and far future (Eno, 1979; Brand, 1999; The Long Now Foundation, n.d.). Sources: Brand, S. (1999). The Clock of the Long Now: Time and Responsibility. Basic Books; Eno, B. (1979). The Big Here and Long Now. [Essay]. Reprinted by The Long Now Foundation; The Long Now Foundation. (n.d.). About the Long Now Foundation. Retrieved from https://longnow.org

3. The concept of upstream thinking has been widely popularised by Dan Heath in his book Upstream: The Quest to Solve Problems Before They Happen (2020), which argues for shifting focus from reacting to crises to preventing them at their source. Source: Heath, D. (2020). Upstream: The quest to solve problems before they happen. Avid Reader Press/Simon & Schuster.

4. The phrase kind politics is not formalised in a single text, but has been exemplified in contemporary leadership — most prominently by New Zealand Prime Minister Jacinda Ardern (2017–2023), whose empathetic, inclusive style was visible in her responses to the Christchurch mosque attacks, child poverty, and the COVID-19 pandemic. Similar currents have been recognised in the leadership of Finland's Sanna Marin and Iceland's Katrín Jakobsdóttir, who foregrounded empathy, trust, and collective wellbeing. Scholars have connected these approaches to the ethics of care tradition in political philosophy (Gilligan, 1982; Tronto, 2013), to human rights frameworks that place dignity at the centre of governance (Sen, 1999), and to anti-oppressive practice in social policy and community development (Dominelli, 2002). Taken together, these strands suggest that "kind politics" is both a contemporary practice and part of a longer intellectual lineage that challenges domination, centres care, and expands the moral horizon of public policy (Wilson, 2020; Lewis, 2020; Manch, 2023). Sources: Dominelli, L. (2002). Anti-oppressive social work theory and practice. Palgrave Macmillan; Gilligan, C. (1982). In a different voice: Psychological theory and women's development. Harvard University Press; Lewis, S. (2020, March 25). Finland is led by five women — here's what the country looks like during coronavirus. Forbes. https://www.forbes.com; Manch, T. (2023, January 19). Jacinda Ardern resigns as Prime Minister of New Zealand. Stuff.co.nz. https://www.stuff.co.nz; Sen, A. (1999). Development as freedom. Alfred A. Knopf; Tronto, J. (2013). Caring democracy: Markets, equality, and justice. New York University Press; Wilson, S. (2020). Pandemic leadership: Lessons from New Zealand's approach to COVID-19. Leadership, 16(3), 279–293. https://doi.org/10.1177/1742715020929151

5. The Power Threat Meaning Framework (PTMF) was developed by clinical psychologists Lucy Johnstone and Mary Boyle for the British Psychological Society's Division of Clinical Psychology. It was designed as an alternative to diagnostic models of mental illness, emphasising how distress is shaped by power, threat, and the meanings people construct in response (Johnstone & Boyle, 2018). Source: Johnstone, L., & Boyle, M. (2018). The Power Threat Meaning Framework: Towards the identification of patterns in emotional distress, unusual experiences and troubled or troubling behaviour, as an alternative to functional psychiatric diagnosis. British Psychological Society.

IT'S TIME TO STAND

1. Inspired by Canada, G. (1996). Take a stand. Do the Right Thing for Kids. Retrieved July 12, 2025, from https://dotherightthingforkids.org/poems-by-geoffrey-canada/poem

PRELUDE

1. A traditional Irish proverb, originally expressed in Irish Gaelic as "Ar scáth a chéile a mhaireann na daoine." The phrase has been widely cited in Ireland and abroad to emphasise human interdependence and the necessity of community. Former Irish President Mary McAleese often invoked it in speeches during the late 1990s and early 2000s, particularly in the context of reconciliation and peacebuilding.
2. paul's choice to write his name in lowercase is a quiet nod to the writer and activist bell hooks, who famously refused to capitalise her own name. For hooks, this was an act of humility and rebellion — a way of putting her ideas, not her identity, at the centre of attention. paul adopted this approach for similar reasons: to focus on collective change rather than individual recognition.

1. THE LAKE

1. "Water is life's matter and matrix, mother and medium. There is no life without water." — attributed to Albert Szent-Gyorgyi, Nobel Prize-winning physiologist best known for discovering vitamin C and advancing understanding of cellular respiration. The quote reflects his belief in the centrality of water to all biological life and has since become widely cited in environmental and ecological discourse. Source: Szent-Györgyi, A. (1972). The Living State: With Observations on Cancer. Academic Press.
2. The subtle hat tip repeated throughout the book is a quiet homage to The Cat in the Hat and its creator, Theodor Seuss Geisel (Dr. Seuss). The tipping of the hat appears throughout the Cat in the Hat series, a gesture that can be read as both greeting and respect. In many ways, it's as if Dr. Seuss is meeting readers where they are — playfully, respectfully — inviting them into the world of reading. For all his whimsy, the gesture carries weight: a nod not just from character to child, but from Ted to the millions who trusted his path and followed his peculiar, poetic journey.
3. The black, fluid mud typical of the Tamar River Yacht Basin is best described as sulfidic estuarine fine sediment (also called monosulfidic black ooze). It accumulates where fine silts and organic matter settle and oxygen is low; sulfate-reducing microbes produce sulfide that combines with iron to form iron monosulfides, giving the mud its colour and "rotten-egg" odour. When kept submerged, it is not acidic; however, if exposed to oxygen (e.g., by dredging or drawdown), it can oxidise and produce acidity, so management follows national acid sulfate materials guidance. In the upper Tamar, sediment builds where tidal energy drops — the Yacht Basin's shape is governed more by Cataract Gorge than by North Esk tidal prism — which is why this fine, sulfidic mud persists there.
4. Tamar Lake Incorporated is a member-funded not-for-profit established in 2010 to explore a barrage at Point Rapid that would create a managed freshwater lake on kanamaluka / the Tamar. Over more than a decade it has commissioned more than twenty studies across hydrodynamics, water quality and sedimentation; ecology

and natural values; engineering concept design and flood-mitigation modelling; and economics. Publicly available work includes a 2012 preliminary technical assessment by BMT Commercial Australia (published under the firm's earlier brand), a 2014 economic impact assessment by Klynveld Peat Marwick Goerdeler, and a 2017 compiled feasibility submission to the Tasmanian Department of State Growth. An updated flood-mitigation study was released in 2024. The organisation's website lists study summaries, a project-status history, and indicates total cash spending in the order of five to six hundred thousand Australian dollars alongside in-kind contributions. Sources: BMT Commercial Australia. (2012). *Tamar Lake preliminary technical assessment* (hydrodynamics, water quality, siltation and flooding). Tamar Lake Incorporated; Klynveld Peat Marwick Goerdeler. (2014). *Tamar Lake economic impact report.* Tamar Lake Incorporated; Tamar Lake Incorporated. (2017). *Tamar Lake feasibility report: Part 1—Strategy and benefits; Part 2—Environmental, technical, economic and funding studies* (submission to the Tasmanian Department of State Growth); Frith, R. (2021, July 13). *Review of the Tamar Estuary and Esk Rivers report (Section 13: Barrages and weirs) with reference to Tamar Lake feasibility studies* (submission to the Tasmanian Department of State Growth); BMT Commercial Australia. (2024). *Tamar Lake flood mitigation study (combined).* Tamar Lake Incorporated; Tamar Lake Incorporated. (2024, November). *Tamar Lake reports* (portal listing feasibility studies and summaries); Tamar Lake Incorporated. (2025). *Project status* (brief history and list of commissioned studies).

5. Emerging in the late 20th and early 21st centuries, the "slow" movements began as a counterpoint to the accelerating pace of modern life. The most widely known, the Slow Food movement, started in Italy in 1986 as a defence of regional cuisine, traditional farming, and convivial meals in response to the rise of fast food. From this seed grew a family of slow philosophies: Slow Cities (Cittaslow), Slow Travel, Slow Fashion, Slow Education, and more — each advocating for quality, sustainability, and human connection over speed, efficiency, and mass production. In a relentlessly fast, hyper-connected world these movements endure as cultural counterweights — reminders that meaningful change and deep satisfaction often require time, attention, and patience.

6. While Dan Heath's Upstream (2020) popularised the idea of prevention in organisational and policy arenas, the metaphor has a longer lineage in public health. The "going upstream" parable — of rescuers pulling people from a river until one finally walks upstream to address the cause — has been widely used to illustrate the shift from crisis response to prevention. In epidemiology, Geoffrey Rose (1985) advanced this logic in his "prevention paradox," arguing that reducing risk at the population level has far greater impact than treating individuals after harm occurs. Upstream thinking, in this sense, is rooted in public health traditions that emphasise structural determinants, long-horizon investment, and equity-focused prevention. Source: Rose, G. (1985). Sick individuals and sick populations. International Journal of Epidemiology, 14(1), 32–38. https://doi.org/10.1093/ije/14.1.32

7. bell hooks (1952–2021) was an American author, feminist, educator, and social critic known for her powerful explorations of race, gender, class, and love. Writing in a style that was both deeply personal and theoretically rigorous, she challenged systems of domination and championed the transformative power of care, community, and education. Her name, intentionally styled in lowercase, honoured her great-grandmother and symbolised a focus on ideas over identity. hooks' work remains foundational in discussions of intersectionality, critical pedagogy, and the politics of love and justice.

2. THE BRIDGE

1. "Bridges become metaphors for everything that connects us." — Jeanette Winterson, quoted in The Independent, 22 July 2004. In an article reflecting on architecture, literature, and symbolism, Winterson highlights the bridge as a powerful emblem of human connection, both literal and metaphorical.
2. In Tasmanian Aboriginal language and culture, the concept often referred to elsewhere as "Dreamtime" or "Dreaming" is instead call paywoota in Palawa Kani. Elder Jim Everett explains, paywoota means "beginning of time" – the ancestral era when creator beings shaped the land, rivers, animals, and social laws.

3. THE CHILDREN

1. Nelson Mandela, Speech at the Launch of the Nelson Mandela Children's Fund, Pretoria, South Africa, May 8, 1995. Full speech archived by the Nelson Mandela Foundation.
2. For sustained critiques of Ruby Payne's A Framework for Understanding Poverty and the associated Bridges Out of Poverty program, see Bomer, Dworin, May, and Semingson (2008), who document how Payne relies on deficit thinking, the discredited "culture of poverty" thesis, and unsupported "hidden rules." Gorski (2008) synthesises these criticisms, describing Payne's work as "uncritical and self-serving scholarship," published through her own for-profit enterprise. More recent scholarship (Smith-Carrier et al., 2021) argues that Bridges perpetuates paternalistic, assimilationist approaches that minimise structural inequities, while Learning for Justice (2016) provides an accessible overview of the stereotypes, deficit framing, and lack of evidence underpinning Payne's claims. Sources: Bomer, R., Dworin, J. E., May, L., & Semingson, P. (2008). Miseducating teachers about the poor: A critical analysis of Ruby Payne's claims about poverty. Teachers College Record, 110(11), 2497–2531; Gorski, P. C. (2008). Peddling poverty for profit: Elements of oppression in Ruby Payne's framework. Equity & Excellence in Education, 41(1), 130–148; Smith-Carrier, T., Kerr, M., Wang, J., Tam, S., & Oelke, N. D. (2021). Bridges out of poverty: Neoliberal poverty governance and the normalization of suffering. Critical Social Work, 22(1), 1–18; Learning for Justice. (2016). A framework for understanding Ruby Payne. Southern Poverty Law Center. https://www.learningforjustice.org
3. See The State of Launceston's Children Report (Anglicare Tasmania, Launceston Child Friendly City Working Group, & Launceston City Council, 2014), which provided a benchmark account of children's wellbeing in the city and helped catalyse subsequent community and policy initiatives. Source:
   Anglicare Tasmania, Launceston Child Friendly City Working Group, & Launceston City Council. (2014). The State of Launceston's Children Report 2014. Anglicare Tasmania. http://nla.gov.au/nla.obj-1374943163
4. According to the Australian Government's Closing the Gap report from 2020–2022, life expectancy at birth was 71.9 years for First Nations males and 75.6 years for First Nations females, while non-Indigenous counterparts were projected at 80.6 and 83.8 years respectively—representing gaps of about 8.8 years for males and 8.1 years for female. Sources: Australian Institute of Health and Welfare. (2023). Life expectancy and mortality—Health status and outcomes (Indigenous HPF). ABS 2023 figures via Indigenous Health Performance Framework. Retrieved from Australian Institute of

Health and Welfare website; Australian Government, National Indigenous Australians Agency. (2020). *Closing the Gap 2020: Life expectancy*. Australian Bureau of Statistics life tables, 2015–2017 data. Retrieved from NIAA website.

5. Failure demand refers to the additional burden placed on services and systems when the initial need or problem is not resolved properly—resulting in repeat requests, escalating crises, and avoidable costs. In other words, failure demand is the workload created by systemic failure to "get it right the first time," rather than by value-adding activity. It is a well-established concept in service economics, originally articulated by John Seddon and increasingly recognised across public policy sectors. In Australia, policy analysts including those at the Social Policy Institute and Centre for Policy Development have identified failure demand as a key driver of avoidable costs—those expenses that would not arise if upstream prevention and early intervention were prioritised and adequately resourced. Source: https://cpd.org.au/wp-content/uploads/2025/06/Avoidable-Costs.pdf

6. Actuarial modelling by the Australian Government Actuary, published in the Department of Social Services' Priority Investment Approach to Welfare valuation reports, estimates the average lifetime social-security cost at around $213,000 per person, but for long-term cohorts the figure rises to between $500,000 and $600,000 — for example, Carer Payment ($592k) and Disability Support Pension ($529k) recipients. These figures exclude additional health, justice, and child-protection costs, meaning the true public expense of entrenched disadvantage is significantly higher. Source: Department of Social Services. (2022). Australian Priority Investment Approach to Welfare: 2022 valuation report. Australian Government. https://www.dss.gov.au

7. Harlem Children's Zone (HCZ), began as a one-block pilot and expanded to a 24-block area in 2000 and 97 blocks by 2007, offering a cradle-to-college pipeline (e.g., Baby College, health supports, and the Promise Academy charter schools). Rigorous lottery-based studies find that attending HCZ's middle school closed the Black-white achievement gap in maths, with large gains in primary years as well; the model later informed the U.S. Promise Neighborhoods initiative. Sources: Dobbie, W., & Fryer, R. G., Jr. (2011). Are high-quality schools enough to increase achievement among the poor? Evidence from the Harlem Children's Zone. American Economic Journal: Applied Economics, 3(3), 158–187; Harlem Children's Zone. (n.d.). Our history & Zone map. https://hcz.org/our-purpose/our-history-zone-map/; Center for the Study of Social Policy. (2025). Harlem Children's Zone. (Brief). https://cssp.org/wp-content/uploads/2025/03/Harlem-Childrens-Zone.pdf

8. Wraparound Milwaukee. Launched in the mid-1990s as a countywide "system of care" with pooled funding across child welfare, juvenile justice, mental health and Medicaid, Wraparound Milwaukee coordinates individualized, home- and community-based services for high-need youth. Evaluations and program reports show sharp reductions in psychiatric-hospital days (from ~5,000/year to <200), major drops in residential treatment placements (average daily census from ~375 to ~50), and substantial cost savings (≈US$3.2–$4.0k per child/month vs. ≈US$8–$10k for residential care). Source: National Wraparound Initiative / CHCS / Milwaukee County DHHS. (various). Wraparound Milwaukee reports and briefs (e.g., hospitalization and cost trends; program overview). https://nwi.pdx.edu/pdf/recommendationsToCMS.pdf; https://county.milwaukee.gov/ImageLibrary/Groups/cntyHHS/Wraparound/Provider-Network/ProviderTraining-Feb12.pdf

9. Social Impact Bonds (SIBs), first piloted in the United Kingdom in 2010, are a form of outcomes-based contracting in which private investors fund preventive or social

programs and are repaid by government if agreed outcomes are achieved (Fraser, Tan, Lagarde, & Mays, 2018). Source: Fraser, A., Tan, S., Lagarde, M., & Mays, N. (2018). Narratives of promise, narratives of caution: A review of the literature on Social Impact Bonds. Social Policy & Administration, 52(1), 4–28. https://doi.org/10.1111/spol.12260

10. Rumble's Quest is an interactive, game-based tool developed by Griffith University researchers to assess social-emotional wellbeing and executive functioning in children aged roughly 6 to 12 years. The platform evolved from an earlier tool, Clowning Around, and has been refined into an engaging digital game that children play on iPads or computers, navigating a narrative quest that incorporates questions and tasks across four wellbeing domains. Results feed into a secure reporting dashboard, enabling schools and service providers to track student wellbeing, plan responsive programs, and evaluate outcomes. Initially developed as part of the "Creating Pathways to Prevention" project with Mission Australia and Education Queensland, Rumble's Quest was trialled in Queensland schools by the Queensland Family & Child Commission, earning praise as a valid, user-friendly alternative to traditional wellbeing assessments. Most recently, RealWell (a Griffith-affiliated social enterprise) has overseen its broader rollout; by mid-2022, over 40,000 Australian children had participated, at a cost of approximately $4 per child per year.

11. Results-Based Accountability (RBA), developed by Mark Friedman in the late 1990s, is a performance framework that distinguishes between population outcomes (broad conditions of well-being for whole communities, such as "all children are healthy and safe") and program or performance outcomes (the measurable results of specific services or initiatives). For example, a population outcome might be improved child wellbeing across a city, while a program outcome could be an increase in immunisation rates within a local health service. By working backwards from the desired population outcome, RBA helps align programs, partners, and measures around shared goals (Friedman, 2005). Source: Friedman, M. (2005). Trying hard is not good enough: How to produce measurable improvements for customers and communities. Trafford Publishing.

12. The original concept of collective impact (Kania & Kramer, 2011) emphasised five conditions for cross-sector collaboration: common agenda, shared measurement, mutually reinforcing activities, continuous communication, and backbone support. In practice, however, critiques emerged that the model underplayed equity, power, and authentic community voice. The updated framework, Collective Impact 3.0 (Cabaj & Weaver, 2016), reframed the approach around "community aspiration" as the starting point, placed equity and engagement at the centre, and emphasised continuous learning and systems change over technical coordination. Source: Cabaj, M., & Weaver, L. (2016). Collective impact 3.0: An evolving framework for community change. Tamarack Institute; Kania, J., & Kramer, M. (2011). Collective impact. Stanford Social Innovation Review, 9(1), 36–41; Christens, B. D., & Inzeo, P. T. (2015). Widening the view: Situating collective impact among frameworks for community-led change. Community Development, 46(4), 420–435. https://doi.org/10.1080/15575330.2015.1061680

13. Economist James Heckman's research demonstrated that early childhood interventions deliver the highest rates of return on investment in human capital. His analyses found benefit–cost ratios of up to 13:1, with long-term gains in education, employment, health, and reduced crime. Source: Heckman, J. J., Pinto, R., & Savelyev, P. A. (2013). Understanding the mechanisms through which an influential early

childhood program boosted adult outcomes. American Economic Review, 103(6), 2052–2086. https://doi.org/10.1257/aer.103.6.2052

14. This phrase originates from Dr. Seuss's Horton Hears a Who! (Geisel, 1954), a children's book that has often been cited for its message of dignity and recognition. Source: Geisel, T. S. (1954). Horton hears a who! Random House.

15. The credit for popularising rain-activated street art in public spaces is often given to projects in Seoul reported in 2015 as "Project Monsoon," which used hydrochromic paint to reveal colourful murals during rain. In parallel, Seattle artist Peregrine Church's Rainworks (2014–2015) pioneered a widely documented approach using hydrophobic coatings to make images appear when wet. This book nods to those public examples.

4. THE PLEDGE

1. Dr. Peter Attia, physician and author of Outlive: The Science and Art of Longevity. Attia's work redefines healthspan as a measure of not just lifespan, but of quality, function, and agency in later life. His approach blends preventative medicine, exercise science, and emotional wellbeing to help individuals live more fully and intentionally. See: Attia, P. (2023). Outlive: The Science and Art of Longevity. Harmony Books.

2. Tasmania has consistently recorded the highest prevalence of overweight and obesity in Australia. In 2017–18, 70.9% of Tasmanian adults were overweight or obese, compared to 67.0% nationally; among children, 28.7% were overweight or obese — also above the national average (Australian Bureau of Statistics [ABS], 2019). Earlier data reported that 32.3% of Tasmanian adults were obese and 67.5% overweight or obese combined, the highest of any state (Atlantis et al., 2017). Overweight and obesity are now the leading cause of preventable disease burden in Australia (8.3% of total), surpassing tobacco use, with impacts concentrated in cardiovascular disease, type 2 diabetes, chronic kidney disease, and several cancers (Australian Institute of Health and Welfare [AIHW], 2024). Additional morbidity includes musculoskeletal disorders, sleep apnea, depression, and reduced mobility (World Health Organization [WHO], 2021). Sources: Australian Bureau of Statistics. (2019). National Health Survey: First results, 2017–18 (Cat. no. 4364.0.55.001).Canberra: ABS. Retrieved from https://www.abs.gov.au/statistics/health/health-conditions-and-risks/waist-circumference-and-bmi/2017-18; Atlantis, E., et al. (2017). Prevalence of obesity in Australia: Trends and regional variations. Obesity Research & Clinical Practice, 11(5), 407–415. https://doi.org/10.1016/j.orcp.2017.07.001; Australian Institute of Health and Welfare. (2024). Australian Burden of Disease Study 2024. Canberra: AIHW. Retrieved from https://www.obesityevidencehub.org.au/collections/impacts/disease-burden-overweight-obesity-poor-diet; World Health Organization. (2021). Obesity and overweight. Geneva: WHO. Retrieved from https://www.who.int/news-room/fact-sheets/detail/obesity-and-overweight

3. The concept of the Preventative Health Survey in this chapter draws inspiration from the real-life Preventative Health Survey conducted by the Geelong Council. This initiative was a pioneering effort to collect data on community health needs and guide public policy, focusing on prevention rather than reaction.

4. This chapter draws on city-led programs with demonstrated uptake and/or evaluation across multiple jurisdictions: Australia — Hobart's My Street neighbourhood parties (TAS); Seniors' Exercise Parks / ENJOY and Walking Football 4 Health

(VIC); 30 km/h Slow Streets (City of Yarra, VIC) and 40 km/h local-area limits (City of Vincent, WA). United Kingdom — parkrun (and the NHS parkrun practice link), GoodGym, Playing Out/PlayStreets, Green Gym, and Walking Football. Colombia — Bogotá's weekly Ciclovía/Open Streets. Spain — Barcelona's Superblocks (Superilles). Singapore — Therapeutic Gardens and Park Prescription trials, the National Steps Challenge, and community Brisk Walking Clubs. United States — Philadelphia PlayStreets. Japan — Radio Taiso daily micro-exercise. Across these examples, the common intent is to raise daily movement and reduce loneliness by: (1) reclaiming or calming streets for people; (2) scaling free/low-cost, hyper-local classes and walking groups; (3) building age-friendly outdoor strength/balance parks; (4) linking health services through social prescribing and GP-led activations; (5) offering modified, inclusion-first team sport; and (6) pairing exercise with civic purpose (e.g., conservation tasks).

5. The social determinants of health refer to the non-medical factors that influence health outcomes — including housing, education, employment, income, social connection, early life experiences, and access to green space, transport, and nutritious food. These conditions shape the environments in which people live, work, and age — and are often more influential on overall health than access to healthcare itself.

6. Heart–Move Index (HMI). The HMI is a simple public-friendly adaptation of the research metric "Daily Heart Rate per Step" (DHRPS). paul inverted DHRPS to make it intuitive and round to a whole number: HMI = steps ÷ average daily heart rate (lower HR and/or more steps → higher HMI → better everyday cardio efficiency). Suggested starter bands (motivational, not clinical): <60 red (getting started; ~3,000–4,500 steps, HR 80–95 bpm); 60–99 amber (building; ~5,000–7,000 steps, HR 75–90); 100–149 green (healthy everyday engine; ~7,500–10,000 steps, HR 60–80); 150+ gold (high everyday efficiency; 10,000–13,000+ steps, HR 45–70). Examples: 10,500 steps ÷ 64 bpm = HMI 164; 3,200 ÷ 88 = 36; 8,000 ÷ 75 = 107. Concept adapted from DHRPS to improve public readability and engagement. Source: Chen, Z., Wang, C. T., Hu, C. J., Ward, K., Kho, A., & Webster, G. (2025). Daily heart rate per step (DHRPS): A wearables metric associated with cardiovascular disease in a cross-sectional study of the All of Us Research Program. Journal of the American Heart Association, e036801. https://doi.org/10.1161/JAHA.124.036801

7. A growing body of research confirms that social isolation and loneliness pose serious health risks—with mortality increases comparable to—or exceeding—those associated with smoking, physical inactivity, and obesity (Holt-Lunstad et al., 2017; Office of the U.S. Surgeon General, 2023). For instance, poor social relationships have been linked to a 29% increased risk of heart disease and a 32% increased risk of stroke across multiple longitudinal studies. In Australia, loneliness is especially pronounced among older men: one survey found 43% reported feeling lonely, with 16% experiencing high levels of loneliness (Healthy Male, 2023). Sources:

Holt-Lunstad, J., Robles, T. F., & Sbarra, D. (2017). Advancing social connection as a public health priority in the United States. American Psychologist; Office of the U.S. Surgeon General. (2023). Our epidemic of loneliness and isolation: The U.S. Surgeon General's advisory on the healing effects of social connection and community. U.S. Department of Health and Human Services; Healthy Male. (2023). Survey on loneliness among Australian men.

5. THE GARDENS

1. The earliest known printed instance of this saying appears in the Cleveland Plain Dealer in March 1967, where it was presented with an anonymous attribution: "Someone remarked that the best time to plant a tree was 30 years ago, and the second best time is now". Despite its uncertain origins, the quote has become widely recognized and is frequently cited to encourage timely action and to emphasize that while the optimal moment for certain endeavors may have passed, the present remains a valuable opportunity to begin.

2. Midnight Oil's Earth and Sun and Moon (1993) reflects on humanity's relationship with natural cycles, invoking themes of renewal, balance, and environmental connection. The song has often been read as a lyrical meditation on grounding and regeneration, aligning with ecological and social themes present in the band's wider body of work. Source: Midnight Oil. (1993). Earth and sun and moon [Song]. On Earth and sun and moon. Columbia Records.

3. Some of the thinking in this chapter is informed by Tom Rath's *Eat Move Sleep: How Small Choices Lead to Big Changes* (2013). Rath highlights the power of environment in shaping daily habits — from the placement of healthy food to opportunities for natural movement and social connection. His emphasis on designing lives and communities that make the healthy choice the easy choice helped inspire aspects of the urban greening and community garden initiatives described here.

4. Inspired by reading: McDonough, W., & Braungart, M. (2002). Cradle to cradle: Remaking the way we make things. North Point Press.

5. Free-range parenting is a term coined by Lenore Skenazy in the early 2000s to describe a style of parenting that emphasizes giving children the freedom to explore and learn independently, often with minimal adult supervision. Inspired by a more traditional, pre-1970s approach to childhood, free-range parenting encourages children to take risks, solve problems on their own, and develop resilience. It challenges modern parenting trends that focus on overprotection and constant supervision. Proponents argue that allowing children to experience more autonomy fosters confidence, responsibility, and critical thinking skills. Critics, however, raise concerns about safety and societal pressures, particularly in an era of heightened fears about crime and danger. Despite these debates, free-range parenting has gained popularity as a response to overly structured, risk-averse approaches to modern childrearing.

6. This passage was inspired by Saul Alinsky's Rules for Radicals. Alinsky saw grassroots organizing as a tool for social and political change. Alinsky emphasizes collective action, persuasion, and direct engagement with those in power, advocating for tactics – including unconventional tactics - that challenge the status quo. His approach prioritizes the realities and needs of the people, aiming to build power from the ground up. This strategic focus on empowerment has influenced movements seeking to create meaningful change from within communities.

7. Urban greening strategies deliver wide-ranging benefits. By reducing ambient temperatures, they help mitigate the urban heat island effect and protect communities from extreme heat. Greener environments are also linked to improved public health outcomes — including fewer heat-related illnesses and better mental wellbeing. Additionally, these initiatives support local biodiversity, enhance neighbourhood character, increase property values, and contribute to tourism by creating more attractive, livable streetscapes.

6. THE WORKERS

1. Rollins Band. (1994). Shine [Song]. On Weight [Album]. Imago Records.
2. Tasmania's Health Workforce 2040 strategy, released in 2021, sets out a clear 20-year plan to build a sustainable and future-ready health workforce. Developed after extensive consultation—including over 120 responses from clinicians, educators and community groups—it addresses key challenges: aligning education to workforce demand, boosting geographic distribution, and supporting workforce wellbeing. The strategy's focus spans six areas—education, recruitment, innovation, planning, wellbeing and workforce shape—to ensure Tasmania has the right people, in the right places, delivering quality care. Its 2024 implementation report confirms ongoing progress and a firm commitment to adapting as needs evolve.
3. A nod to a former colleague (WF), who's attention to detail, methodical approach to work, and friendship I miss.
4. The Cynefin framework, developed by Welsh researcher Dave Snowden in 1999 while working at IBM, offers a sense-making model to guide decision-making in complex systems. It categorises situations into five domains: Clear (obvious), Complicated, Complex, Chaotic, and Confused (later renamed Aporetic). Each domain suggests a different leadership approach. For example, in Clear contexts, best practices can be followed. In Complex ones, however, outcomes emerge through experimentation and learning — a concept that influenced upstream thinking models, especially in areas like workforce reform, where cause and effect aren't easily predicted. The strength of Cynefin lies in recognising which type of problem you're facing — and adapting your response accordingly.
5. The headlines presented in this section are drawn from actual newspaper and media reports. They have been lightly adapted for flow and readability within the narrative.
6. The phrase "It's the economy, stupid" was coined by James Carville, a lead strategist for Bill Clinton's 1992 U.S. presidential campaign. It originated as one of three key reminders posted on a sign in the campaign headquarters in Little Rock, Arkansas: 1. Change vs. more of the same; 2. The economy, stupid; and 3. Don't forget health care. Though intended as internal guidance, the phrase quickly became a defining message of the campaign and entered the global political lexicon as a shorthand for prioritising economic concerns.

7. THE BOOM

1. Coretta Scott King spoke and wrote often about the power of compassion, justice, and community — continuing the legacy of her husband, Dr. Martin Luther King Jr., while also building her own legacy as a civil rights leader, author, and advocate for peace.
2. Warden, J. (2021). Regenerative futures: From sustaining to thriving together. The RSA. https://www.thersa.org/wp-content/uploads/2021/10/from-sustaining-to-thriving-together-final.pdf Source: Royal Society for Arts, Manufactures and Commerce. (n.d.). Regenerative futures. The RSA. Retrieved September 17, 2025, from https://www.thersa.org/regenerative-futures/
3. The integration of solar panels and sheep grazing — known as agrivoltaics — allows farmland to generate renewable energy while continuing agricultural use. Sheep are ideal grazers under solar arrays, helping manage vegetation without

damaging equipment. This dual-use model improves land productivity and supports the transition to clean energy.

4. Doughnut Economics is a model developed by economist Kate Raworth, proposing a safe and just space for humanity. It visualises a circular zone — the "doughnut" — between two boundaries: the social foundation, where everyone has access to life's essentials, and the ecological ceiling, which we must not overshoot to protect Earth's systems. The goal is to meet human needs without breaching planetary limits. See: Raworth, K. (2017). Doughnut Economics: Seven Ways to Think Like a 21st-Century Economist. Chelsea Green Publishing.

5. Northern Tasmania has seen rapid growth in large-scale solar energy projects. In 2025, George Town Council approved the $700 million Cimitiere Plains Solar Farm, featuring more than 600,000 panels across 454 hectares of grazing land. Nearby, the $500 million Northern Midlands Solar Farm near Cressy is expected to be operational by 2027, generating enough electricity to power around 70,000 homes.

6. Pollinator-friendly solar farms integrate wildflower meadows and native grasses beneath and around solar panels. These habitats support bees, butterflies, and other pollinators by providing food and shelter, helping reverse biodiversity loss while enhancing nearby crop yields. It's a win–win for clean energy and ecological health.

7. Some solar farms are designed to create cool, shaded microclimates ideal for cultivating mushrooms. These "shadowed mushroom" rows make use of the lower-light spaces beneath panels, enabling high-value food production without additional land use.

8. Solar panels can be installed above vineyards on elevated structures, allowing grapevines to grow underneath. This dual-use approach provides shade during extreme heat, reduces water stress on the vines, and generates renewable energy — enhancing both resilience and productivity.

9. Floating solar farms are installed on the surface of dams or reservoirs, generating clean energy while reducing water evaporation, limiting algae growth, and preserving valuable land. They're especially effective in sunny regions with high water storage needs.

10. This passage was inspired by engineer and entrepreneur Daniel Stack. His TED talk introduced the breakthrough potential of "electrified bricks" — a form of thermal battery made from low-cost firebricks that can be heated to over 1,500°C using excess solar or wind energy. These bricks store and release high-temperature heat on demand, enabling 24/7 clean energy access for heavy industry. By making renewable energy dispatchable, the technology reduces reliance on fossil fuels and eases pressure on hydroelectric systems. Stack, D. (2023, June). The surprising solution to industrial heat that's already here [Video]. TED Conferences. https://www.ted.com/talks/daniel_stack_the_surprising_solution_to_industrial_heat_that_s_already_here

11. Bell Bay, in Northern Tasmania, has been identified as a promising site for green hydrogen production due to its deep-water port, industrial zoning, renewable energy capacity, and proximity to high-quality water sources from the Tamar Valley. Multiple feasibility studies and industry proposals have pointed to its potential to become a key hub for exporting green hydrogen produced using solar, wind, and hydro power.

12. The creation of a freshwater lake in the Tamar Valley would open significant opportunities for recreational fishing, particularly with the introduction of species such as trout and native freshwater fish. Similar artificial lakes in Tasmania and mainland Australia have supported thriving fishing tourism, local tackle and guiding indus-

tries, and community events. With careful ecological management and water quality monitoring, a freshwater lake could become both an environmental asset and a recreational drawcard.

13. In 2018, Australia faced a major food contamination crisis when sewing needles were found hidden in strawberries, prompting widespread recalls, consumer panic, and severe financial losses for growers. The incident led to harsher penalties for food tampering, tighter supply chain protections, and investments in tamper-evident packaging. It also sparked public solidarity campaigns like #SmashAS-trawb, and became a turning point for traceability and safety in Australia's fresh food sector.

14. Cricket farming involves raising insects in controlled environments where they are fed a plant-based diet — often made from food-grade waste streams or fast-growing crops like lettuce or leafy greens. Crickets are typically harvested within 6–8 weeks, then cleaned, dried, and milled into a fine, high-protein powder rich in essential amino acids, iron, and B12. It is plausible that leafy greens and unsellable strawberries could be repurposed into feed for crickets, creating a closed-loop model that turned crisis into innovation. Compared to traditional livestock, cricket protein has a much smaller environmental footprint — requiring minimal land, water, and feed while producing negligible methane emissions.

15. It is plausible that a small, efficient industry like cricket protein farming could emerge in a region like the Tamar Valley and supply the World Food Programme (WFP). Cricket farming requires minimal land and water, produces low emissions, and yields a highly nutritious powder rich in protein, iron, and B12. The WFP has trialled insect-based nutrition in several contexts and actively supports innovative, locally sourced protein solutions. It also accepts in-kind donations at scale, particularly when aligned with its goals for sustainable, climate-resilient food systems.

8. THE GROWTH

1. Kate Raworth, a British economist and Senior Associate at the University of Oxford's Environmental Change Institute, is best known for developing the Doughnut Economics framework — a model that envisions a safe and just space for humanity, balancing essential social foundations with ecological ceilings. The approach critiques traditional growth-centric economics and seeks to align human prosperity with planetary boundaries. Source: Raworth, K. (2017). Doughnut economics: Seven ways to think like a 21st-century economist. London: Random House Business Books.

2. The goal is to transitioning all public transport to electric by 2035. The strategy referenced here aimed to reduce emissions, lower operational costs, and improve air quality — particularly in the CBD and densely populated corridors. Early investments in electric buses and charging infrastructure began in the late 2020s, paving the way for a fully electric, quieter, and cleaner transport network within a decade.

3. Park-and-ride facilities allow commuters to park on the outskirts of the city and transfer to public transport for the final leg of their Willowurney. By intercepting car traffic before it enters the CBD, these hubs reduce urban congestion, lower transport emissions, and ease the demand for expensive city parking infrastructure. For commuters, they offer cost savings, less time spent in traffic, and a more relaxed arrival into work or study. For cities, they're a practical piece of upstream design — shifting daily behaviour while reclaiming central space for people rather than cars.

4. The City of Launceston 10-year Strategic Plan projects a net increase of only 1,500 residents between 2025 and 2035.

5. Seven generation thinking is a principle rooted in Indigenous knowledge systems. It invites decision-makers to consider the impact of their actions not just on the present, but on the wellbeing of people seven generations into the future. Unlike election cycles driven by short-term wins, this long arc of responsibility reframes leadership as an act of stewardship. It asks us to be good ancestors — to design systems, cities, and cultures that our descendants will thank us for. For more, see: Haudenosaunee Confederacy. (n.d.). Values. https://www.haudenosauneeconfeder acy.com/values/

6. To grow Tasmania's population to the scale signaled in this book a strategy combining skilled immigration with the compassionate resettlement of displaced people would be required. A kind policy like this would give freedom and hope to those fleeing war, persecution, and protracted stays in refugee camps. It would also giveTasmania the population bump it needed to accelerate its transformation. This is not without precedent. After World War II, Tasmania welcomed thousands of migrants from war-torn Europe. Many of them helped build the state's hydro-elec-tric dams, railways, and key infrastructure — laying the foundations of modern Tasmania. The same principle underpins this chapter: welcome those in search of safety and purpose, and you renew Tasmania itself. Migration is both a humani-tarian act and a practical strategy — with the potential to enrich the state's culture, economy, and future.

7. The "1 in 5" principle — allocating one in every five homes in new suburbs for social or affordable housing — is grounded in a social justice logic that recognises housing as both a human right and a foundation for wellbeing. By embedding social housing seamlessly within mixed-income communities, the approach prevents the creation of isolated "poverty pockets," fosters social inclusion, and ensures equitable access to new amenities, schools, transport, and green spaces. It also disrupts cycles of disadvantage by giving lower-income families the same opportunity to live in safe, thriving neighbourhoods. Long-term, this integrated model reduces the costs associ-ated with inequality — including health, education, and justice system burdens — while building stronger, more diverse communities.

8. Medium-density housing — such as townhouses, low-rise apartments, and duplexes — strikes a balance between detached homes and high-rise towers. When embedded in new suburbs, it offers multiple social and environmental benefits. It allows more people to live closer to transport, schools, shops, and community services, reducing car dependence and social isolation. Environmentally, it curbs urban sprawl, protects surrounding farmland and bushland, and enables more effi-cient use of infrastructure like water, energy, and public transport. As social policy, medium density creates housing diversity that suits different life stages and income levels — from downsizing retirees to young families and essential workers — helping to build inclusive, connected communities.

9. Inclusive design is not an afterthought — it's a foundation. When new suburbs are planned with universal design principles from the outset, accessibility is built in, not bolted on. Footpaths are wide and gently graded, crossings intuitive, signage read-able, and public spaces welcoming to all — including people with disability, older residents, parents with prams, and those with temporary injuries. The cost of inclu-sion is lowest when embedded early, and the benefits ripple widely: more indepen-dence, more participation, and a stronger sense of belonging. In this imagined

future, inclusive design wasn't framed as 'special needs' — it was simply how good design was done.

10. Neighbourhood batteries are shared energy storage systems that collect surplus solar power from local rooftops during the day and redistribute it to homes at night. Typically serving 50–200 households, they reduce pressure on the grid, lower energy bills, and improve access to clean energy — even for renters or those without solar panels. Pilots across Australia (including in Victoria, New South Wales, and Western Australia) have demonstrated their ability to support energy equity, maximise rooftop solar use, and accelerate the transition to net-zero.

11. The Passivhaus (or Passive House) standard, developed in Germany, sets one of the world's most rigorous benchmarks for energy efficiency and thermal comfort. It is especially well-suited to cool climates like Tasmania, where maintaining warmth in winter is critical. Passivhaus buildings use high-performance insulation, airtight construction, triple-glazed windows, and heat recovery ventilation to create a stable indoor climate year-round. While construction costs are modestly higher, the life-time energy savings — through drastically reduced heating and cooling bills — more than offset the upfront investment. The result: healthier, quieter, more comfort-able homes with minimal environmental impact.

12. Rainwater harvesting delivers long-term environmental and economic benefits — especially when installed during construction. Integrated systems reduce costs and allow rainwater to be used for gardens, cooling trees, washing, and flushing toilets. In some designs, hand basins are built into cisterns so water used for handwashing is captured for reuse. Over a home's lifetime, this lowers bills and conserves treated mains supply. The practice echoes post-WWII Launceston, when backyard tanks were common — catch the water, feed the garden.

9. THE CREATIVITY

1. Buckminster Fuller (1895–1983) was an American architect, systems theorist, inventor, and futurist best known for his pioneering work in sustainable design and holistic thinking. He popularised the concept of "Spaceship Earth", urging humanity to recognise the planet as a single interconnected system requiring careful stewardship. Fuller is credited with inventing the geodesic dome and championed the idea of "doing more with less" — advocating for innovation, design science, and resource efficiency to solve global challenges. His work continues to influence environmentalists, architects, and changemakers around the world.

2. The Royal Society of Arts (RSA) introduced the concept of *Teenagency* to describe how young people's creative self-efficacy links to their capacity for social action. The RSA emphasises that effective youth-led change requires four enabling conditions: young people must be allowed to identify the issues, design their own solutions, lead the response, and reflect on the impact. When these conditions are met, social action delivers a "double benefit"—communities are strengthened, and young people themselves develop confidence, skills, and purpose (Partridge, Sapsed, & Puttick, 2018). Source: Partridge, L., Sapsed, J., & Puttick, R. (2018). Teenagency: How young people can create a better world. Royal Society for the encouragement of Arts, Manufactures and Commerce (RSA). Retrieved from https://www.thersa.org/globalassets/pdfs/reports/teenagency-rsa-2018.pdf

3. Mulford, B. (2015, April). Broadening what counts as good schooling: The criteria employed to judge the success of Tasmanian school education—Time for review and broadening (Submission to The Hothouse). University of Tasmania.

4. Inspired by: Stroud, G. (2018). Teacher: One woman's struggle to keep the heart in teaching. Allen & Unwin.
5. Inspired by: Biddulph, S. (2021). Fully human: A new way of using your mind. Bluebird.
6. Inspired by: Duckworth, A. (2016). Grit: The power of passion and perseverance. Scribner.
7. Inspired by: Wyn, J. (2007). Learning to 'become somebody well': Challenges for educational policy. *The Australian Educational Researcher, 34*(3), 35-52. https://doi.org/10.1007/BF03216864
8. The organising idea for Changemaker High is informed by the Japanese concept of oubaitori (ōbaitōri) — meaning "cherry–plum–peach–apricot", which holds that each person blooms in their own season. Accordingly, the school resists ranking and comparison, and focuses on cultivating each learner's strengths and pace.

10. THE SPORT

1. Ido Portal, movement teacher and founder of the Ido Portal Method, emphasises the body's adaptive capacity in response to use or disuse. Source: Portal, I. (n.d.). Movement 1. Retrieved from https://www.benmedder.com/movement-1
2. In ancient Greece and Rome, a palaestra was a public space for exercise, wrestling, and social interaction. More than a gymnasium, it served as a centre for physical training, conversation, and civic life, often adjoining baths or other communal facilities.
3. Some of the insights in this chapter were inspired by Peter Attia's book Outlive: The Science and Art of Longevity (2023), which emphasises the importance of physical activity, metabolic health, and proactive prevention in extending both lifespan and healthspan. His work helped shape the case for movement-friendly environments as a form of upstream investment.
4. Tasmania consistently records poorer health outcomes compared to the rest of mainland Australia. The state has the oldest median age of all jurisdictions (43.1 years vs. 38.5 nationally), a higher burden of chronic disease, and the highest proportion of people living with disability per capita. Rates of obesity, smoking, and preventable hospitalisations are significantly above the national average. According to the Australian Institute of Health and Welfare, Tasmanians are more likely to experience multiple health conditions and less likely to report good health overall. These compounding factors place additional strain on the health system and highlight the critical importance of upstream, preventative policy interventions.
   Source: Australian Institute of Health and Welfare (AIHW), Australia's Health 2022: State and Territory Health Performance.
5. The 2025 state and federal election cycles in Australia saw a clear political pattern: major parties across jurisdictions secured victories with strong commitments to downstream health investments. Campaigns frequently centred on pledges for new hospitals (or hospital upgrades), shorter emergency wait times, more bulk-billing doctors, and reduced out-of-pocket costs for medicines. In Tasmania, Queensland, and Victoria, for example, party leaders toured hospital construction sites and announced regionally targeted funding packages for GP training, rural health services, and specialist appointments. While these promises responded to genuine public concern — particularly amid post-pandemic system strain — they also reinforced a reactive model of health policy. Preventative and upstream strategies (such as active transport, healthy food access, and community-based early

intervention) received comparatively little attention during the 2025 campaign cycle, despite mounting evidence of their long-term cost savings and social benefit. Source: Grattan Institute (June 2025), Budgeting for Better Health: The Case for Prevention.

6. Evidence from countries such as Mexico, the UK, and cities like Philadelphia shows that a well-designed sugar tax can reduce consumption of sugary drinks, encourage healthier choices, and ncentivize manufacturers to reformulate products. These policies not only improve dietary behaviour but also raise revenue for public health initiatives. While flat taxes can be regressive, using the revenue to subsidise healthier foods and water access can offset equity concerns and enhance the overall impact.

7. Social prescribing is a practice where health professionals, particularly GPs, refer patients to non-clinical supports such as exercise groups, community activities, volunteering, or arts programs — rather than relying solely on medication. It is used in countries like the UK, Canada, and parts of Australia to address the social and lifestyle factors that influence health. Evidence shows it can improve wellbeing, reduce loneliness, and ease pressure on primary care and mental health services.

8. This passage is inspired by the quote: "Never doubt that a small group of thoughtful, committed citizens can change the world. Indeed, it is the only thing that ever has." This quote is widely attributed to Margaret Mead (1901–1978). It is consistently associated with her philosophy and advocacy for grassroots social change.

9. Blue zones are population regions identified by demographers and popularized by National Geographic research where unusually high proportions of people reach very old ages (often 100+) with lower rates of chronic disease. Commonly cited examples include Okinawa (Japan), Sardinia—especially Ogliastra (Italy), Ikaria (Greece), the Nicoya Peninsula (Costa Rica), and Loma Linda, California (USA). See Poulain, Herm, and Pes for the academic framing and Buettner/National Geographic for the public synthesis. Sources: Poulain, M., Herm, A., & Pes, G. (2013). The Blue Zones: Areas of exceptional longevity around the world. Vienna Yearbook of Population Research, 11, 87–108. https://www.researchgate.net/publication/255508953; National Geographic Staff. (2025, July 15). What are 'blue zones'? Five places on Earth where people live the longest. National Geographic. https://www.nationalgeographic.com/premium/article/5-blue-zones-where-the-worlds-healthiest-people-live; Blue Zones. (n.d.). Original Blue Zones explorations. https://www.bluezones.com/exploration/

10. The concept of "PlayMetrics" draws on principles of gamification to boost engagement with physical activity. By blending digital feedback with real-world play, playmetrics can motivate children and young people through goals, challenges, and intermittent rewards — helping bridge the gap between screen time and movement. Sensor-enabled equipment also allows for anonymous data collection on usage patterns, supporting evidence-based investment in community infrastructure and ensuring that spaces evolve with actual need and demand.

11. The economic cost of physical inactivity in Australia has been estimated at $33 billion per year, including direct health costs, lost productivity, and premature mortality. According to the Australian Institute of Health and Welfare, nearly 40% of the national chronic disease burden is preventable, with inactivity being a maWillowr contributor. Source: Australian Institute of Health and Welfare (2021). Chronic conditions and multimorbidity. https://www.aihw.gov.au/reports/chronic-disease/chronic-conditions-and-multimorbidity

12. A VicHealth report from the 2020s found that $4.40 was returned for every $1 invested in walking and cycling infrastructure in Melbourne, through improved

health, reduced congestion, and stronger local economies. Source: VicHealth (2023). Creating Healthier Places through Active Design. https://www.vichealth. vic.gov.au

13. Global studies from the World Health Organization and others place the benefit-cost ratio between 5:1 and 13:1, depending on the city and scale of intervention. World Health Organization (2018). Source: Health economic assessment tool (HEAT) for walking and cycling. https://www.euro.who.int/en/health-topics/environment-and-health/Transport-and-health

14. Launceston has a long rowing tradition, with regattas held at Stephenson's Bend on the Tamar River from the 1840s. The Tamar Rowing Club was established in 1876, and school regattas, including the "Head of the River," were held on the river until the early 1940s. However, variable tides, limited spectator facilities, and ageing infrastructure led to a decline in maWillowr events. By the late 20th century, competitive school and state regattas had shifted to Lake Barrington — a purpose-built venue offering more reliable conditions. In recent years, despite the state of the river, rowing has seen a quiet revival in Launceston, with the return of community events like the Launceston & Henley Regatta and the Tamar Masters Regatta.

11. THE CELEBRATIONS

1. Helen Keller, American author, disability rights advocate, and lecturer, highlighting the transformative power of collective effort. Source: Keller, H. (1924). Speech at the American Foundation for the Blind, Washington, D.C.

2. The confluence of the North and South Esk Rivers with the kanamaluka / Tamar Estuary has long been a place of gathering for the Palawa people. For thousands of generations, this meeting place was a site of trade, ceremony, conflict resolution, and connection — where multiple clans of Aboriginal Tasmanians came together to share knowledge, culture, and custodianship of Country. Today's civic gatherings in this region echo that deep history of relational place-making.

12. THE ATTRACTION

1. Peter Hughes, British historian and commentator on public art, on the role of monuments in civic life. Source: Hughes, P. (2020, June 14). Why statues are important. The Sunday Post.

2. The concept of celebrating each birth publicly draws inspiration from traditions in northern Italian towns—such as those around Cremona—where church bells have rung at births for centuries. Today, many of these communities still ring bells to welcome new life—a small, profound ritual that brings people together in shared recognition. This enduring practice informed the imagined design of Launceston's Statue of Equity, as a way to honour new arrivals not with names or fanfare, but with light and tone, uniting the city in a moment of collective belonging.

AUTHOR'S REFLECTION

1. Inspired by: Sutton, R. I. (2007). The no arsehole rule: Building a civilised workplace and surviving one that isn't. Piatkus.

www.ingramcontent.com/pod-product-compliance
Lightning Source LLC
Chambersburg PA
CBHW062204270326
41930CB00009B/1638

9 781764 292207